LANGUAGES OF WITCHCRAFT

Illustration taken from the title page of Henning Gross: Magica de Spectris et Apparitionibus Spirituum ..., published 1656, British Library Shelfmark 231.k.34. Reproduced by permission of The British Library.

LANGUAGES OF WITCHCRAFT

Narrative, Ideology and Meaning in
Early Modern Culture

Edited by
Stuart Clark

First published in Great Britain 2001 by

MACMILLAN PRESS LTD
Houndmills, Basingstoke, Hampshire RG21 6XS and London
Companies and representatives throughout the world

A catalogue record for this book is available from the British Library.

ISBN 0–333–79348–X hardcover
ISBN 0–333–79349–8 paperback

First published in the United States of America 2001 by

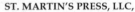

ST. MARTIN'S PRESS, LLC,
Scholarly and Reference Division,
175 Fifth Avenue, New York, N. Y. 10010

ISBN 0–333–79348–X (cloth)
ISBN 0–333–79349–8 (paper)

Library of Congress Cataloging-in-Publication Data

Languages of witchcraft: narrative, ideology & meaning in early modern culture / edited by
Stuart Clark.
    p. cm.
   Includes bibliographical references and index.
   ISBN 0–333–79348–X – ISBN 0–333–79349–8 (pbk)
    1. Witchcraft–Europe–History–16th century–Congresses. 2. Witchcraft–Europe–History–17th
century–Congresses. 3. Witchcraft–Europe–History–18th century–Congresses. I. Clark, Stuart.

BF1584.E85 L36 2000
133.4'3–dc21   00–033302

This book is printed on paper suitable for recycling and made from fully managed and
sustained forest resources.

10   9   8   7   6   5   4   3   2   1
10   09 08 07 06 05 04 03 02 01

Copy edited and typeset in *Book Antiqua* by Password, Norwich, UK.
Printed in China

In memory of

Gareth Roberts

Contents

Preface

In September 1998 the History Department of the University of Wales, Swansea, held a conference devoted to recent trends in witchcraft research and to the issues raised by the concept of 'reading witchcraft', both as a style of interpretation and as an aspect of the subject itself. The conference focused largely on witchcraft in Europe between the sixteenth and eighteenth centuries, and it brought together the great majority of the scholars currently working on this subject in Britain and some of the most important overseas experts. This volume consists of essays arising from papers delivered at the conference, grouped according to the three themes that dominated our discussions. My thanks go to all those who participated in the original meeting, which lived up to the reputation that witchcraft studies have justifiably gained for promoting originality, liveliness, and good humour. My task as editor was also eased considerably by the speed and efficiency with which the authors of the papers turned them into publishable essays. For financial assistance towards the costs of the conference, we are all grateful to the following: the British Academy, the Royal Historical Society, the Society for Renaissance Studies, and the History Department at Swansea.

Through a sad irony, Gareth Roberts was due to give a paper on demonology and *The Comedy of Errors* at the conference, but a family illness intervened. His sudden death in February 1999 shocked and bewildered us all, and deprived witchcraft research and Renaissance studies generally of one of their most subtle exponents. Fortunately, his work on witchcraft in early modern Scotland, in collaboration with Lawrence Normand, was virtually complete and will soon be published. Gareth was universally admired and respected as a scholar and teacher and cherished as a friend. He was a person of great humanity and generosity, with an expansive Welshness that endeared him to everyone. We dedicate this volume to him in affectionate memory of the man and in acknowledgement of his many achievements.

Chapel Hill, NC
November 1999

Contributors

Jonathan Barry is Senior Lecturer in History and Head of the School of Historical, Political and Sociological Studies at the University of Exeter. Among his publications on the social and cultural history of early modern Britain, he has co-edited *Witchcraft in Early Modern Europe* (Cambridge University Press, 1996) and is preparing a collection of essays on witchcraft and demonology in south-west England.

Robin Briggs is a Senior Research Fellow of All Souls College, Oxford. He is the author of *Early Modern France, 1560–1715* (Oxford University Press, 2nd edn 1998), *Communities of Belief: Cultural and Social Tensions in Early Modern France* (Oxford University Press, 1989), and *Witches and Neighbours: The Social and Cultural Context of European Witchcraft* (Harper Collins, 1996). He is currently working on a study of 'The Witches of Lorraine'.

Stuart Clark is Professor of Early Modern History at the University of Wales, Swansea. He has published *Thinking with Demons: The Idea of Witchcraft in Early Modern Europe* (Oxford University Press, 1997), and is co-editor of the 'Athlone History of Witchcraft and Magic in Europe' series. At present he is writing a book on visual reality in the early modern period.

Peter Elmer is a Staff Tutor and Lecturer in the history of science at the Open University. He is currently chairing a new course on the Renaissance which is being co-published by Yale University Press. He is also completing a book on the seventeenth-century miracle healer, Valentine Greatrakes, which focuses on the relationship between politics, medicine, and demonology in Restoration England.

Malcolm Gaskill is Fellow and Director of Studies in History at Church-ill College, Cambridge. He has written several articles, essays, and re-views concerning witchcraft and popular beliefs, and is the author of *Crime and Mentalities in Early Modern England* (Cambridge University Press, 2000). He is currently working on a history of English witch-craft.

Marion Gibson lectures in English Literature at the University of Ex-eter and on its BA in English programme at Truro College, Cornwall. She is the author of *Reading Witchcraft: Stories of Early English Witches* (Routledge, 1999), and her edition of English witchcraft pamphlets from the period 1566–1621 will be published by Routledge in 2000.

Katharine Hodgkin lectures in Literature and History in the Depart-ment of Cultural Studies at the University of East London. She has published articles on various aspects of autobiographical writing, gen-der, and unreason in early modern England. She is currently working on autobiographical accounts of madness in the seventeenth century, and on an edition of Dionys Fitzherbert's manuscript.

Diane Purkiss is Professor of English at the University of Exeter. She is the author of *The Witch in History* (Routledge, 1996), and is working on a full-length study of fairies for Penguin Books.

Thomas Robisheaux is Associate Professor of History at Duke Uni-versity, Durham, North Carolina. His current work is a microhistory about a peasant witch and the end of the witch trials in south-west Germany.

Peter Rushton is Reader in Historical Sociology at the University of Sunderland. He has published on different areas of early modern so-cial history such as family life, the community, the poor law, and the treatment of the mentally ill and disabled. He is co-author (with Gwenda Morgan) of *Rogues, Thieves and the Rule of Law: The Problem of Law Enforcement in North-East England, 1718–1800* (University College of London Press, 1998).

María Tausiet received her doctorate at the University of Zaragoza in 1997. Her publications include several essays on witchcraft, magic, and religion in sixteenth- and seventeenth-century Spain, and she is the author of *Ponzoña en los ojos: Brujería y superstición en Aragón en el siglo XVI* (Institución Fernando el Católico, 2000).

David Wootton is Professor of Intellectual History at Queen Mary and Westfield College, University of London. He has recently edited Locke's political writings for Penguin, and edited and translated Machiavelli's *The Prince* and More's *Utopia* for Hackett.

Introduction[*]

Stuart Clark

The fact is that the nature of witches and the acts they are believed to carry out cannot be determined without taking into account the concept of reality of the times and circles in which they move ... This is the essential problem for those who investigate witches and witchcraft. What is the nature of reality in a world where there are witches? Above all, what do those who believe themselves to be the victims of witchcraft believe to be real?[1]

n 1995 the world of witchcraft studies lost one of its most influential modern pioneers, the celebrated Spanish anthropologist and social historian Julio Caro Baroja. Nearly 40 years ago, and already an authority on Basque ethnography, he published *Las brujas y su mundo*, recounting how, during his boyhood, he had spoken with believers in witchcraft in the region where he grew up. It seems that these encounters had a profound effect on Caro Baroja's book. They taught him to focus on the radically different conceptions of the world that made witchcraft possible in some societies and periods and impossible in others. Ultimately, he said, the history of witchcraft raised an issue that was fundamental to philosophy and science as well – 'the nature of reality itself'. Between the notions of reality produced and made significant during the centuries of modern science and those of 'prescientific' peoples there was obviously an enormous gulf. Even so, it was imperative for historians to grasp the point of view of those who accepted witchcraft as a real threat, and to do this by analysing both their mentalities and the demands made upon them by the

---

*   While writing this Introduction I was able to benefit from conversations with Laura Gowing, who very kindly also read it in draft.

structural characteristics of the societies to which they (and their witches) belonged. In this respect, they should aim to emulate anthropologists like Edward Evans-Pritchard and Bronislaw Malinowski.[2]

Caro Baroja was not, in fact, a thoroughgoing relativist; nor would Evans-Pritchard have approved of his psychological theories of religion (he did not approve of Malinowski's either). *Las brujas y su mundo* begins by arguing that, in many different societies and periods, a 'rudimentary' everyday experience of the natural environment had imprinted itself on the minds of 'primitive' peoples – looking at the world, so to speak, for the first time – in the form of the same emotionally grounded religious and mythical beliefs, amongst which was the notion of magic.[3] Nevertheless, Caro Baroja's idea that the problem of witchcraft was ultimately a conceptual one – in effect, an epistemological one – was rich in possibilities. His solution was to concentrate not on what witches did, but on what they were *said* to do; the reality of witchcraft was a consequence of beliefs and embodied in language. These beliefs were necessarily communal in nature and they structured the experiences of those who feared witches, giving them, for example, a particular view of what was possible in the physical world, as well as a whole set of religious and legal sanctions. 'However arbitrary such a view of life may appear', Caro Baroja repeated, 'and however hard our task, it is clear that certain distinctions and qualifications have to be made between one kind of consciousness and another …'[4] The story told in his book is, indeed, of the changing forms of consciousness that accompanied, first, the rise of witchcraft prosecutions in Europe and, later, their decline. The age in between, he said, was, not unlike the present one, an age of *angst*, whose witch-believers might for this reason be better understood. But Caro Baroja concluded as he had begun – with a radical dissimilarity between their idea of reality and ours.[5]

This statement of witchcraft's 'essential problem' and how it should be dealt with seems even more relevant today than it was in 1961. The points that Caro Baroja was making seem somehow to be the right ones, bearing in mind the assumptions and aims that most cultural anthropologists and cultural historians now take for granted. There is, after all, something fundamental about the idea that human life is irreducibly constituted by the terms in which it is known, even though this is a knowledge that must always remain multiple and contested, and always generate its own forms of uncertainty and ignorance – of not knowing. This is the reason why the category of experience –

experience no longer raw and unmediated, but discursively formed – has been at the forefront of so much social analysis in the last decade, even among those who, like the historians associated with the tradition of the *Annales* 'school', would previously have rejected it.[6] Since past lives are what historians seek to interpret, the ways in which these were experienced do now seem to have become the inescapable foundations of historical thinking. 'Belief' will certainly not account for everything we mean by experience; nevertheless, we seem to know what Caro Baroja was saying when he argued that the beliefs of those who experienced witchcraft ought to be given priority in any attempt to understand its role in their lives. Beliefs about 'reality', likewise, did not exhaust what witchcraft meant to these people; but, again, we can agree that their attitude to it must have depended largely on what they felt to be possible and impossible in the real world.

What is striking about the intervening years, then, is the extent to which Caro Baroja's advice was so largely forgotten – at least in the study of the witchcraft trials of early modern Europe. It is almost as if the experiences of those most immediately involved became the last things to consider, not the first – their 'point of view' the least significant component, not the most. Instead, all manner of other explanatory frameworks were adopted, drawn mostly from what he called a different 'form of consciousness'. These were able to account successfully for how modern people might have experienced early modern witchcraft, if they had been living at that time, by drawing on theories about how modern societies do in fact experience what are taken to be the equivalent phenomena. Thus, over the years, historians of witchcraft have appealed to social-anthropological functionalism, to labelling theories of deviance, to revolutionary feminism, to acculturation theory, to the sociology of state-building, to the Gramscian notion of hegemony, to Freudian and Kleinian psychoanalysis, to theories of collective psychological trauma and psychosis, and to psychosomatology and the science of hallucinogens. Mostly, this has made for a freshness and liveliness of debate that few other fields can match. As a topic, witchcraft has stretched our theoretical resources and challenged us to experiment in undoubtedly exciting ways; it has become, as Katharine Hodgkin has written in another context, 'a place where history asks questions about itself'.[7] Even so, one occasionally yearns for restraint – indeed, for the kinds of limits set by Caro Baroja's notion of consciousness. In 1988, for example, it was suggested that witchcraft prosecutions could be linked to the impact of syphilis on sixteenth-century European society.[8] In 1990 it was argued that they were a contribution to the 'mass production' of deviance by the 'social control system' of the early modern state, which was itself comparable to the terror in revolutionary France, Stalin's purges, the Holocaust, the cultural revolution in China, and the McCarthy era in America.[9]

Why was Caro Baroja's advice replaced by this fever for explanation? How did we get from the witch trials of early modern Europe to Senator McCarthy in one easy step? One reason lies in the dominance of a particular model of the history of witchcraft that distorted the subject and led to false expectations – as historical models do from time to time. The notion of a 'European witch craze' suggested that the whole continent was caught up in a massive panic, during which the church and state in each region or area orchestrated a ruthless campaign to eradicate thousands of innocent people on the spurious grounds that they were 'witches'. An episode so all-embracing and so dramatic required a comparable explanation, which only the overarching, largely social-scientific theorizing that was so influential at the time could provide. Recently, of course, this model has been steadily dismantled. The evidence has been reconsidered, expectations have been revised, and a strikingly different picture has emerged. We have indeed rethought the subject. There now seems to have been nothing 'European' about the witch trials, little to suggest church- or state-promoted campaigns to 'hunt' witches, and no overall atmosphere of 'craze' or panic or ruthless persecution. What emerges from a study like Robin Briggs's *Witches and Neighbours* is that the 'common currency' of witchcraft, as it was typically experienced, was not the devil or the 'sabbat', but a very real fear of *maleficium*, driven by the quarrels and rivalries that emerged among villagers when ill-will and resentment replaced the sense of good neighbourliness that normally kept their communities together. This was an everyday drama, constructed from their own affairs and beliefs, to which the courts and the judicial élites often responded with scepticism and restraint.[10] In England, in particular, excepting the exceptional activities of Matthew Hopkins and his helpers in the 1640s, there was a steady trickle of mostly minor prosecutions for a crime that assumed hardly more legal prominence than any other felony, and which becomes intelligible as soon as we pay attention to the ordinary fears and anxieties, and ordinary beliefs and prejudices, expressed by people in everyday situations. There was no coordination and no campaign, either in church or state, beyond the passing of, again, largely unexceptional statutes, which neither the judiciary, nor any other section of the aristocracy (which was, in any case, divided on the issue) showed any uniform desire to put into effect.

There is, however, a more fundamental reason for the search for explanations that has marked witchcraft research since the 1960s and it takes us back to Caro Baroja's 'essential problem'. What are historians supposed to do with beliefs and practices that appear to them to have no basis in reality? His answer, as we have seen, was to treat reality as a cultural variant; in this respect, he resembled not so much the anthropologists whom he cited, but the late nineteenth-century philosopher and historical theorist, Wilhelm Dilthey, for whom, also, the real world presented itself to human consciousness as lived experience. Generally, the researchers who followed Caro Baroja made a different kind of conceptual adjustment. For them, witchcraft could not be traced to a different version of reality, but only condemned as unreal in relation to their own. They therefore made an almost unconscious switch from dealing with things that were obviously genuine and solid (like wars, revolutions, and price rises) to dealing with things that seemed faulty and incorrect. This is why so many accounts of the subject have tried to explain it in terms of something more real – for example, some set of social, political, or psychic conditions – and also why so many of them have been couched in the language of pathology.[11] The assumption has been that the men and women who believed in witchcraft and wanted witches to be punished did so because there was something wrong with them and the societies in which they lived. They were suffering from collective fears and anxieties brought on by traumatic social and cultural changes; they were in the grip of a collective psychosis; they were scapegoating; they were trying to come to terms with the arrival of syphilis; the men were at war with the women; or, most common of all, they were simply irrational. At one time it was extraordinarily difficult to find any account of why early modern Europeans believed in witchcraft or promoted witchcraft prosecutions that did not speak about abnormalities, or inadequacies, or mistakes of one kind or another. Even the celebrated and highly influential hypothesis of Alan Macfarlane and Keith Thomas concerning the link between witchcraft accusations and changing attitudes to indigence in Tudor and Stuart village communities was derived from the view that these communities were experiencing severely strained social relationships – of which witchcraft accusations were a kind of gauge and which they served functionally to resolve.[12] Caro Baroja himself, it has to be admitted, spoke of the age as one of *angst*.

What has occurred more recently, by contrast, is a return to something like his priorities. In place of the social scientific approaches of previous decades, with their search for explanation – which, in effect, meant explaining witchcraft away – recent research has concentrated on witchcraft as a cultural phenomenon with a reality of its own. There has been a significant convergence of views towards a more interpretative model aimed precisely at the lived experiences of those originally involved in witchcraft cases, whether as participants or commentators. Their view of the matter is now much more likely to be privileged. In *Witches and Neighbours*, Robin Briggs speaks of needing to focus on ordinary people and on the climate in which their beliefs flourished – of hearing them 'talking about their everyday lives, their hopes and fears, their families'.[13] This kind of approach has led to a renewed interest in witchcraft episodes as expressions of beliefs, values, and fantasies; to greater emphasis on witchcraft as an ideological and cultural resource; and, above all, to an awareness of witchcraft's great symbolic and metaphoric power not only in literature and drama, but in the general world of religion and politics, and in the life of communities. In this way, questions to do with the original meaning and significance of witchcraft, and with witchcraft as a category in language, have come to the fore.

There is a certain methodological economy at work here – a recognition that the real world can take many forms without being any the less real for that, a feeling that our investigations ought to be restrained by the historical limits to which meaning and behaviour are, in consequence, always subject, and a decision that those who experienced witchcraft historically ought to be listened to first. But putting these aims into practice should not be thought of as anything but highly complex. Caro Baroja spoke simply of concepts of 'reality' and of 'the world', yet every student of witchcraft is now becoming aware of how varied, how controversial, and how fought over these were in early modern societies. Witchcraft was contested terrain not simply in the courtroom, but in every community where it occurred and every text where it was discussed. Between the real and the unreal were many things that partook of both or were difficult to apportion to either, as Diane Purkiss very effectively shows in her essay in this collection on the stories told about fairies in seventeenth-century Scottish courtrooms. To focus on experience is also to focus on something manysided and elusive, even inchoate; something that historical agents, like ourselves, could not always understand or express. This, indeed, is one of the reasons why applying psychoanalytic theory to witchcraft cases still seems to many historians such a useful interpretative strategy to adopt, despite the theory's own almost aggressive modernity. But in any case, the shift from explanation to interpretation is in no sense a movement back to some kind of theory-free history. Paying attention to the way witchcraft was constructed, imagined, and represented, to its ability to carry meanings, and to its political, moral, and psychological significance in the lives of individuals and communities might be a different way of approaching it from that adopted in the past, but this approach itself owes much to theoretical assumptions about the relationships between belief and behaviour, language and reality, and the historian and the past.[14]

What has changed is the feeling, once so strong among commentators, that witchcraft was a fundamentally enigmatic element of early modern history that only a very special kind of explanation can account for.[15] A great deal of research and an abundance of publications has made us well aware of the difficulties in generalizing about a subject that manifested itself in so many ways in virtually every region of Europe. In some contexts it was sensational and produced responses that were extraordinary even for the period; in others – the vast majority – it was an essentially ordinary, indeed routine, part of community life. But, whatever form it took, we no longer think of it as resistant to the kinds of enquiries that we would usually make regarding any other aspect of early modern culture. Previously, it was singled out for attention among other phenomena that, intellectual prejudice apart, might have been deemed just as mysterious, just as intractable, and just as unreal – many aspects of orthodox religious belief and behaviour, and of early modern scientific and medical practice, for example. Now all alike are expected to yield to the sort of analysis that mixes a faith in the capacity of early modern people to make sense of their own world in their own way with a degree of cultural relativism regarding the results. 'Making sense', it must be stressed again, is a far from simple or uniform thing to attempt or achieve; Katharine Hodgkin reminds us in her essay in this volume of its historiographical limitations as well. But it is what human beings do with their lives and, in this fundamental respect, we are no different from those who believed in witchcraft and acted on their beliefs. This, at least, is the way we now tend to formulate Caro Baroja's idea that 'reality' is always construed differently in every time and society.

What then is the best way to focus on such issues? In the 1960s, as he indicated, the answer lay in arguments about the nature of rationality conducted by anthropologists, philosophers, and social theorists. Indeed, at that time no discussion of rationality was complete without its witches. These were not the witches of Europe; they came instead from the pages of Evans-Pritchard's study of the Azande. But they served the crucial purpose which these debates had – of pointing to the often dramatic differences in beliefs about reality that seemed to distinguish Western from 'other' cultures, the difficulties (even the impossibility) of doing anthropology in these circumstances, and the problem of whether Evans-Pritchard himself had lived up to his own aim of not imposing scientific criteria of rationality on Zande magic.[16] Today, the relevant debates occur not in the philosophy of the social sciences, but in critical theory and cultural history, and the issues raised are to do with the primacy of language, the irreducibility of experience, and the referentiality of texts. A particularly good example is the way in which historical investigation is increasingly being treated, in conceptual terms, as a kind of reading. This serves to emphasize that historians are, first and foremost, interpreters, and that historical understanding is achieved by approaching the past in much the same manner as a reader confronts a text – that is, by exploring patterns of meaning rather than causal relationships. It assumes that historical agents, too, were interpreters and that, in trying to make sense of their world and act in it, they were also reading it, and in ways that deserve prominence in any account that we might give of what they were up to. Finally, it recognizes the textual character not merely of the historical record itself, but also of the actions recorded in it – in the sense that the latter, while not literally texts, are, again, intelligible (or otherwise) in terms of patterns very like those found generally in language.

The implications of this kind of approach for witchcraft studies are important. To make sense of witchcraft beliefs and the accusations, prosecutions, and punishments associated with them – if possible through the eyes, minds, and imaginations of those involved – is rather different from explaining them in terms of prevailing social conditions or large institutional forces or general psychological states. It does not, of course, dispense with the social, the political, or the psychic as categories; rather, it turns them into idiomatic aspects of the life-worlds of the participants – things they experienced and expressed. Here, the concept of reading the past captures well the dialogic relationships that make these various aspects of experience mutually dependent on each other. Witchcraft scholars have always been well aware of the actual texts in which their subject seems to be described – trial records, pamphlets, treatises, plays, and the like. But they are now thinking in terms not of textual description, but of textual construction, abandoning, for example, the assumption that trial documents can be read transparently as materials for empirical social analysis. For reading itself has changed and 'reading' witchcraft is changing also. We now have much greater insight into the relationship between witchcraft beliefs and other areas of early modern European thought, debates about witchcraft in the context of religious, political, or other controversies, the cultural production, transmission, and contesting of notions of witchcraft, the filtering of witchcraft episodes in terms of gender and race, and, above all, the 'language' or 'rhetoric' of witchcraft – its symbolisms, idioms, classifications, and vocabularies, its metaphorical extensions, its narrative features, and so on. All this has served to make it a lot less startling than it once was, yet at the same time a lot more revealing of the world in which it occurred.

*   *   *

The essays collected in this volume illustrate these recent trends in witchcraft research, and in historical research in general, as well as engaging critically with them. The collection starts, indeed, with one of the topics central to the re-conceptualizing of witchcraft that is currently taking place – the role of narrative in the actions and descriptions of those who immediately confronted it. Given what has been said, this is clearly the natural place to begin, even if witchcraft historians have been slower than others to do so. Once we decide to privilege the experiences of historical agents and to see them as active in the construction and interpretation of their worlds, we cannot avoid looking carefully at what they themselves said and did. And the power of narrative to influence both language and action is now thought to be overwhelming. This has been persuasively argued by anthropologists like Victor Turner and Renato Rosaldo, psychologists like Jerome Bruner, and philosophers like Paul Ricoeur.[17] But it is empirically discoverable in what historians mostly read and it was classically enshrined in Natalie Zemon Davis's treatment of sixteenth-century French pardon tales in her influential book of 1987, *Fiction in the Archives*. From other directions, then, and by reflecting on what they themselves confront and on the nature of memory, historians have learned that narrative not only gives form to human actions as told but to the acting of them as well. It shapes the way we express ourselves, our communities and our culture, and is also constitutive of each of these. Here, too, the notion of experience is central, both as something lived and as something known. Important to Ricoeur, for example, is the assertion, as Rosaldo phrases it, that 'time becomes human when shaped by narrative form, and narrative becomes meaningful when it depicts human experience in the flow of time. Narratives shape temporal experiences, and temporal experiences in turn embody narratives.'[18] This intertwining of history and story has nowhere been more vividly demonstrated than in Miri Rubin's account of how Christian communities in later medieval Europe acted and re-enacted the especially potent mythical narrative of host desecration by Jews. 'People act through narratives', she writes, 'and they remember through narrative. Willed acts are probably both conceived narratively and also understood and used as such.'[19]

The dramatic consequences of *Fiction in the Archives* for social historians have been such that it is now impossible, whatever their period of study, for them to treat the narratives contained in judicial or other similar records as more-or-less transparent 'documentary' accounts of various social facts, from which findings can be straightforwardly gleaned. Instead, most attention is now given to their shape and style – the forms they were in some sense required to take for them to succeed in doing whatever it was that they were told *for* in the particular context of their telling. Rather than illustrative, albeit distorted, accounts of social reality – accounts with 'contents' that have to be separated out from their unfortunately fictional trappings – they have become texts that construct and represent the socially real, without any sacrificing of the notions of agency and practice – or indeed, of reality. Their historians, likewise, have been transposed from analysts of causes and structures into readers of plots and tropes – experts in 'cultural narratives'.[20] In this new guise, the courtroom stories of early modern England, in particular, have become the basis of innovative analyses of the workings of sex, gender, and honour in the daily experiences of women, and of the nature and representation of domestic and sexual violence.[21]

The potential benefits of reading witchcraft narratives in the same terms are comparable, though as yet only partially realized. Certainly, a very powerful case has recently been made by feminist historians and historians of gender for seeing them as evocations of the world of the household and the anxieties of motherhood. In this respect, witchcraft history now intersects with feminism in a much more fruitful way than was initially the case.[22] But in 1995, in one of the first attempts to look at the role of narrative conventions in deciding matters of truth and fact in witchcraft cases, Frances Dolan argued that critics had still 'barely begun to consider how stories operated as evidence in witch trials and the processes by which the legal system adjudicated among competing narratives'.[23] Part 1 of this volume offers examples of what has been achieved since these words were written. In each of the four chapters, what was said by or about witches during the legal process or in the pamphlet literature associated with it is no longer regarded as reasonably raw description. Instead, its content and meaning is seen as contingent upon the circumstances of its production and use. If, as Peter Rushton makes particularly clear for northern England in Chapter 1, testimony was built around certain kinds of story-types and featured particular themes and arguments, it was because these were formally required for judicial procedures actually to work; these procedures had to begin, continue, and reach a conclusion and carry conviction with those involved at every stage. In this sense, judicial protocols – whether strict rules or looser conventions – demanded that the right kind of story be told, not that it be simply descriptive of some objectively ascertained situation. The truth about witchcraft – its reality – was created rather than reflected by the legal process. Something similar happened with the narratives told in the printed pamphlets which historians, assuming them to offer a uniform record, have so often in the past made the basis of their studies of English witchcraft. As representations of witchcraft, they were subject to variations of genre. Their form was a function of, first, their reliance on the stories told by victims and accused, and produced largely by the legal process, and then, from the 1590s onwards, their adoption of third-person narratives of a non-legal kind. What they said about witches varied accordingly. In what respect, then, was the classic pattern of the witch's revenge following a refusal of charity a reflection of a single social reality? Among the most striking of Marion Gibson's arguments on the subject in Chapter 2 are her suggestions that this was itself a story-type, that it was shaped in accordance with a particular kind of legal accusation and source, and that it was bound to reproduce itself by shaping 'perceptions of future encounters and subsequent narrations of these as accusations' (p. 46).

It should not be thought, however, that the rules and conventions of telling stories about witches simply dictated what came to be said. In their essays, both Malcolm Gaskill in Chapter 3 and Diane Purkiss in Chapter 4 illustrate how the testimony of witnesses and the confessions of the accused, however stylized in accordance with legal requirements, contained strategies for being heard, not simply formulaic patterns that satisfied only their listeners. Through the adoption of narrative themes, idioms, and motifs of their own and of their culture, they were able to give voice to their interests and suspicions, their feelings and desires, all within the formal setting of persuasive legal storytelling. The way depositions were structured thus allows access to the mental and psychological worlds of the people who made them, not just the expectations of those who demanded them or wrote them down. This helps us, as Gaskill puts it, to understand witchcraft from within. In the cases of Elspeth Reoch and Janet Weir, whose confessions to Scottish courts mingled the themes of fairies and incest – the first seeming to help shape their memories of the second – there is the likelihood, even, that this setting permitted them to talk about things that they could not say or that could not be said in any other. This may not seem like power, but storytelling may well have provided a form of it to otherwise powerless and inaudible people.

In Part 2 of the collection, three further essays explore the need to read witchcraft belief and disbelief, and in the first example witchcraft trials too, in a very much broader context than has hitherto been the case. This, again, reflects an important change of emphasis. One product of the puzzlement that witchcraft used to cause was a tendency to treat contemporary discussions of it in isolation. Witchcraft was a strange phenomenon in that it was difficult to absorb into familiar versions of the early modern world. It could not be connected to anything so lofty as philosophy or political theory, and certainly not to the sciences; it was related to religion and theology only as 'superstition', and to law only as legalized persecution. Today, with much of that world rendered unfamiliar and all of it desegregated, nothing is allowed to stand apart from its larger symbolic order or from its other components. We have come to realize that witchcraft encroached upon, and was in turn influenced by, a wide range of contemporary cultural phenomena and, to be intelligible, must be located in relation to them. These included, potentially, the whole sweep of religious and political change and controversy in the early modern centuries. Here, demons and witches appeared not just in literal terms as threats and enemies; they were also vehicles for ideology and propaganda. Believing in them or denying them had uses and implications across the spectrum of affiliations in church and state. To work out the historical significance of any particular enunciation of opinion in these circumstances is to write a much broader kind of witchcraft history than has usually been attempted.[24]

For Peter Elmer in Chapter 5, writing on England, it embraces, in principle, the entire range of views on public affairs, from the local to the national level. The fate of witchcraft, he writes, 'both as a body of ideas and as a crime, was inextricably bound up with the demands of contemporary religious and political debate' (p. 115). Between the accession of Elizabeth and the Restoration of the Stuarts and beyond, its uneven distribution over time and by region, and the manifold forms it took, correlate to the manner in which the prevailing political élites and their factions envisaged national and communal order, the nature of authority, and the need for change. In this sense, witchcraft was a kind of idiomatic resource, infinitely flexible and put to often contradictory uses, in terms of which political and religious communities confronted their ever fluctuating condition. The trials that occurred, including those associated with the activities of Matthew Hopkins in the 1640s, bear the marks of this, arising as and when the peculiar chemistry that was involved 'primed' those responsible for turning accusations into legal proceedings.

For David Wootton in Chapter 6 and Jonathan Barry in Chapter 7, the starting point is the personal position and the individual text, yet these turn out, again, to be deeply implicated in the very broadest issues of the day. The demonological scepticism of Reginald Scot and the demonological orthodoxy of Arthur Bedford, separated by nearly 150 years of history, were moments of the intersection of similar things, notably the social and moral values pertaining to different religions or to different conceptions of the place of religion in English affairs. In the case of Scot, disbelief in witchcraft stemmed from unorthodox ways of reading the Bible, thinking about sin, and talking about devils – ways that link him, via Wootton's exciting new 'intellectual microhistory', first to Abraham Fleming (beloved by generations of student readers of Scot's *Discoverie of witchcraft* as 'Gnimelf Maharba') and then to the Elizabethan Family of Love. At stake in this theological affinity with the Familists, and perhaps even a personal commitment to them, were matters central to the state of the church and its relations with dissent, the religious proclivities of the Elizabethan regime, and the place of communitarianism and egalitarianism in contemporary

social and religious thought. In the early eighteenth century, Arthur
Bedford's moral campaign was aimed at the playhouses of Bristol, not
witchcraft trials, but he blamed the theatre both for diabolism in
England and for the diabolizing *of* England. Quite simply, there were
too many plays that depended on the presence of demons, textual or
actual. In the vocabulary of traditional demonology, Bedford saw the
theatre as an anti-church, embattled against, and thereby helping to
define, the true version. But, again, the setting for this polemic could
not have been more contemporary – a contest for power and authority
in an urban community still living in the aftermath of revolution, and
divided politically and morally by the 'reformation of manners' and
the maintenance of the 'godly state'. Clearly, the devil remained as
relevant to this contest as he was to its Elizabethan equivalent.

Readings of this sort make intelligible the attitudes to demonology
of those who would otherwise remain oddities – the man who seems
too extreme a disbeliever in one age and the man who seems too
extreme a believer in another. In this way, refusing to draw boundaries
around the subject of witchcraft helps us to make better sense of
particular instances in its history. On the other hand, by looking
microhistorically at individuals like Scot and Bedford, we obtain access
by a sometimes surprisingly direct route to the central debates of their
cultures. This is because we are now able to view witchcraft in terms
of its power to shape and reflect larger ideologies – what Ian Bostridge
has called 'the function which the notion of the witch played within
the ideologies of the educated'.[25] Indeed, all the essays in Parts 1 and 2
of this volume concentrate on the way *our* interpretative habits have
changed. In Part 3, however, we turn more precisely to the ethnographic
question of how men and women living at the time of the witchcraft
prosecutions or taking part in them tried to understand these episodes
for themselves. The things that historians interpret are always already
interpretations; we do not examine an unmediated past. In this sense,
our reading of historical phenomena now can never be separated from
the way they were read at the time. In the case of witchcraft, this was
done from certain positions and with certain purposes, with or without
certain skills, and in terms of certain categories and assumptions. While
the subject was often bizarre to those involved, they were not bereft of
interpretations of it or ways of coming to terms with it and fitting it
into a scheme of things. How was this done and what issues and
arguments were at stake?

The final group of essays suggests some answers. Each of them is rich in illustrative detail concerning the first-hand experience of witchcraft, and allied things, in a different area of Europe – Lorraine, Aragón, south-west German, England. Each, too, enables us to see how different readings of witchcraft were achieved. First in line were the families and neighbours of both victims and witches, especially the women of the community, who, in Thomas Robisheaux's essay (Chapter 10), for example, interpreted the death of Anna Fessler in terms of cognitive perceptions moulded by a particular culture of mothering and childbirth, considerations of status and credibility, intimate knowledge of village enmities, and a sensitivity to the rituals of time. In Chapter 9 María Tausiet treats this complex act of interpretation as one of translation too. Faced with the deaths of children, the villagers of Aragón, as well as the defence lawyers for their witches, knew that more or less intentional infanticide by the parents might explain them – it was even, she says, a 'well-established parental custom' (p. 184). They often chose instead to invoke the traditional stereotype of the child-killing witch, in an easy and convenient switch from one language to another. The next layer of involvement was that of the local experts – magical healers and other 'cunning folk' – who specialized in detecting witchcraft and identifying its sources, but who in Chapter 8 end up in Robin Briggs's archival sources as accused witches themselves. Here was another group with the techniques and the power to influence the course of witchcraft episodes by reading one set of meanings into a particular situation rather than another. Indeed, the metaphor is peculiarly apt in their case, since they evidently thought that 'everyday events had multiple meanings, that virtually everything was full of significance …'. 'Witch doctors' could be decisive in this respect, since not unnaturally, they saw witchcraft in terms of diagnosis and cure, rather than accusation and prosecution; for them, and presumably for their many clients, it was 'a natural idiom in which to understand and manage sickness' (pp. 176–7). Finally, operating not only in a different cultural environment, but also on a different time-scale, were the interventions of legal and medical academics and professionals who, for example, tried to decide whether Anna Fessler's death was really due to witchcraft or to poisoning. In the context of the increasing use of autopsies in criminal cases and a developing legal caution about witchcraft cases in particular, the activity of dissecting her body and inspecting it for signs became an especially critical form of public reading and debate – *forensic* medicine indeed.

The last contribution to this volume, Chapter 11 by Katharine

Hodgkin, tackles these same issues arising from the patterns and problems of contemporary interpretation, but also returns us to our start, and in a sense to Julio Caro Baroja – though with some additional question marks. Linked to witchcraft in her essay are the two allied cases of visionary prophecy and madness taken from the experiences of Anna Trapnel and Dionys Fitzherbert. These are allied cases because they too invite us to consider both what our own response should be to what often seems like irrationality in the past and how those immediately involved responded to unreason themselves. They too involve phenomena whose reality was taken for granted by some at least at the time, but which to the historian seem impossible. One solution to this is to identify historically all the various possible explanations of irrationality available to contemporaries, and the criteria for making them, and leave things at that. Prophecy and madness, after all, were no less contentious subjects than witchcraft, and contemporaries were no less divided about them. Each encounter with unreason, as this essay makes clear, entailed arguments about how to read the behaviour and how to assign it, perhaps uneasily, to a category – was it a divine, a demonic, or a natural disturbance, or a mixture of these? To appreciate the alternatives available, means invoking the various discourses of medicine, theology, philosophy, and so on, together with the kinds of individual judgements and choices that might be made when confronting strange actions – including those made by the subjects themselves. The merit of this approach is that it is symmetrical with regard to the forms that reason and unreason, reality and unreality, could take in the past; essentially, it is what Caro Baroja had in mind. The difficulty with it, and with the cultural relativism to which it leads, is that it may diminish the sense of strangeness and downright impossibility that nevertheless attaches itself to some historical events. Here, again, we may need to employ the concept of 'making sense' with caution. For although witchcraft will probably always be linked in some way to the bizarre, our reactions to it might well be blunted if it were not.

Notes

1. Julio Caro Baroja, *The World of the Witches*, trans. O. N. V. Glendinning (London, 1964), p. xiii.
2. Ibid., pp. xi–xiv.

3. Ibid., pp. 3–14; cf. E. E. Evans-Pritchard, *Theories of Primitive Religion* (Oxford, 1965), pp. 20–47.
4. Caro Baroja, *World of the Witches*, p. 13.
5. Ibid., p. 257.
6. See the collection by Bernard Lepetit (ed.), *Les Formes de l'expérience: Une autre histoire sociale* (Paris, 1995) and the essay review by Gareth Stedman Jones, forthcoming in *Annales: Histoire, Sciences Sociales*. The issues for historians were summarized in the early pages of John E. Toews, 'Intellectual History after the Linguistic Turn: The Autonomy of Meaning and the Irreducibility of Experience', *American Historical Review*, 92 (1987), 879–907, and for anthropologists in Victor Turner and Edward Bruner (eds), *The Anthropology of Experience* (Urbana and Chicago, IL, 1986), see esp. Bruner's introduction, 'Experience and its Expressions', pp. 3–30. The concept of experience is decisively reformulated, but not abandoned by Joan Wallach Scott, *Gender and the Politics of History* (London, 1988).
7. Katharine Hodgkin, 'Historians and Witches', *History Workshop Journal*, 45 (1998), 272.
8. Stanislav Andreski, *Syphilis, Puritanism and Witch Hunts: Historical Explanations in the Light of Medicine and Psychoanalysis with a Forecast about Aids* (London, 1989).
9. Jon Oplinger, *The Politics of Demonology: The European Witchcraze and the Mass Production of Deviance* (London, 1990). The latest example is Laurie Winn Carlson, *A Fever in Salem: A New Interpretation of the New England Witch Trials* (Chicago, IL, 1999), which attributes the Salem trials to an epidemic of encephalitis.
10. Robin Briggs, *Witches and Neighbours: The Social and Cultural Context of European Witchcraft* (London, 1996), *passim*; cf. his essay '"Many Reasons Why": Witchcraft and the Problem of Multiple Explanation', in Jonathan Barry, Marianne Hester, and Gareth Roberts (eds), *Witchcraft in Early Modern Europe: Studies in Culture and Belief* (Cambridge, 1996), pp. 49–63.
11. For telling points relating to explaining witchcraft and the supernatural away, see Diane Purkiss, *The Witch in History* (London, 1996), ch. 3 'The Witch in the Hands of the Historians', esp. pp. 61, 77–9.
12. This view formed only a small part of *Religion and the Decline of Magic*, as is made clear by Jonathan Barry, 'Introduction: Keith Thomas and the Problem of Witchcraft', in Barry et al. (eds), *Witchcraft in Early Modern Europe*, pp. 1–45.
13. Briggs, *Witches and Neighbours*, p. 10.
14. For discussions of some of these issues, see the review feature 'Witchcraft and the Historical Imagination', *History Workshop Journal*, 45 (1998), 265–77.
15. Briggs, *Witches and Neighbours*, p. 13: '[Witchcraft] no longer seems a strange aberration, calling for some very special explanation, but an integral part of past European society.'
16. See the essays in the collections by Bryan R. Wilson (ed.), *Rationality* (Oxford, 1970); and Martin Hollis and Steven Lukes (eds), *Rationality and*

Relativism (Oxford, 1982), esp. Peter Winch's contribution to the first volume, 'Understanding a Primitive Society', pp. 78–111.

17. Renato Rosaldo, *Culture and Truth: The Remaking of Social Analysis* (Boston, MA, 1989), esp. ch. 6 'Narrative Analysis'; Jerome Bruner, *Actual Minds, Possible Worlds* (London, 1986); Paul Ricoeur, *Time and Narrative*, trans. K. McLaughlin and D. Pellauer, 3 vols (London, 1984–88).

18. Rosaldo, *Culture and Truth*, p. 135.

19. Miri Rubin, *Gentile Tales: The Narrative Assault on Late Medieval Jews* (London, 1999), pp. 2–3.

20. Sarah Maza, 'Stories in History: Cultural Narratives in Recent Works in European History', *American Historical Review*, 101 (1996), 1493–515.

21. Laura Gowing, *Domestic Dangers: Women, Words, and Sex in Early Modern London* (Oxford, 1996), esp. pp. 42–58, 232–62; Frances E. Dolan, *Dangerous Familiars: Representations of Domestic Crime in England, 1550–1700* (London, 1994); Miranda Chaytor, 'Husband(ry): Narratives of Rape in the Seventeenth Century', *Gender and History*, 7 (1995), 378–407. For other explorations of narrative in the context of crime, see Lincoln B. Faller, *Turned to Account: The Forms and Functions of Criminal Biography in late Seventeenth- and early Eighteenth-Century England* (Cambridge, 1987); David Lindley, *The Trials of Frances Howard: Fact and Fiction at the Court of King James* (London, 1993); and Judith Moore, *Appearance of Truth: The Story of Elizabeth Canning and Eighteenth-Century Narrative* (London, 1994).

22. See particularly, Lyndal Roper, *Oedipus and the Devil: Witchcraft, Sexuality, and Religion in Early Modern Europe* (London, 1994); Diane Purkiss, 'Women's Stories of Witchcraft in Early Modern England: The House, the Body, the Child', *Gender and History*, 7 (1995), 408–32; and Deborah Willis, *Malevolent Nurture: Witch-Hunting and Maternal Power in Early Modern England* (London, 1995). Malcolm Gaskill, 'Reporting Murder: Fiction in the Archives in Early Modern England', *Social History*, 23 (1998), 1–30, deals in part with witchcraft cases. Robin Briggs speaks of witchcraft presenting itself as 'an overlapping set of narratives, which might be envisaged as comprising a mosaic, that contain both smaller and larger patterns': *Witches and Neighbours*, p. 12.

23. Frances E. Dolan, '"Ridiculous Fictions": Making Distinctions in the Discourses of Witchcraft', *Differences: A Journal of Feminist Cultural Studies*, 7 (1995), 82–110.

24. This has become most apparent, perhaps, in relation to demonology; see Ian Bostridge, *Witchcraft and Its Transformations, c.1650–c.1750* (Oxford, 1997); Stuart Clark, *Thinking with Demons: The Idea of Witchcraft in Early Modern Europe* (Oxford, 1997); and Jonathan L. Pearl, *The Crime of Crimes: Demonology and Politics in France 1560–1620* (Waterloo, Ontario, 1999).

25. Bostridge, *Witchcraft and its Transformations*, p. 4.

Part One

History and Story in Witchcraft Trials

Chapter One
Texts of Authority: Witchcraft Accusations and the Demonstration of Truth in Early Modern England*

Peter Rushton

istorians may no longer see themselves as storytellers, despite the return to narrative styles of writing, but they have always relied upon stories from the past for their sources. The interpretation of these recorded stories has become problematic in the years since the 'linguistic turn' in historiography. This is not the place to review the problems of treating history as text, nor deal with the uncertainties and dilemmas this new direction caused.[1] However, one useful outcome was that the production and reception of historically recorded statements became a major focus. In research into the legal system, however, the new linguistic or literary perspectives had a limited impact. Clearly, literary analysis can enrich the understanding of some judicial sources, as Natalie Zemon Davis showed in *Fiction in the Archives*.[2] However, she has been criticized for attempting the impossible task of recovering the authors' original *intentions*, rather than trying to uncover the 'meaning the text or story can produce in particular contexts'.[3] Intention

*   I would like to thank Stuart Clark and the participants at the 1998 Swansea conference for their helpful responses to an earlier version of this paper, and particularly Jim Sharpe and Malcolm Gaskill for comments and pointers to vital sources.

is naturally difficult to establish given poor or fragmentary evidence, but equally meanings within the judicial context cannot be easily inferred from a simple outline of the legal processes and courtroom setting. Yet unless we understand more of the rules governing the process of forming and communicating legal stories, and the way this shaped the narrative forms adopted, we shall misread our evidence. The pioneering work of Davis and Peter King, looking at stories told to secure reprieves or pardons by highlighting the factors which influenced the granting of mercy by the powerful, revealed the rules of what Pieter Spierenburg calls the 'game with pardons'. 'Game' is too strong a word, but its use does indicate an important aspect of judicial statements: they are not freely chosen or constructed without constraint. There were, and are, rules governing the forms of legal texts, even if they are not explicitly stated at all times.[4]

It is therefore important to examine the influence of the legal process on the forms of story told before, and in, court. Even Keith Thomas has been castigated for failing 'to allow sufficiently for the shaping of the evidence we have by its status as legal evidence'. So we should be aware of the judicial framework within which our texts were produced. As Brook Thomas remarks, 'we can read a legal text *as if* it were literature, but doing so deprives it of its legal function.'[5] Studies of modern law courts have frequently noted that storytelling is integral to adversarial judicial processes, with lawyers and judges alike adopting a narrative style in presenting or summing up evidence.[6] Therefore we should not be surprised by the use of stories in the early modern legal context. In many ways, the following analysis is heavily influenced by parallel developments in recent social science which reinforce scepticism about the objectivity of texts, while simultaneously seeking to examine how the social relations and context of their production affect the forms they take.

Textualization and the Historical Record

The meaning of archival texts, far more than that of the printed word, is bound up with the context of their production and use. Yet historians have tended to address the conditions under which their documents have been produced, copied or published only where their reliability has been in question. But the processes lying behind the creation of many historical documents mark a fundamental shift in social modes

of self-presentation, the inevitable outcome of increasingly pervasive
literate bureaucracies. The development of surnames, familiarity with
public and official processes of manor and parish, techniques of
recording the events of personal life in records, growing skill in
presenting evidence in courts, all point to the impact of literacy on
self-identification, particularly in the early modern period.[7] This has
been described as the *textualization* of social life, in which we are forced
to place our lives, relationships, experiences, duties and obligations,
and so on, in publicly-available texts. It is comparable to reification in
that we are required to produce evidence in a material form. The
resulting text, of course, must also be a truthful account, in the sense
of being socially or officially verifiable. Textualization, so common
today, has led some commentators to conclude that it is a product purely
of modernity, but this may be to confuse the modern with the new. As
Dorothy Smith puts it, 'the texts' capacity to transcend the essentially
transitory character of social processes and to remain uniform across
separate and diverse local settings' allows its transfer from the local
context to a wider world. Legal records, especially the statements by
witnesses and accusers, are typical transferable texts, making the
individual available to someone – anyone with authorized access – in
another location, as well as to the state.[8]

Textualization demands personal expression, producing its highest
form in the growing numbers of early modern autobiographies.[9] But
in the official forums of early modern society, individuals became
accustomed to rendering an account of their lives, their experiences,
and their very identities. This was probably gender biased: it is highly
likely that men were not only more literate, but more expert in grasping
the technicalities of the law and its forms of self-presentation. It is
notable that more men were likely to have indictments against them
dismissed at the preliminary stage, declared 'no true bill', or 'quashed'
on technical grounds, perhaps reflecting their greater skill at issuing
challenges.[10] Legal records are therefore one product of compulsory
textualization, which occasionally reveal the deep emotions and private
details of personal lives. The transference of spoken words into written
form raises the question of the precise relationship of speech to text. In
a highly verbal culture, what Jack Goody calls 'the substitution of the
text for utterance' was as yet incomplete. However, as Brian Stock
suggests, in certain circumstances 'texts were not always written down,
but they were invariably understood as if they were'.[11] The resulting
documentation makes up official records, what James Scott calls the

public transcripts which conform to a dominant culture, but they may also reveal the *hidden* transcripts of personal, communal, and perhaps nonconformist beliefs.[12]

Oaths, Statements, and the Performance of the Law

Judicial decisions resulted from public performances of narrative accounts, which, by being accepted, became authoritative versions of reality. In this sense, truth was 'constructed' in what was called *courts of record*, those with final authority – the final word, in fact: 'One may affirm a thing, and another deny it, but if a Record once saye the word, no man shall be received to averre (or speake) against it', said William Lambarde.[13] The process of achieving this level of public certainty was tortuous. Those appearing before the law were subject to various requirements, one of which was accountability: giving an account of yourself was the essence of subordination to legitimate authority. Vagabonds and incorrigible rogues, such as Northumberland's gypsies, the 'Faws', were transported in the eighteenth century because they could 'give no account of themselves'. More generally, being uncooperative under examination by magistrates provided considerable ammunition for the prosecution. It may have been a popular belief that witches revealed themselves by silence under questioning: 'for it used to be so among the witches, they could not speak before the magistrate', recorded Anna Trapnell, a Fifth Monarchist, who by contrast could not stop talking when hauled before the justices.[14] Secondly, statements had to be given on oath: without one, magistrates would not regard a case as seriously established. Possibly, by the seventeenth century, oaths in general 'were not taken as seriously as they had been in earlier centuries', but it was equally true that early modern society was 'littered with oaths'. Perjury had the wider meaning, not just of changing a story in court, but breaking an oath of office, in effect dereliction of duty.[15] Oaths had a political function, particularly in demonstrating loyalty, but at the local level, justices of the peace used them as a means of weeding out bad from good stories. Even in the middle of the eighteenth century, the oath remained important. Accusers had to stand by their oaths, and the accused could be cleared by them if given with convincing vehemence. In this local judicial culture, the oath was a public demonstration of sincerity and truth, a kind of test comparable to ancient ordeals.[16]

Public testimony was therefore subject to a number of requirements before formal proceedings were started. Subsequently, in the trial, standing by your text was the essence of court appearance, involving performance under oath of your statements in a testing public reaffirmation. The relation of the oral testimony given in court to the documents created in the pre-trial processes is obscure in criminal cases at this time. Holdsworth records that it was a general rule in the sixteenth and early seventeenth centuries, particularly in civil law, that the contents of a written document could not be varied by oral evidence. Consistency through repeated questioning and recording testimony under oath was often regarded as proof of truthfulness: of Anne Whittle (known as Old Chattox) in Lancashire in 1612, it was said:

> She lived in the Forrest of Pendle amongst this wicked company of danger-
> ous Witches. Yet in her Examination and Confession, she dealt always very
> plainely and truely: for upon a speciall occasion being oftentimes examined
> in open Court, shee was never found to vary, but alwayes to agree in one,
> and the selfe same thing.[17]

It is unknown whether, in the early modern period, all witnesses were required to undergo this type of assessment through repetitive examination, a procedure which led Unsworth to designate the English system 'sub-inquisitorial', more closely resembling some continental practices. Barbara Shapiro comments that the turning point seems to have been in 1563, when legislation made it possible to compel witnesses to attend the trials and rendered perjury (in effect, the alteration of a text) a crime. The process of trial increasingly became a *documentary* one of witnesses or victims and their statements in writing, all of which had to be assessed for truthfulness and trustworthiness.[18] This shift may have been completed only by the end of the seventeenth century. It is striking to see the contrast between Edward Coke, who asserted that 'evidence of witnesses to the jury is no part of a criminal trial, for trial is trial by jury, not by witnesses', compared with Matthew Hale 70 years later, demanding testimony from 'credible and authentic witnesses'.[19] The question arises whether witchcraft prosecutions were allowed greater scope in producing testimony, and, in encouraging the use of statements from witnesses as well as victims, witchcraft trials placed greater reliance on circumstantial evidence. Hale cited witchcraft cases as examples where testimony of very young witnesses had been allowed, an exception to the rule that people under 14 were usually unable to understand the importance of an oath and the nature of truth.[20] Was witchcraft exceptional, therefore, not as a crime, but in its type of trial? The Elizabethan witchcraft statute coincided with the new law on witnesses, and both witnesses and witchcraft figured more prominently after the 1560s. In the Lancashire trials, the judge made careful efforts to have evidence given orally, so that the defendants could hear each detail, and told them on their conviction that they could not be unhappy with the proceedings, 'nor with the witnesses who have been tried, as it were, in the fire'.[21]

Analysing Stories: Content, Connections, and Expectations

Witchcraft trials involved what, by today's standards, seem extraordinary stories. In some ways, the contents of English trial narratives were predictable, the result of expectations fuelled by theological teachings, popular beliefs, famous cases, and the print literature which grew from the late sixteenth century onwards. In northern England the evidence suggests that a number of themes were continually stressed in accusations (see Malcolm Gaskill's chapter in this volume). The aim here, however, is not to examine the content so much as the structure of the testimonies. We should not mistake narratives of this kind for purely factual chronological accounts, what Hayden White terms mere chronicles. What distinguishes narratives is the use of structures or plots which, by selecting significant elements for emphasis, also construct a model of causation leading to a convincing conclusion. Despite the use of the term 'narrative' for the opening section of Kenneth Starr's report on the case against President Clinton, it is clearly an argumentative and carefully-structured *accusation*.[22] As in the past, no prosecutor's narrative is an innocent account of events. Content analysis is certainly one way of approaching the problem of why some accusations worked. It is probable that testimony which drew upon the established elements of witchcraft stood a greater chance of being believed. This is to see legal narratives as drawing upon a kind of cookbook of convincing ingredients of 'phrases, motifs and images'.[23] In north-east England – the location for the narratives used for analysis here – it is likely that a handful of early cases set the character of local beliefs, and that some of the themes were then repeated in many others. One frequent element was the vision of the witch appearing, usually at night, to the victim and other witnesses.

This spectral bewitchment was found in half the 'little' cases occurring outside the two great outbreaks of 1649–50 and 1673.[24] Two of the earliest pamphlets produced by people from the region contained spectral appearances, tormenting of the victim, and confirmatory witnesses, suggesting that there was a long established tradition. A 1641 pamphlet, *Most Fearefull and Strange Newes from the Bishoppricke of Durham*, has distinctly religious overtones, with the power of prayer demonstrated by the defeat of the devil who appeared in several guises, most commonly as a headless bear (no named witch seems to have been involved). The other, which recounts the bewitching of the children of Mrs Mary Moore in 1650, and was probably in her own words, involved spiritual battles between her daughter's angels and an attacking dragon. It seems to have been motivated by resentment that one of the accused, Dorothy Swinow, widow of a Colonel Swinow, escaped to Berwick where the authorities refused to arrest her. Curiously, the pamphlet, while recording the death in gaol of one of the accused, John Hutton, ignores the execution of another, Jane Martin, the miller's wife of Chatton, hanged in Newcastle in August 1650. One key witness, Margaret White, confessed that she had served the devil for five years (having sexual intercourse with him twice), possessed a familiar, and had been told by him that she would never want: yet she seems to have escaped any penalty. The group of accused women had met the devil in a house to eat and drink and make merry.[25] The resemblances between these early cases and the post-Restoration accusations suggest the existence, for about 40 years, of a consistent set of anxieties about witchcraft, with some frequently-repeated characteristics, and a congruity between the printed versions, the judicial storytellers' accounts, and their audience's expectations. Whether it was memory alone or possession of printed accounts which perpetuated this culture, it is impossible to establish, but clearly narrators were providing what they already knew their local listeners would believe.[26]

Testimony as Argument: Stories in Court and in Law

Credible contents were not sufficient to establish the legal validity of witnesses' narratives:

> Those who chose to employ the official machinery against witches were
> obliged to shape the local fears and rumours from which the prosecution

emanated to the formalities of the law as defined by the statutes and to the reading of these by magistrates and judges.[27]

We need therefore to distinguish stories which were popularly credible from those which were judicially acceptable. Many accounts were unconvincing, not because they omitted suitably terrifying components, but because they did not add up to a workable accusation.

Witchcraft narratives need to be examined as persuasive arguments, and can for this purpose be classified in various ways according to their argumentative structure and testimonial purpose. One common type is the account which justifies the definition of a situation as stemming from witchcraft: this necessitates a switch from normal to abnormal. Mary Douglas argued that in witchcraft accusations there are social restraints on perception, determining how a case is acknowledged. The problem for analysis is therefore how perceptions are publicly altered and sustained.[28] Zande forms of reasoning famously show that such changes in definition have to be justified by rational argumentative procedures. For example, termites will inevitably undermine a granary, even that of a competent builder, in the end: so only a premature, unpredicted collapse of a well-built building, in effect, an undeserved misfortune, can be due to witchcraft. This suggests that witchcraft has to be argued rather than just asserted, by telling an *extraordinary* story. Christianity saw suffering as a normal state, 'the just punishment of a just God for particular sins', so 'the practice of medicine tended to affirm that all human maladies, including disease, were traceable to God or the devil.'[29] A challenge to the divine interpretation of suffering required what Barthes calls a *shifter*, whereby demonstrable evidence was monitored, evaluated, and new conclusions drawn.[30] In witchcraft cases this may be the point when collective experience defined the situation as *unnatural*, where, to use Erving Goffman's term, the *frame* changed. In the case of Isobel Story, this unnatural explanation was the last resort when all else has failed. Both the victim and a helpful visitor came to a common conclusion: Nicholas Johnson recorded –

That being consulted about the health of Mr Robert Johnson of Newcastle, after he had seen his water told him that he would send or bring him something that he would apply to his leggs and armes which accordingly he did, but the sayd Robert Johnson told him that several such things he used but to no purpose yet he applyed them; and which time the foresayd Robert Johnson told the sayd Nicholas Johnson he conceaved that he had some wrong done him (meaneing by witchcraft), to which the said Nicholas answered 'Now so you have, and that by Bely Story', and further affirmed that she was an arrant witch, and further desired him the sayd Robert Johnson to distraigne hir from any employment that might relate to him ... and bid him not doubt that within a short time he should recover.[31]

Victims might diagnose or suggest witchcraft, but were not freely allowed to make accusations until the community agreed: then they became a divining rod, and the community the approving watchers of successful detection and accusation. External opinion was sometimes central in either initiating or confirming the shift in definition. Some consultants may have been magical specialists, 'orthodox' medical practitioners, or simply the better educated.[32] Alexander Nickle in 1653 told Lady Widdrington that his sick child had cried out that Margaret Stothard was pressing out her heart and likely to break her back. Widdrington replied that 'she could not understand the distemper unless she was bewitched'. This formed one of several of convincing-sounding pieces of testimony against Stothard, including a spectral appearance at the foot of John Mill's bed, and (in her practice as a healer) an effective cure for Jane Carr's child by sucking out the illness and transferring it to a calf. In other circumstances ministers or doctors provided the external validation, as happened in the Throckmorton case in Warboys in 1593, where the doctor consulted by the family concluded rather weakly that 'all surely cannot be well'.[33] With the witch identified, organized confrontations between victim and accused, particularly those entailing the drawing of blood from the 'witch' (above the breast), then become a staple part of the confirmation of the identification and subsequent testimony.

It was most important in this switch of frame from natural to unnatural that, firstly, effective public opinion was marshalled. Secondly, it needed what was to some extent a properly 'rational' procedure, to use an anachronistic term, but one which signifies processes paralleled by those of the Azande. Alternative theories had to be demonstrably false, and the condition clearly anomalous, for an accusation to be made. Irrespective of whether the actual events followed this pattern in reality, this kind of narrative testimony provided a summation and an argumentative justification of the process by which suspicion hardened into accusation.

Victims and Witnesses

A group of depositions by victims of spectral witchcraft attack suggests that victims' stories have their own dynamic. The victim, sometimes through the mouth of a close relative, had to provide a dramatic narrative of innocence, suffering, and survival which led to only one conclusion, the truth of both the bewitchment and the witch's identity. This kind of story may have had an established format, to judge from some of the repeated features in north-east sources, although there may be parallels in a longer history of Christian stories of travail and redemption. Significantly, the power of prayer or faith is stressed in the printed as well as unpublished accounts, establishing by implication the godly character of the victims or witnesses. Many victims of this kind of possession were not in positions of social power. Through bewitchment, suggests Harley, they 'became the focus of attention, able to wreak vengeance on even more marginal individuals if they wished'. But their role in these dramas is of uncertain origin, acquired, perhaps, from the reactions and indications provided by a susceptible audience. As Stephen Greenblatt puts it: 'those selected to play the possessed in effect learn their roles without realizing at first that they are roles.'[34]

When identifying the witch, it was essential to demonstrate an *absence of malice*, or even a reluctance to believe ill of that person, which made the accusation more convincing because it was the conclusion of a process of investigation, of discovery and proof, not an instant decision derived from personal resentment.[35] An interesting example of the confirmatory witness's account of spectral bewitchment is that of Anthony Hearon, baker and brewer of Newcastle upon Tyne, against Jane Simpson and Isabel Atkinson. The action started with a dispute between Jane Simpson, a huckster (street-seller), and his wife Dorothy over the price of a pound of cherries. Within days, Dorothy Hearon was ill, 'most strangely and wonderfully handled', and in her sickness sometimes 'rageing madd, other tymes in a laughing and singing condicion, other tymes in a dispareing and disconsolat condicion, and att other tymes in a very solitary and mute condicion'. The crucial turn was the appearance of the witch at the bedside:

> And upon Saturday last aboute three of the clocke in the morning she took a most sad and lamentable fitt crying out to this informer who was lyeing in bedd with her that one Isabell Atchieson and Jane Simpson did afflict and torment her body and were aboute the bedd to carry her away, and this

Informer had much to doe to hold and keep her in bedd and did persist with her cry, saying to this informer doe you not see them, looke where they both stand and the said Dorothy putt by the curten this informer did visably and clearly see the said Isabel Atchieson standing att the beddside in her owne humane and bodyly shape, clothed in a green waistcoate and in the same habitt she dayly weares and this informer calling upon the Lord to be present with him, the said Isabell did vanish and disappeared.

Anthony Hearon then sent for the two women, so that the victim could 'take blood of them', and afterwards she recovered, rose from her bed and called for food, to the astonishment of all observers.[36]

A narrative of this kind depends on a number of shared understandings. While the aim is to lead us into the world of the speaker, into the experiences endured and the conclusions drawn, the means is a narrative of suffering and survival, of accusation and action. Above all, there is more than one witness. While almost all the New England colonies adopted 'some version of the two-witness rule', this essentially scriptural requirement was never incorporated into English law (though Robert Boyle thought it was).[37] Nevertheless, while it was a rule of English law that only one witness was sufficient, it was perhaps harder in practice to call more than one person a liar. *Confirmation of sighting* was therefore useful in cases of familiars or spectres: in the north-east the evidence of co-witnesses, remembering convincing details such as the accused's clothing, was provided in at least half of the 'spectral bewitching' cases. The youth of many of the victims invited legalistic scepticism, so the provision of additional witnesses was an important adjunct to the accusation.[38] Any *strangeness* of the victim's condition, being 'strangely handled in her lyms', had to be diagnosed as devilish, as did the visions seen in the midst of sickness. An accused might artfully reply to an allegation of spectral appearance, as Isobell Atkinson did when confronted by her victim, that 'it was not her but the Devill that was there', suggesting diabolical delusion. This kind of response had to be effectively countered by showing the vision to be genuine rather than the outcome of illness.[39] Testimony could be supported by distinctly odd or terrifying events, the appearance of the witches as animals, the accompanying noises, the flash of fire in the empty chimney, and so on. Such preternatural events had to be more than just wonders, but *signs* of the diabolical.[40]

Participants as Ethnographic Reporters

The third type of story is rare in England: the witnesses participated in witches' gatherings, then acted as ethnographers of the mysterious and narrators of the devilish. All ethnography, it has been realized, is a narrative which constrains what passes for facts: it depends above all on public trust. 'The feet of the natives are large', says (Sir) Raymond Firth of the people of Tikopia, and of course we believe him.[41] Unlike the modern anthropologist, the witchcraft ethnographer was a reporter from a far country to which listeners did not *wish* to travel, but about which they had to know. Eyewitnesses had to be innocent participants, not implicated in what was observed. Nevertheless, some trials relied on treachery among witches. 'Who but Witches can be proofes, and so witnesses of the doings of Witches, since all their Meetings, Conspiracies, Practices, and Murthers, are the workes of Darkeness?' remarked Thomas Potts of the 1612 Lancashire trials in which the accused turned on each other, and a nine-year-old child (Jennet Device) provided crucial evidence. In Scotland, certainly, criminal associates (*socii criminis* or infamous persons) were specifically encouraged to testify in witchcraft trials.[42]

Ethnography is a form of rhetoric: the details must be convincing, and the overall analysis conclusive;

> The text cannot simply transcribe or report, but it must also persuade. The reader must be drawn into its own frame of reference, and come to share the perspectives of the text; it must be found plausible and engaging, arresting or novel ... It needs to reproduce a recognizable world of concrete detail, but not appear to be a mere recapitulation of it ... The anthropologist constructs himself as a credible *witness*, using graphic description to convey the credibility and authenticity of his account.[43]

The same has always been true of witnesses who report their participation – traitors, innocent victims or *agents provocateurs* alike. Anne Armstrong in Northumberland in 1673 went to the witches' meetings (ridden by the witches using an enchanted bridle). There, she saw their activities, and could analyse their organization. What emerges is almost a classical piece of anthropological reportage, derived from intense personal experiences.[44]

Anne Armstrong, 12 May 1673 before John Ridley JP at Willimontswick

Story	Structure
That she hath been sore troubled and tormented and many times taken away by wicked people called witches to there meetings at severall places where there was severall Companies of them and in every Company thirteen witches and every Company there devill (whom they called there Protector) whoe they discoursed with and made there confessions to him what harme and evill they had done, and those that confessed the doing of moste harme the devill made most of them, and those that made but small confession of hurt the devill punished them.	**[A] GENERAL ALARM** 1. Establishes general threat. 2. Asserts personal expertise as objective if reluctant ethnographer. 3. Gives convincing detail of witches' local organization.
And some of the witches she knew, and others she knew not, but she thinkes she can know there faces when she sees them.	**[B] EXPRESSION OF FALLIBILITY**
And the last meeting she was att amongst the witches was upon the second of May last at night when they carried her to Berwicke Bridge end (as they called it) where she see a great number of them: amongst the reste she see one Anne Parteis of Hollisfield, and heard her make her confession and declare to the devill that she did enter into the house of one John Maughan of the parish of Haydon in Northumberland, and found his wife's rocke lying upon the table (and her name was Anne). And she tooke up the rocke to spinne of it, and by the spinneinge of the rocke she had gotten the power of the said Anne that she should never spinne more, and would still torment her till she had her life.	**[C] DIRECT OBSERVATION** 1. Dated offence. 2. Observation of specific acts of deviance.
And this woman now standing before her at the time of giveing this Information is the same woman she heard confess to the Devill she had bewitched Ann Maughan wife to John Maughan.	**[D] DIRECT ACCUSATION**

Significantly, Armstrong establishes her credibility in different ways, appearing both a reluctant participant and ignorant of the people involved prior to the meeting. Moreover, while giving a detailed and thorough analysis of the social organization of witches, she admits the possibility of her own fallibility, perhaps adopting a deliberately disingenuous use of 'powerless speech' to disarm local critics.[45] In the overall structure, she establishes the power of the narrative by moving from the *general* to the *particular*, starting with the general situation in the county, alarming her audience, and then moving with increasing specificity to time, place, and individual action. This movement is found in other narratives from other periods: indeed, it is rather reminiscent of Stanley Cohen's classic model of moral panics, in which doom-laden general warnings are convincingly fulfilled through later individual incidents. A similar internal structure of general/particular contrasts is also found in some of the printed eighteenth-century criminal narratives: the general scene was set in a convincing way, but one which lacked any specific features which could be subjected to criticism. Armstrong does the same, with perhaps a greater tendency to become more specific. Her numerous depositions probably have a sequential structure as well as an internal one, with each building on the previous accusations.[46] Testing this kind of text in court was always difficult, the main attack being directed at the identification of the accused. For example, by courtroom tricks (placing others between the accused and demanding repeated identification of those seen at the meetings), Jennet Device was tested at the Lancashire trials in 1612. She passed, though failure by the Bury St Edmunds girls did not affect the trial's outcome.[47]

Conclusion

With their careful structures of narrative argument, depositions provided a formidable story, which was, perhaps, difficult to oppose. We cannot know the consequences of the north-east cases discussed here, as evidence of verdicts and sentences is mostly lacking. Consequently, textual analysis must dominate the discussion. There are few examples of alternative textualizations, at least by the condemned, although some continued to protest their innocence all the way to the gallows (dying 'impenitent').[48] In the north-east some resisted in the dreadful year of 1650: in Durham one accused woman refused to be searched, and yet was acquitted, while in Newcastle, Eleanor Loumsdale was accused of suborning a witness against one of those executed in August. Moreover, some scepticism was evinced by the stepfather of the Muschamp children as their visions burgeoned. In the only Restoration case of opposition, Daniel Stranger attacked one of the witnesses against his wife Dorothy, apparently in the courtroom itself. But Daniel Stranger had stood surety for one of the women hanged in Newcastle in 1650. Probably he had had bitter experiences, while the public retained a long memory of his involvement.[49]

That violence and illicit acts were needed for opposition suggests that words were still 'deadly', whether written or spoken: they retained their power in the mouths of both supposed witches and their accusers, stubbornly resistant to opposing versions.[50] Historians are equally unable to provide alternative readings of witchcraft accusations in terms of the silences and the unspoken contents. Unlike, say, rape accusations, there is no 'reality' available for us with which to begin a sympathetic reading.[51] 'Bewitchment' is constituted in the depositions themselves: we cannot go behind the testimonies to find another source. There can be no real distinction drawn between facts and evidence, that is, between the accounts of reality and the legal use made of them.[52] If accusations took an appropriately legalistic form, were framed within a convincing narrative structure, and were supported in court by testimony from authoritative witnesses, contemporary criticism could be disabled, the accused left only with blank denials. Words were therefore still powerful: in law and witchcraft alike, they could, in the right framework, still kill their victims.

Notes

1. Robert F. Berkhofer, *Beyond the Great Story: History as Text and Discourse* (Cambridge, MA, 1995).
2. Natalie Zemon Davis, *Fiction in the Archives: Pardon Tales and their Tellers in Sixteenth-Century France* (Stanford, CA, 1987); Malcolm Gaskill, 'Reporting Murder: Fiction in the Archives in Early Modern England', *Social History*, 23 (1998) 1–30.
3. Diane Purkiss, *The Witch in History: Early Modern and Twentieth-Century Representations* (London, 1996), p. 75.
4. P. Spierenburg, *The Spectacle of Suffering: Executions and the Evolution of Repression: From a Preindustrial Metropolis to the European Experience*

(Cambridge, 1984), p. 101; Peter King, 'Decision-Makers and Decision-Making in the English Criminal Law', _Historical Journal_, 27 (1984), 25–58.

5. Jonathan Barry, 'Keith Thomas and the Problem of Witchcraft', in J. Barry et al. (eds),_Witchcraft in Early Modern Europe: Studies in Culture and Belief_ (Cambridge, 1996), p. 9;. Brook Thomas, 'Reflections on the Law and Literature Revival', _Critical Inquiry_, 17:3 (1991), 510–39, see especially p. 533.

6. W. Lance Bennett and Martha S. Feldman, _Reconstructing Reality in the Courtroom_ (London, 1981); Bernard S. Jackson, 'Narrative Theories and Legal Discourse', in Christopher Nash (ed.), _Narrative in Culture:The Use of Storytelling in the Sciences, Philosophy and Literature_ (London, 1990), pp. 28–30; William O'Barr, _Linguistic Evidence: Language, Power and Strategy in the Courtroom_ (New York, 1982), p. 32 suggests narrative styles are seen as more convincing by naive jurors.

7. Christina Larner, _Enemies of God: The Witch-Hunt in Scotland_ (Oxford, 1981), p. 193; Stephen Wilson, _The Means of Naming: A Social and Cultural History of Naming in Western Europe_ (London, 1998).

8. Dorothy E. Smith, _Texts, Facts, Femininity: Exploring the Relations of Ruling_ (London, 1990), pp. 167–8.

9. See Roy Porter (ed.), _Rewriting the Self: Histories from the Renaissance to the Present_ (London, 1997); Jack Goody, _The Logic of Writing and the Organization of Society_ (Cambridge, 1986), ch. 4.

10. See G. Morgan and P. Rushton, _Rogues, Thieves and the Rule of Law: The Problem of Law Enforcement in North-East England, 1718–1800_ (London, 1998), ch. 3.

11. Goody, _The Logic of Writing_, p. 165; Brian Stock, _Listening for the Text: On the Uses of the Past_ (Baltimore, MD, 1990), p. 20.

12. James C. Scott, _Domination and the Arts of Resistance: Hidden Transcripts_ (New Haven, CT, and London, 1990).

13. Jack K. Weber, 'The Power of Judicial Records', _Journal of Legal History_, 9:2 (1988), 180–200, see especially p. 180.

14. Anna Trapnell, 'Report or Plea etc.', reprinted in Elspeth Graham et al. (eds), _Her Own Life: Autobiographical Writings by Seventeenth-Century Englishwomen_ (London, 1989), quotation p. 80; see Morgan and Rushton, _Rogues, Thieves and the Rule of Law_, ch. 4.

15. Contrasting quotations from Barbara J. Shapiro, _Probability and Certainty in Seventeenth-Century England: A Study of the Relationships between Natural Science, Religion, History, Law and Literature_ (Princeton NJ, 1983), p. 186; and John Spurr, 'Perjury, Profanity and Politics', _The Seventeenth Century_, 8:1 (1993), 29–50, see especially p. 30; James Oldham, 'Truth-Telling in the Eighteenth-Century English Courtroom', _Law and History Review_, 12:1 (1994), 95–121.

16. _The Justicing Notebook of the Reverend Edmund Tew, 1750–64, Rector of Boldon_, edited and introduced by G. Morgan and P. Rushton, Surtees Society forthcoming; cases at 5 and 6 August 1763, 14 December 1754; Theodor Reik, 'The Euro-American Trial as Expiatory Ordeal', in Alison Dundes

Rentels and Alan Dundes (eds), *Folk Law: Essays in the Theory and Practice of **Lex Non Scripta**,* 2 vols (Madison, WI, 1995), vol. 1, p. 480.

17. *The Wonderfull Discoverie of Witches in the Countie of Lancaster. With the Arraignment and Triall of Nineteene notorious Witches, at the Assizes and generall Gaole deliverie, holden at the Castle of Lancaster, upon Munday, the seventeenth of August last, 1612 etc.*, Thomas Potts, originally London 1613, introduced and notes by James Crossley, Chetham Society, vol. 6 (Manchester, 1845), p. D2.

18. Richard Godbeer, *The Devil's Dominion: Magic and Religion in Early New England* (Cambridge, 1992), p. 100; C. R. Unsworth, 'Witchcraft Beliefs and Criminal Procedure in Early Modern England', in Thomas G. Watkin (ed.), *Legal Record and Historical Reality* (London, 1989), p. 86. See Shapiro, *Probability and Certainty*, pp. 176 and 180; John H. Langbein, *Torture and the Law of Proof: Europe and England in the Ancien Régime* (Chicago, IL, 1977); see W. Holdsworth, *The History of English Law* (London, 1906–82), vol. 1, 1956, p. 335, and vol. 9, 1982, p. 185; Adam Fox, 'Custom, Memory and the Authority of Writing', in Paul Griffiths et al. (eds), *The Experience of Authority in Early Modern England* (London, 1996), pp. 90–1.

19. Coke in John Bellamy, *Criminal Law and Society in Late Medieval and Tudor England* (Gloucester, 1984), p. 52; Hale in Shapiro, *Probability and Certainty*, p. 180.

20. Holdsworth, *History of English Law*, vol. 9, p. 188; for a recent study of the Bury St Edmunds case, see Gilbert Geis and Ivan Bunn, *A Trial of Witches: A Seventeenth-Century Witchcraft Prosecution* (London, 1997).

21. J. H. Baker, 'The Refinement of English Criminal Jurisprudence, 1500-1848', in *Crime and Criminal Justice in Europe and Canada*, L. A. Knafla (ed.), (Waterloo, Ontario, 1981), pp. 17–42; Shapiro, *Probability and Certainty*, p. 178; *Wonderfull Discoverie of Witches in the Countie of Lancaster*, p. V3. Note Marianne Hester, *Lewd Women and Wicked Witches: A Study of the Dynamics of Male Domination* (London, 1992), p. 127.

22. Hayden White, *The Content of the Form: Narrative Discourse and Historical Representation* (Baltimore, MD, 1987), pp. 21–5; *Clinton: The Starr Report*, foreword by Henry Porter (London, 1998).

23. Malcolm Gaskill, 'Reporting Murder', p. 8.

24. The 1649-50 outbreak in Newcastle and Northumberland involved 39 accused, of whom 17 or 18 were executed (lists differ); 31 were accused in 1673 (by Anne Armstrong). The remaining 29 accused are often poorly documented (105 in all, 99 between 1649 and 1680); Peter Rushton, 'Crazes and Quarrels: The Character of Witchcraft in the North East of England', *Durham Local History Society Bulletin*, 31 (1983), 2–40.

25. *Most Fearefull and Strange Newes from the Bishoppricke of Durham* (London: printed for John Thomas, 1641), and M. A. Richardson, *Reprints of Rare Tracts*, no. 9 (Newcastle upon Tyne: M. A. Richardson, 1843); Mary Moore, *Wonderfull News from the North, or a true relation of the sad and grievous torments, inflicted upon the bodies of three children of Mr George Muschamp, late of the county of Northumberland, by Witch-craft etc.* (London, 1650), p.

25; the miller's wife p. 10; Tyne and Wear Archives Service, MF279, p. 46.

26. Peter Rushton, 'Crazes and Quarrels', pp. 22–5.

27. Clive Holmes, 'Women: Witnesses and Witches', *Past and Present*, 140 (1993), 45–78, p. 76.

28. Mary Douglas (ed.), *Witchcraft Accusations and Confessions* (London, 1970), Introduction, p. xiv.

29. G. Tourney, 'The Physician and Witchcraft in Restoration England', *Medical History*, 16 (1972), 143–55, p. 154; Larner, *Enemies of God*, p. 172.

30. E. Evans-Pritchard, *Witchcraft, Oracles and Magic among the Azande*, abr. edn, (Oxford, 1976), p. 22; Roland Barthes, 'Historical Discourse', in Michael Lane (ed.), *Structuralism: A Reader*, (London, 1970), p. 146.

31. Nicholas Johnson, 26 March 1661, against Isabel Story of Seaton Delavel, Public Records Office, ASSI 45/6/1/134–5, ASSI 44/8; Erving Goffman, *Frame Analysis: An Essay on the Organization of Experience* (Harmondsworth, 1975).

32. See Marijke Gijswijt-Hofstra, 'The European Witchcraft Debate and the Dutch Variant', *Social History*, 15:2 (1990), 189; Michael MacDonald (ed.), *Witchcraft and Hysteria in Elizabethan London: Edward Jorden and the Mary Glover Case* (London, 1991).

33. C. H. L. Ewen, *Witchcraft and Demonianism* (London, 1933), pp. 323–4. Apparently, the only source for the depositions against Stothard is E. Mackenzie, *An Historical, Topographical and Descriptive View of the County of Northumberland etc.*, 2nd edn, (Newcastle upon Tyne, 1825), vol. 2, pp. 33–6. The Throckmorton case is in Barbara Rosen (ed.), *Witchcraft in England, 1558–1618* (Amherst, MA, 1991), p. 242; see also Anne Reiber de Windt, 'Witchcraft and Conflicting Visions of the Ideal Village Community', *Journal of British Studies*, 34 (1995), 427–63.

34. Four cases involved prayers, of 12 in all, two printed, two unpublished; victims in the north-east were two adult men, the rest were seven women and nine children or young people; five of the women were married; of 18 known in all. D. Harley, 'Mental Illness, Magical Medicine and the Devil in Northern England, 1650–1700', in R. French and A. Wear (eds), *The Medical Revolution of the Seventeenth Century* (Cambridge, 1989), p. 143; MacDonald, *Witchcraft and Hysteria*, p. xxxvi; Stephen Greenblatt, *Shakespearean Negotiations: The Circulation of Social Energy in Renaissance England* (Oxford, 1988), p. 107.

35. Dorothy Smith, 'K is Mentally Ill', in *Texts, Facts, Femininity*, originally in *Sociology*, 12 (1978), 23–53.

36. PRO, ASSI 45/7/1/7, 20 July 1664.

37. Edgar J. McManus, *Law and Liberty in Early New England: Criminal Justice and Due Process, 1620–1692* (Amherst, MA, 1993), p. 35; B. Shapiro, 'The Concept "Fact": Legal Origins and Cultural Diffusion', *Albion*, 26:2 (1994), pp. 231 and 247, note 84.

38. Holdsworth, *History of English Law*, vol. 9, pp. 206–7; J. A. Sharpe, 'Disruption in the Well-Ordered Household: Age, Authority and Possessed Young People', in Griffiths, *Experience of Authority*, pp. 187–212. See

Godbeer, *The Devil's Dominion*, pp. 162 and 222.

39. Ronald C. Sawyer, '"Strangely Handled in all Her Lyms": Witchcraft and Healing in Jacobean England', *Journal of Social History*, 22:3 (1989), 461–85; Rosen, *Witchcraft in England*, p. 352; Isabel Atkinson, 1664, ASSI 45/7/1/7 and 8.

40. Lorraine Daston, 'Marvelous Facts and Miraculous Evidence in Early Modern Europe', *Critical Inquiry*, 18:4 (1991), 106.

41. Raymond Firth, *We the Tikopia: A Sociological Study of Kinship in Primitive Polynesia*, 2nd edn (Boston, MA, 1963), p. 14.

42. *Wonderfull Discoverie of Witches in the Countie of Lancaster*, p. P3; Larner, *Enemies of God*, p. 180.

43. Paul Atkinson, *The Ethnographic Imagination: Textual Constructions of Reality* (London, 1990), pp. 15, 27.

44. PRO ASSI 45/10/3/45.

45. O'Barr, *Linguistic Evidence*, pp. 61–5.

46. S. Cohen, *Folk Devils and Moral Panics: The Creation of the Mods and Rockers* (St Albans, 1972). Miranda Chaytor's forthcoming study of this outbreak should help us here.

47. *Wonderfull Discoverie of Witches in the Countie of Lancaster*, p. P2; and Geis and Bunn, *A Trial of Witches*, p. 224.

48. *Wonderfull Discoverie of Witches in the Countie of Lancaster*, p. Y, Jennet Preston.

49. Durham gaolbook, PRO ASSI 47/20/6, f. 393; Eleanor Loumsdale suborning for Margaret Browne, TWAS 540/1, f. 33v; R. Gardner, *England's Grievance Discovered in Relation to the Coal Trade etc.* (London, 1655), pp. 107–9; Mary Moore, *Wonderfull News from the North*, p. 15; Daniel Stranger, TWAS 540/2, f. 8, £20 surety for Isabella Browne; and PRO ASSI 47/20/1 f. 297.

50. J. A. Sharpe, *Witchcraft in Seventeenth-Century Yorkshire*, p. 9–10; J. Favret-Saada, *Deadly Words: Witchcraft in the Bocage*, trans. Catherine Cullen (Cambridge, 1977).

51. See Miranda Chaytor, 'Husband(ry): Narratives of Rape in the Seventeenth Century', *Gender and History*, 7:3 (1995), 378–407, and Garthine Walker, 'Rereading Rape and Sexual Violence in Early Modern England', *Gender and History*, 10:1 (1998), 1–25; also Diane Purkiss, *The Witch in History*.

52. Daston, 'Marvelous Facts and Miraculous Evidence', pp. 93–4.

Chapter Two
Understanding Witchcraft? Accusers' Stories in Print in Early Modern England

Marion Gibson

eginning an essay about witchcraft and truth with a quotation from *Macbeth* might give an impression of cosy familiarity (no pun intended). Here are the weird sisters, safely fictional and well-known:

> ... Oftentimes to win us to our harm
> The instruments of darkness tell us truths,
> Win us with honest trifles to betray's
> In deepest consequence[1]

But this essay opens with this quotation (neatly incorporating the title of Jim Sharpe's comprehensive guide to the history of English witchcraft) because I want to concentrate on the second part of the famous warning, and examine in anxious detail some of our sources for understanding what witchcraft was. When we look closely, it can be seen that some of the 'honest trifles' – legal documents and pamphlets concerning witchcraft cases – which we use as part of our foundation for understanding witchcraft are seriously (but interestingly) flawed as data-sources. Some of them are as fictional as *Macbeth* itself. In these cases, they are less likely to 'tell us truths' than they are to 'betray us'. This article will look briefly at how some of these sources represent witchcraft to us, and why it is represented by them in these ways. My suggestion is that the sources from which information about witchcraft comes, and the ways in which that information is used by the legal system and by witchcraft pamphlets, determine in part our understanding of witchcraft. I shall concentrate here on informants (victims and other witnesses) and their stories.

In primis, then, there is a change in the representation of witchcraft in witchcraft pamphlets in the 1590s. I shall suggest here that this is because of a change in the type of accuser and the type of source used. When these change then so does the historical stereotype of the witch, and with it our understanding of what witchcraft was. Such a clear connection between the source of the story and the type of represent-ation of witchcraft should make us careful in reading stories about witchcraft as if they were 'historical truth'. Whilst the producers of most accounts of witches and their activities believed both that they were telling the truth and that they were describing real events, Jeanne Favret-Saada's comment in her book, *Deadly Words,* suggests the difficulty of telling and evaluating a story about an unverifiable (even impossible) crime: 'any information on the subject [of witchcraft] is not informative, but only moments in a strategy'.[2] In this important sense, there is no such thing as historical 'data' about witchcraft. Therefore, I shall suggest that it is not only the *magical* details in stories of witchcraft which we can no longer accept as factual; 'facts' such as physically possible events, places, persons, and chronologies are often also misrepresented, or, to speak less judgementally, are represented in many different ways – ways which change over time, especially in the 1590s. If we assume for the moment that we are looking only at representations of witchcraft, and not data about it, we can look in a sharper and more interrogative way at what is being said: why, by whom, for whom and in what context.

Some of these questions can be answered simply by reference to legal procedures against felons in early modern England. Most early printed accounts of witchcraft begin with the documents produced when a witch was informed against and arrested. The victim would complain of the suspected felon to a Justice of the Peace, who would record the accusation as a written 'information'. The witch was then questioned by the Justice, and her or his response to the accusation was recorded as an 'examination'. These pre-trial legal documents are often printed in pre-1590 witchcraft pamphlets. But there are more subtle negotiations behind these basic conditions of production than is immediately obvious, and there are also the pamphlets produced after 1590 to be considered.

There are, in fact, two categories of witchcraft pamphlet, with two resultant categories of information about witchcraft. The first uses almost exclusively legal documentary sources. These pamphlets, almost all dating from before 1590, can only be dismissed as 'sensational' (a curiously common description of news pamphlets about witchcraft) if we decide that either the legal documents which they use are an unreliable source, or that whilst the documents would have been a good source in their original form, pamphleteers have misused and altered them.[3] The other type of witchcraft account does not use legal documentary sources, or uses them in a very minor way. Almost all the pamphlets of this kind date from after 1590 and they are basically third-person narratives of witchcraft. J. S. Cockburn is right to say of some of them that 'the reliability of the pamphlets is heavily qualified by both carelessness and fabrication'.[4] Some have a 'literary flavour'.[5] Some are just plain dishonest. A pamphlet of 1592, *A most wicked worke of a wretched witch*, plagiarized a long extract from a play, Robert Greene's *Friar Bacon and Friar Bungay*, inserting incidents from it into the story of a Middlesex farmhand.[6] These pamphlets give a wholly different idea of witchcraft from that given by legal documentary pamphlets. Legal documentary and narrative pamphlets are thus two distinct *genres* telling stories of different shape, and they are more or less chronologically separated by the date of 1590. And here is the first difference – that of source – which gives us a different stereotype of the witch after 1590. Witches in legal documents are usually represented quite differently from witches in narrative accounts.

There is a concise example of the choice of the two different kinds of source, and the effects of the use of different sources, in a pamphlet of 1589 which uses both types. Legal documentary information merges with narrative. In *The Apprehension and confession of three notorious Witches*, the 'witch' Joan Cunny's examination seems, from its opening 'Imprimis' and calm list of crimes, to be transcribed from a documentary original. But the tone suddenly changes:

> And beeing further examined, she confesseth that although her saide spirits at some time can have no power to hurt men, yet they may have power to hurt their Cattell. This Joane Cunny, living very lewdly, having two lewde Daughters, no better then naughty packs, had two Bastard Children: beeing

> both boyes, these two Children were cheefe witnesses, and gave in great
> evidence against their Grandam and Mothers, the eldest being about 10 or
> 12 yeeres of age. Against this Mother Cunny the elder Boye gave in this
> evideoce [*sic*] which she herselfe after confessed ... [7]

The second sentence is narrative, full of opinion, adjectives and
comment – a completely different type of representation from the
legalistic factuality of the first sentence. The examination is framed by
notes in the same vocabulary as the addition to the examination:

> This witch had nine Spirits 2 of them were like unto a black dog, having the
> faces of a Toade. These spirits belonging to this witch, did sucke commonly
> upon a sore leg which this mother Cunny had. She had fower principall spir-
> its. The first was Jack. The second was Jyll. The third was Nicholas. The
> fourth was Ned. Jack killed mankinde. Jyll killed women-kinde. Nicholas
> killed horses. Ned killed Cattell[8]

The witch is described colloquially as 'Mother Cunny', and dismissively
with the judgmental 'this witch', by a 'voice' who appears, from a trial
report concluding the pamphlet, to have attended the trial. This 'voice'
possesses extra information on Cunny which the examination does not
contain, and offers us a different view of the witch. Thus, in the
examination she is described as a woman of 'fourscore yeeres, or ther-
abouts', working with two spirits to harm her neighbours and the
town's minister, whilst in the added comment she is called 'lewd' and
held up by an excited moralist to our censure, as leading a family of
sexually transgressive women. These are two entirely different images
of what a witch was thought to be, given by two different writers. The
first image is produced by the legal context: a questioning magistrate,
responding witch, and recording clerk. The second image is produced
by a pamphleteer, reporting events in court and putting a spin on them
for his readership. Scholars have traditionally synthesized the different
portrayals into one image, or stressed only one of its elements: for
example Marianne Hester's emphasis on Joan as the victim of an attack
by witch-hunters on a sexual 'deviant', or Keith Thomas's understanding of Joan 'Cony' in the context of religion and magic, as the
kind of witch who was 'eighty years old and ... presumably ... brought
up a Catholic'.[9] Historians like Jim Sharpe have seen this kind of
conflicting evidence as 'complementary'.[10] I would argue that it is

actually an interesting shattering of our image of the witch, and that it is worth exploring in other cases which type of writer – magistrate's clerk or pamphleteer – produces which type of image of witchcraft.

It is also important to consider what the originators of the stories of witchcraft – accusers and witches – intended to convey to their audiences. The most authoritative analysis of accusers' stories about witches is still that pioneered by Reginald Scot and George Gifford in the sixteenth century, and taken up by Keith Thomas in the twentieth. Scot parodies this usual pattern of accusers' narrations when, using the voice of the accuser, he says of an imaginary witch:

> She was at my house of late, she would have had a pot of milke, she departed in a chafe bicause she had it not, she railed, she curssed, she mumbled and whispered, and finallie she said she would be even with me: and soone after my child, my cow, my sow, or my pullet died, or was strangelie taken[11]

To demonstrate Scot's accuracy, here are some informations from the 1582 St Osyth pamphlet, *A true and just Recorde*, and the 1579 *A Detection of damnable driftes*:

> The sayde Joan saieth, that in sommer last, mother Manfielde came unto her house and requested her to give her Curdes, shee saith that answere was made that there was none, and so shee departed. And within a while after some of her cattell were taken lame …[12]

> Item, she [Mother Staunton] came on a tyme to the house of one Richard Saunder of Brokewalden, and beeyng denied Yeest, whiche she required of his wife, she went her waie murmuryng, as offended with her aunswere, and after her departure, her yonge child in the Cradle was taken vehemently sicke[13]

Scot's parody serves its purpose as ammunition against accusers, but it also suggests that their stories are stereotyped. It is in itself an analysis of their stories. Scot declares that no magic happened, and that therefore the shape of the story is a false one, based on the false creation of a narrative of cause and effect (victim offends witch, victim suffers harm). But his parodic story might make us question not just the stereotyped shape of accusers' stories, but also all the material contained within such stories in legal documents or pamphlets. In Scot's terms, if the stories are not true in one respect (no magic happened), then why should they be true in other, supposedly more verifiable ways? Why should we accept unquestioningly that Elleine Smithe of Maldon quarrelled over money with her stepfather, who then died (according to an unnamed witness), or that John Wade offended Annis Herd and his sheep died?[14] I am not suggesting that informants brazenly lied, although some may have done, but that, as Jean-Noel Kapferer says, stories 'organise our perception to validate themselves', and 'what we sustain sometimes reflects more our mental stereotypes than what we have really seen'.[15] Victims see what they expect to see after a quarrel with the witch, and their perception thus adjusts reality even before their articulation of the incident in words further shapes their experience into a neat, coherent tale. Even the description of an initial falling out can be suspect: John Wade, for example, provides no evidence at all in his information that his fair and carefully explained refusal of help was taken in ill part by Herd – but we do know that when the encounter took place, Wade was aware that she was suspected of using witchcraft against others. When problems beset his sheep, a ready explanation would present itself, and a discussion of resources might become 'a falling out'. The story of the witch taking revenge for a refusal of neighbourly help is thus bound to reproduce itself once it has become part of the cultural complex surrounding witchcraft, because it will shape perceptions of future encounters and subsequent narrations of these as accusations. Jonathan Barry has also argued that the usual shape of the story – the witch revenging a wrong – would have provided the court with a testimony which would be likely to secure conviction, on the basis that this account clearly showed plausible evidence of criminal motive – offence taken, revenge enacted, result.[16] Thus, if we believe without nuance the typical accuser's story, as recorded in legal documents, printed in pamphlets, and discussed by theorists from Scot and Gifford to Thomas and Macfarlane, we are basing our view of what witchcraft was on both a convenient legal fiction and a narrational stereotype.

I want to add to this simple statement (that in both legal documents and pamphlets we are reading a shaped story, not an account of 'real events') with the idea that the whole pattern of accusers' stories as represented in witchcraft pamphlets develops over time, with the important change coming in the 1590s as a consequence of the change in sources. In other words, our view of witchcraft changes because the narrative genre, rather than any inaccessible reality, changes over time. Most pamphlets no longer use legal documents in the period after 1590 – for reasons which are totally unclear. Thus, after 1590 we no longer have access to the traditional story of witchcraft taken from informations, and a new story from a different source takes its place. In the Scot/Gifford/Thomas/Macfarlane version of accusers' stories, we have the version which appears in witchcraft pamphlets before 1590, and it is shaped as it is partly because they use legal documents as sources. Before 1590, nearly all the pamphlet stories about witches show the witch taking revenge for an injury or insult, or else being denied something. In a story of witch's revenge, the victim injures the witch, the witch swears he or she shall repent it, and therefore the victim suffers losses, falls ill or dies. The story of witch's revenge is a classic pattern identified, as representing the reality of witchcraft, by such writers on witchcraft as King James and Thomas Potts.[17] Thomas accepted and discussed it in *Religion and the Decline of Magic* and Macfarlane in *Witchcraft in Tudor and Stuart England*. The other main genre of stories about witches in witchcraft pamphlets dating from before 1590 is the denial narrative. The denial narrative was first recognized as an accusatory generic stereotype – rather than a reflection of reality – by sceptical or semi-sceptical demonologists such as Scot and Gifford, who enumerated its contents, and noted its cause-and-effect shape based on motive.[18] In a narrative of the denial of charity, the victim refuses help to the witch, the witch retorts, and therefore harm comes to the victim. Joan Cheston's narrative about Mother Manfield, quoted earlier, is a good example. The witch is portrayed as having successfully punished her uncharitable neighbour. Thomas identified the denial narrative as the most common pattern of stories about English witches in the sixteenth and seventeenth centuries, and Alan Macfarlane analysed its significance.[19] The story of witch's revenge and the story of denial are thus the basis of current witchcraft research, springing – as much of it still does – from Thomas and Macfarlane's work.

But when sources change, the story of witchcraft changes too. The major change is this: that victims begin to deny that they provoked the witch. For example in *The Most strange and admirable discoverie of the three Witches of Warboys*, published in 1593, the victims of witchcraft are described:

devising with themselves for what cause it should be wrought upon them or their children, they could not imagine, for they were but newly come to the towne to inhabite, which was but at Michaelmas before, neither had they given any occasion (to their knowledge) either to her [the witch] or to any other, to practise any such malice against them[20]

The pamphlet moves from their refusal to believe they are bewitched to their shocked reiteration that they have done nothing to deserve this witchcraft, and that they had always treated the witch well. *The Witches of Northamptonshire* (1612) also fits this pattern. The author describes how Joane Vaughan, being in company with the gentlewoman Mistress Belcher:

> whether of purpose to give occasion of anger to the said Mistris Belcher, or but to continue her vilde, and ordinary custome of behaviour, committed something either in speech, or gesture, so unfitting, and unseeming the nature of woman hood, that it displeased the most that were there present: But especially it touched the modesty of this Gentlewoman, who was so much mooved with her bold, and impudent demeanor, that she could not containe her selfe, but sodainely rose up and strooke her, howbeit hurt her not[21]

Although Mistress Belcher is the aggressor, the incident is represented as the witch's fault because of her unacceptable unwomanliness. Mistress Belcher did not hurt her, reassures the pamphleteer, who cannot know this. Thus, when Mistress Belcher is afflicted by the witch, the reader must pity her, the victim. Abuse is heaped on the witch, who is 'a maide (or at least unmaried)' and a 'trull', and on her mother Agnes Browne, who was 'of poore parentage and poorer education', had 'an ill nature and wicked disposition, spightfull and malitious', and was 'hated, and feared among her neighbours', 'both of them as farre from grace as Heaven from hell'.[22] In most pamphlets after 1590 victims are constructed as completely innocent, even where, as with Mistress Belcher, they clearly are not so.

So why is there a change in the type of story told about witches in pamphlets from the 1590s? If there was a general contemporary shift in the perception of what witchcraft was, it should be reflected in legal documents of the time – in informations. Since they have not survived in any quantity, we cannot tell for certain whether such a change took place, but surviving legal documents from later periods, and the only surviving Elizabethan documents, concerning the Trevisard family, suggest that no such change is recorded in legal representations of witches. So is the change perceived by us, as readers, simply because we are reading pamphlets, and because after 1590 they provide a different representation of witchcraft from a different source? Barbara Rosen, who noted some of the changes in pamphlets after 1590, offers a partial explanation:

> Almost exactly in 1590, there is a marked change in the prose literature of English witchcraft which may reflect a change in the type of author as much as a change in the temper of the times. Reporters of straight news had already begun to drift to those forms which foreshadow the first real newspapers ... Witchcraft reporting fell into the hands of amateurs, or professionals writing reports on commission. Ministers justify their beliefs; rich families protect their local reputations by 'authentic versions' of events; doctors defend their professional competency; judges display their own models of procedure[23]

Type of author may be a factor in some cases, although most pamphlets are anonymous, so internal evidence is our only guide. But more important than a change in authorship, although related to it, is the realization, already mentioned, that we are clearly now reading material from a non-legal source. The 1593 Warboys pamphlet, already quoted, is not based on informations and examinations, but is a third-person narration by someone apparently connected with the victims who were wealthy landowners.[24] Exactly the same is true of *The Witches of Northamptonshire*.[25] A third factor in changing stories of witchcraft by accusers is thus that we are looking at stories by a different type of victim/accuser. New circumstances of source and class may have produced the new type of story, because such families, producing their own accounts of their suffering, would not admit they had wronged the witch. The best example of this pattern, a story of 'motiveless' attack on well-born innocents, is a pamphlet written by someone sympathetic to even richer and nobler victims, the Earls of Rutland:

> After the Right Honourable Sr. Francis Manners succeeded his Brother in the Earledome of Rutland: and so not onely tooke possession of Beaver [Belvoir] Castle, but of all other his demeanes, Lordships, Townes, Mannors, Lands, and Revenues appropriate to the same Earledome: hee proceeded so

honourably in the course of his life, as neither displacing Tenants, discharg-
ing servants, denying the accesse of the poore, welcoming of strangers, and
performing all the duties of a noble Lord, that hee fastened as it were unto
himselfe the love and good opinion of the Countrey ... his honourable
Countesse marched arme in arme with him in the same race ... one Joan
Flower, with her Daughters Margaret and Phillip were not onely relieved at
the first from thence, but quickly entertained as Chair-women, and Margaret
admitted as a continuall dweller in the Castle, looking both to the poultrey
abroad and the wash-house within dores: In which life they continued with
equall correspondency, till something was discovered to the noble Lady,
which concerned the misdemeanour of these women ... . Concerning
Margaret, that shee often resorted from the Castle to her Mother, bringing
such provision as they thought was unbefitting for a servant to purloyne,
and comming at such unseasonable houres, that they could not but conjec-
ture some mischiefe between them, and that their extraordinary ryot &
expences, tended both to rob the Lady, & to maintaine certaine deboist [de-
bauched] and base company which frequented this Joane Flowers house the
mother, & especially her youngest Daughter ... untill the Countesse
misconceiveing of ... Margaret, and discovering some undecencies both in
her life and neglect of her businesse, discharged her from lying any more in
the Castle, yet gave her 40s a bolster, & a mattresse of wooll: commanding
her to go home, untill the slacknesse of her repayring to the Castle, as shee
was wont, did turne her love and liking toward this honourable Earle and
his family into hate and rancor[26]

It is explicitly denied that the Earl discharged servants, yet Margaret
Flower was at least partially dismissed, and in her examination, printed
alongside the narrative, she says that 'turning her out of service' caused
her malice. Her sister Phillip says in her examination 'that her mother
and her sister maliced the Earle of Rutland, his Countesse, and their
Children, because her Sister Margaret, was put out of the Ladies service
of Laundry, and exempted from other services about the house'.[27]
Margaret describes her motive in the usual witch's revenge narrative:
she was told to 'lye at home, and come no more to dwell at the Castle;
which she not onely tooke in ill part, but grudged at it exceedingly,
swearing in her heart to be revenged'.[28] But the narrative will not admit
this traditional representation of witch's revenge, taken as usual from
legal sources, to be the legitimate interpretation. The pamphleteer

prefers to construct the Earl and Countess as blameless, attacked by ungrateful, evil atheists for no reason. The two stories of witch's revenge and denial of charity have been superseded by a narrative of motiveless attack as the official publishable narrative of witchcraft. We have a new view of witches and why they attack.

This deliberate construction of witchcraft as a motiveless attack contradicts Thomas's assertion that witchcraft accusations all grew out of the accuser's feeling,

> not merely that the witch bore a grudge against him, but that the grudge was a *justifiable* one. The witch, in other words, was not thought to be acting out of mere vindictiveness; she was avenging a definite injury ... The important point is that, paradoxically, it tended to be the witch who was morally in the right and the victim who was in the wrong[29]

Clearly, the victims, Mistress Belcher or the Earl of Rutland, might have felt guilt which they skilfully concealed in their narrative of events, but the different emphasis in the representation of relations between witch and victim is clear. The difference from the earlier information-based representation of witches' motives can be seen in a comparison of two similar sets of circumstances represented in dissimilar ways – the Jacobean dismissal/demotion of Margaret Flower narrated in the third person, and the Elizabethan sacking of Margaret Ewstace reported in a printed version of a victim's information. In his information, Robert Sannever, Ewstace's employer, said in 1582 that:

> about xv yeeres past, ther dwelt with him the daughter of Elizabeth Ewstace, and that for some lewde dealynges, and behaviour by her doone, hee saieth, hee used some threatning speeches unto her, beeing his servaunt: And that shortlye after shee wente home to her sayde mother, and telled her of her maysters using of her: and the nexte daye hee saieth, as hee was a sitting by his fire side, his mouth was drawne awrye ... whereuppon ... hee sent presently to one of skill to come unto him, who ... tooke a lynnen cloath, and covered his eyes, and stroake him on the same side with a strong blowe, and then his mouth came into the right course: and hee sayeth that hee willed this Examinate to put awaye his servaunt, and that out of hand: the which he saieth he did ... iii yeres sithence his brother Crosse was taken very sickly, and ... tolde him that Margaret Ewstace had bewitched him ... his wife had a most straunge sicknes, and was delivered of childe, which within short

time after dyed ... his beasts did give downe blood in steede of milke ... his
hogges did skippe and leape aboute the yarde in a straunge sorte: And some
of them dyed[30]

This is a conventional witch's revenge narrative. Sannever explains
how he injured the witches, and what the result was. His representation
could have lessened the offence committed by him against his maid,
but instead he elaborates it, describing 'threatning' and dismissal 'out
of hand [immediately]', rather than attempting to present himself as
an injured innocent. Thus the witch's motivation is very clearly
represented and she is shown to have some justification for anger. But
the pamphleteer of *Wonderful Discoverie* (1619) will not admit any guilt
on the employer's behalf and portrays him instead, in the new type of
pamphlet and the new type of story, as the perfect feudal patriarch.
The change is decisive, and it is reflected in almost all pamphlets dating
from after 1590.

In summary, then, the story of motiveless witch attack was not told
in pamphlets made up from legal documents, which told stories of
denial of charity and witch's revenge. There are a few examples of the
older type of story lingering after 1590 – Thomas Potts's *Wonderfull
Discoverie of Witches* of 1612 is the bulkiest, made up from legal
documents, the traditional source of the traditional story. There is only
one example of the story of motiveless malignity before 1590, Richard
Galis's aptly titled *A Briefe Treatise conteyning the most strange and
horrible crueltye of Elizabeth Stile*. In that pamphlet the story of
unprovoked 'crueltye' is, as we would now expect, a narrative, by the
gentlemanly victim himself. We may therefore deduce from this simple
pattern some general guidelines for reading stories of witchcraft in
legal documents and witchcraft pamphlets. Firstly, stories of witchcraft
from a non-legal, narrative context are more likely to exonerate the
victim from blame in bringing witchcraft on themselves by unpleasant
behaviour, whilst documents from a legal context are likely to blame
the victim and, in doing so, find a motive for the witch. Secondly, a
story of motiveless witch attack is more likely to be told by upper-
class victims, whilst ordinary villagers tell the story we have come to
expect and accept blame for angering the witch. Thirdly, after 1590 as
victims get more blameless, witches get wickeder – they are condemned
in pamphlets as atheists, sinners, lechers, and antisocial outcasts. We
therefore have to treat accusatory stories of witchcraft with care because

the type of victim/author determines the type of story, and the recorder/author of the story adds to this distorting effect. We cannot treat stories of witchcraft as 'data' or 'evidence' without enquiring whose stories we are reading, and in what context they were told and recorded.

Notes

1. W. Shakespeare, *Macbeth*, ed. S. Wells and G. Taylor (1623; Oxford, 1988), 1.3.121–4
2. J. Favret-Saada, *Deadly Words: Witchcraft in the Bocage*, trans. C. Cullen (Cambridge and Paris, 1980), p. 25.
3. There are exceptions to the rule dividing pamphlets into pre-1590 (documentary) and post-1590 (non-documentary) categories. Thomas Potts,*The Wonderfull Discoverie of Witches* (London, 1612) is documentary; whilst Richard Galis, *A Briefe Treatise conteyning the most strange and horrible crueltye of Elizabeth Stile* (London, 1579) is narrative. See the final paragraph of this chapter.
4. J. S. Cockburn, *Calendar of Assize Records. Home Circuit Indictments. Elizabeth I and James I. Introduction* (London, 1985), p. 98. Examples of the non-documentary type include *The most strange and admirable discoverie of the three Witches of Warboys* (London, 1593);*The Witches of Northamptonshire* (London, 1612); and *Witches Apprehended* (London, 1613).
5. W. Notestein, *A History of Witchcraft in England* (1911; New York, 1968), p. 356.
6. See M. Gibson, 'Greene's *Friar Bacon and Friar Bungay* and *A Most Wicked Worke of a Wretched Witch*: A Link', *Notes and Queries*, new series 44 (March 1997), 36–7 for a full account of this.
7. *The Apprehension and confession of three notorious Witches* (1589), sig. A4.
8. Ibid., sigs. A3–A3v.
9. M. Hester, *Lewd Women and Wicked Witches* (London and New York, 1992), p. 186; K. Thomas, *Religion and the Decline of Magic* (1971; Harmondsworth, 1978), p. 592.
10. J. A. Sharpe, *Instruments of Darkness* (London, 1996), p. 172.
11. Reginald Scot, *The Discoverie of Witchcraft*, ed. Brinsley Nicholson (1584; London: 1886), 'Epistle to Sir Thomas Scot'.
12. *A true and just Recorde* (London, 1582), sig. E2.
13. *A Detection of damnable driftes* (London, 1579), sig. A7v.
14. Ibid., sig. A5 v; *A true and just Recorde*, sigs. E6 v-E7.
15. J.-N. Kapferer, *Rumors: Uses, Interpretations and Images*, trans. B. Fink (1987; New Brunswick, NJ, and London, 1990), pp. 26–7, 77.
16. See J. Barry, 'Introduction: Keith Thomas and the Problem of Witchcraft', in J. Barry, M. Hester and G. Roberts (eds),*Witchcraft in Early Modern Europe* (Cambridge, 1996), pp. 9, 43–4.

17. James VI and I, *Daemonologie* (Edinburgh, 1597), bk 1, ch. 2, and bk 2, ch. 3; Potts, sig. O3.
18. See S. Anglo, 'Reginald Scot's *Discoverie of Witchcraft*', and A. Macfarlane, 'A Tudor Anthropologist', in Anglo (ed.),*The Damned Art* (London, Henley and Boston, MA, 1977), pp. 106–39, 140–55.
19. Thomas, *Religion and the Decline of Magic*, pp. 604, 659–663; Macfarlane, *Witchcraft in Tudor and Stuart England* (1970; Prospect Heights, IL, 1991), pp. 170–6, 205–6. Thomas argues that 'the overwhelming majority of fully documented witch cases fall into this simple pattern.'
20. *The Most strange and admirable discoverie*, sig. A4.
21. *The Witches of Northamptonshire*, sig. B2v.
22. Ibid., sigs. B2–B2v.
23. B. Rosen, *Witchcraft in England 1558–1618* (1969; Amherst, MA, 1991) p. 213.
24. On this case, see M. Tatem, *The Witches of Warboys* (Cambridge, 1993); and A. Reiber de Windt, 'Witchcraft and Conflicting Visions of the Ideal Village Community', *Journal of British Studies*, 34 (1995), 427–63.
25. On this case, see M. Gibson, 'Devilish Sin and Desperate Death: Northamptonshire Witches in Print and Manuscript', *Northamptonshire Past and Present*, 51 (1998), 15–21.
26. *The Wonderful Discoverie of the Witchcraftes of Margaret and Phillip Flower* (London, 1619), sigs. C2–C4v.
27. *The Wonderful Discoverie*, sigs. Gv, F3.
28. Ibid., sig. F4.
29. Thomas, *Religion and the Decline of Magic* p. 659.
30. *A true and just Recorde*, sigs. C7–C7v.

Chapter Three
Witches and Witnesses in Old and New England*

Malcolm Gaskill

I

arly modern historians have long recognized the value of legal depositions (the informations of accusers and examinations of the accused) for reconstructing contexts of crime and criminal justice.[1] In contrast to European states observing inquisitorial procedure, however, in England depositions were neither meticulously constructed nor routinely preserved as official records. More indictments have survived but, because their content is brief and formulaic, invariably they conceal an intricate substratum of circumstances at parish level which, due to the accusatory nature of English justice, determined not only the course of a trial, but whether an accusation reached the courts in the first place. Depositions also throw light on more general aspects of life, demonstrating, *inter alia*, the dynamics of social relationships, and popular thinking in action. The most enlightening examples concern witchcraft, not just because witchcraft exposes a belief alien to modern

*   I am grateful to Stuart Clark and other participants at the 1998 Swansea conference for their comments on an earlier version of this chapter, and to Brian Levack, Alexandra Walsham, Caroline Oates, and Peter Rushton who supplied me with valuable references.

western mentalities (at least in terms of legal responses), but because it generated meanings which were contested and so changed over time.[2] Of these, there are especially few due to the modest scale of English witch trials. Yet more could be made of what we do have by asking questions concerned less with *why* people made witchcraft accusations and more with *how* they formalized those accusations at law. This approach shifts the focus away from the traditional preoccupation with the ecological causes of accusations, and towards an exploration of their inner meaning in terms of social psychology and culture.

There is no need to rehearse the arguments for and against the reliability of depositions as historical sources; suffice it to say that all literate élite compositions tend to misrepresent the experience of the unlettered poor.[3] Yet it would be wrong to assume that written testimony possessed no vernacular authenticity whatsoever. Even if it did not faithfully reflect plebeian opinion, its form and content did not belong wholly to formal procedure either. Most depositions were not only produced at a pre-trial stage where information was usually freely volunteered, but were also only intended to be a guide at most trials, where witnesses were required to repeat their evidence before both grand and petty juries.[4] A Marxian interpretation whereby magistrates manipulated testimony to bolster their authority seems improbable in most instances, especially where serious felonies were concerned.[5] An overlooked source of distortion were the people themselves, whose interests could be well-served by having their words committed to writing and forwarded to the assizes.[6] 'Depositions deserve close attention,' Miranda Chaytor has argued, 'and attention not just to their content but to language and form: to the way the narrative is structured, to imagery, emphases and ... to evasions and gaps.'[7] Judges and juries were influenced by such things: expressions of local sentiment affected verdicts and sentences to a greater extent than might be expected.[8] In this sense, legal witnesses were more than just passive puppets of state administration: they were storytellers, and their storytelling had a kind of power.[9] Stories help people to interpret existence, make judgments, and solve problems, and, in a specifically legal setting, 'engage widely shared cognitive routines' which enable them to participate successfully in the complex procedures of the courtroom.[10]

More than for any other crime, depositions – and, by extension, the pre-trial process – enhance an understanding of witchcraft since here 'the process of transmutation whereby suspicion became prosecution is opaque'.[11] Perhaps the most important collection originates from the Northern Circuit assizes (1646–78).[12] Also rich are the Ely diocesan records which contain testimony relating to prosecutions in Cambridgeshire and the Isle of Ely, mostly from the 1640s.[13] Pleadings and proofs from the Jacobean Court of Star Chamber help to locate witchcraft within broader social tensions and conflicts.[14] Isolated depositions survive from various other assize circuits, palatinate jurisdictions, quarter sessions, and borough courts, scattered between record offices, libraries, and national and private collections.[15] Although the voluminous Continental records can be used to flesh out what we learn about English witnesses and witches from these sources, differences of judicial procedure impose limitations upon the extent to which one can extrapolate, even if England was a variant of the 'European pattern' rather than its exception.[16] Depositions from early America, however, are ideal for eking out the English material.[17] Not only were they produced by people whose culture belonged to the Old World as much as the New[18] – not least their magical beliefs[19] – but the colonial authorities applied English accusatory justice, where the onus for prosecution was on private complainants and suspects were examined without torture on presumption of innocence.[20] Furthermore, the Salem depositions from 1692 alone are as numerous as all extant English examples.[21]

Admittedly, the English trials of the mid-1640s were an unrepresentative episode due to the interventions of witchfinder Matthew Hopkins; and comparable distortion is apparent at Salem, the forum for which was a special court where 'the zeal and commitment of the magistrates guaranteed that the terms of prosecution would no longer conflict with the terms of accusation.'[22] That said, not only did Hopkins mostly exploit pre-existing village tensions and fears, but behind the hysteria at Salem lies prosecutorial behaviour which seems more rational if one peels away the 'layers of myth' and takes testimony on its own terms.[23] Moreover, what both instances lose by historical peculiarity, they gain from deponents' emotional intensity – an intensity which brings us close to the way they thought. Heightened persecuting fervour amplified and lapidified the dialogue between high and low, allowing the voices of ordinary people – and the mentalities which informed them – to transcend barriers of modern secular, empirical thinking in which 'class', 'industry', 'state', and 'proof' have come to mean more than 'interest', 'land', 'community', and 'faith'. The Salem records evoke a world of neighbourly conflict in a context of magical belief, conflict which boiled over in the presence of zealous and uncompromising examiners at a time of acute social anxiety – essentially what happened in East Anglia in 1645–7.[24]

This chapter does not seek to explain the witch-panics in Salem, East Anglia, or anywhere else. Instead, it exploits New English materials to explore further the storytelling strategies of ordinary people recorded by English magistrates, but for which comparatively little evidence survives.[25] Many witnesses, consciously or unconsciously, structured their testimony according to fictive motifs, of which four have been chosen: apparitions, dreams, miracles, and stock-dramas. Most examples concern providential intervention, illustrating a mental environment in which the supernatural was not only a means of explaining misfortune – the usual focus for historians of witchcraft – but a popular idiom by which witches were identified and accused.[26] We also learn that witchcraft was more than just a matrix of persecution, but an offence of which even the accused could believe themselves guilty. Hence the testimony of witnesses and witches alike leads us not just into an arena of social conflict and its resolution, but the broader plains of popular mentalities.[27]

II

Despite godly objections, apparitions continued to be taken seriously after the Reformation because they were central to folklore, lingered on the margins of orthodox theology, and served a range of social needs.[28] For witchcraft accusations, they were a means by which unseen dangers were perceived, interpreted, and expressed. Susan Barber of New Romney (Kent) testified in 1617 that her landlord William Godfrey's familiar spirits 'like three rugged black spaniel dogs' invaded her home, and that one night Godfrey himself 'came behind her and gave her a great punch upon the back, and then she looking about for him, she could see nobody'.[29] Similarly intimidated was John Greenliff of Beverley (Yorkshire) who informed a Justice of the Peace in 1654 that Elizabeth Roberts had appeared before him, 'and vanishing turned herself into the similitude of a cat' which brushed against his legs, then vanished itself. Thereafter, he fell sick and was menaced by a bee which he swore was Elizabeth Roberts in another transmutation.[30] There can be little doubt that many witnesses were afraid. In 1661 at Newcastle-on-Tyne, a man brandishing a rapier chased an apparition of a witch until it slipped beneath a bed where two afflicted children lay screaming; other witnesses claimed that the witch disappeared up the chimney in a ball of fire.[31] At Rossendale (Lancashire) in 1681, John Nuttall's daughters were traumatized by witch-apparitions, one of which a hysterical Elizabeth Nuttall lashed out at with a sword.[32]

Apparitions manifested the intangible malice of opponents. In 1606 the minister of Radwinter (Essex) complained that his enemies conjured evil spirits 'to haunt and walk about the ... church and churchyard and visibly to be seen, sometimes in the shape of a man, sometimes of a cat, dog or suchlike'.[33] Regardless of sincerity, such a claim was more compelling than a mere report of a threat, assuming that a threat had even been made. Stories certainly got things going. In 1612 a Northampton minister ordered that suspects be searched after a man told him that an apparition had 'appeared to him naked above the middle with a knife in each hand, inciting him to deliver the one to his sister ... to kill herself, and to murder himself with the other'.[34] Deponents thus distanced themselves from their stories, emphasizing their own innocence and passivity. Disembodied voices at Taunton (Somerset) in 1626 allegedly informed Edward Dynham that he was bewitched by 'a woman in green clothes and a black hat with a long poll, and a man in a grey suit with blue stockings', just as the witch chased by the Newcastle man wore a red waistcoat and green petticoat.[35] At Salem, Samuel Gray described the apparition of Bridget Bishop, but claimed not to know who she was; only later did he identify her by her clothes.[36] In these cases, to have named a suspect may have been too explicit: better to let JPs and jurors put two-and-two together, however obvious those deductions might seem.[37] Witnesses less equivocal in their accusations may have been more confident. Richard Coman recognized Bridget Bishop by 'her Red paragon Bodys and the rest of her cloathing that she then usually did ware', adding that he 'knowing of her well also the garb she did use to goe in'.[38] Similarly, Bernard Peach related how Susannah Martin entered his bedchamber 'in her whud & scarf and the same dress that shee was in before at metting the same day'.[39]

Apparitions could become protagonists in set-piece battles between good and evil. In 1641 the devil in the shape of a headless monster was exorcized from a Durham household in the name of God, whereupon 'a thing like unto a little child, with a very bright shining countenance' appeared, which flooded the room with light. Witches at a Newcastle house dematerialized when a strange voice ordered them to depart with the words: 'whosoever trusted in that rock Christ Jesus shall never perish'.[40] More often spectres oiled the wheels of temporal justice. In the mid-1640s a Northumberland girl saw angels struggle with the witches that tormented her, and was promised that if magistrates did not act, they would 'appear like a man and a woman, and justifie the truth'.[41] At Salem, Hannah Putnam deposed that she saw the apparitions of two victims, wrapped in winding sheets, who threatened to tear her to pieces unless she told a magistrate that John Willard had bewitched them. To confirm matters, Willard's apparition also confessed. Susanna Sheldon, too, saw apparitions of Willard and his victims, who 'turned As Red As blood And turning About to look on mee they turned As pale as deth'. A spectral drama then unfolded. Willard's apparition threatened to cut Sheldon's throat if she informed, the ghosts to break her head if she did not. Later, a 'shineing Man' ordered her to testify, whereupon Willard appeared, but vanished when the shining man raised his hand. When Sheldon asked to see the victims' wounds, an angel lifted their winding sheets.[42] Testimony blended folk beliefs, Protestant dogma, legal obligation, and social needs. Ann Putnam senior said six spectral children told her a witch had murdered them, and charged her 'to go and tell these things to the magistrates or else they would tear me to pieces, for their blood did cry for vengeance'.[43]

Apparitions were important in Old and New England because they exemplified the power of divine providence, and were believed to bring secret murderers to justice in essentially unpoliced societies. Their function in this context, then, was both doctrinal and judicial. Even after 1700, the belief in walking spirits was defended on the grounds that everyone who witnessed them could not be deluded and that, in any case, by exposing criminals they performed God's will.[44] This expository function was essential if the civil authorities were to fight – and be seen to fight – the devil on earth by punishing those he most corrupted. In general, a magistrate was advised to write down sufficient evidence to prove the felony; but for witchcraft this was vague.[45] Nor did the 1604 Witchcraft Act or the 1641 Massachusetts statute offer any guidance.[46] In fact, magistrates were advised not to expect direct proof in witchcraft cases because, as a work of diabolic darkness, it rarely left eyewitnesses or material evidence.[47] Along a chain of social communication, therefore, apparitions linked the accuser's suspicion with formal confirmation before authority. Even though spectral evidence did not always constitute conclusive legal proof, it provided grounds for suspicion and was admitted at the committal and trial stages for that reason.

It is striking how many apparitions were seen at night in the bedchamber. Modern studies have shown how easily people misinterpret visual stimuli in dim light, often in spectacular fashion.[48] If afraid or bereaved (as many witch-victims were), then the tendency to see apparitions in the shadows, or even to hallucinate in daylight, increases dramatically.[49] In 1661 a Yorkshireman deposed that his neighbour, in distress from passing gallstones, cried out: 'oh she tears me in pieces, and this informant demanding of him who, he answered Helen Gray and said: there she sits on the chimney-top, but this informant could not see her'.[50] A simpler explanation is that many witnesses were asleep at the time of their experiences, a theory supported by a sceptic in 1680 who observed that people who dream about witches were usually the same as claimed to be bewitched.[51] Among these may have been the victim tormented 'with dreams and fearful visions in his sleep, and hath been twice bewitched', the delirious Suffolk minister who bit a spectral hand from his sick-bed, and the Salem man who saw a witch as he lay, in his own words, 'between sleepeing & wakeing'.[52] The distinction between the two states of consciousness is unclear, but was less important than the fact that the dream-world was what Byron romantically termed 'a wide realm of wild reality'. Like apparitions, this realm conveyed messages between nature and super-nature, thus assisting providential ideology and criminal investigations.[53]

Some cases suggest nightmares informed by specific fears. In 1650 Dorothy Rodes of Bolling (Yorkshire) testified that on hearing her newly-awoken daughter Sara 'quaking and holding her hands together, she asked her what she ailed and that she answered: ah mother, Sikes wife came in at a hole at the bed's feet and ... took me by the throat.' Asked why she had not cried out, the girl replied that the witch's grip had prevented her.[54] 'I saw the apparition of Sarah Goode', Sarah Bibber told a Salem court, 'standing by my bedside, and shee pulled aside the curtain and turned down the sheet and Looked upon my child 4 years old and presently upon it the child was stracke into a great fit that my hausband and I could hardly hold it.'[55] One can easily imagine how the mother's dream could have been invaded by the child's crying, and how illusion and reality had fused on waking. The same overlap is apparent in confessions. Sarah Osborne declared 'that shee was frighted one time in her sleep and either *saw or dreamed* that shee saw a thing like an indian all black which did prick her in her neck and pulled her by the back part of her head to the dore of the house'.[56] By contrast, a witch at Lincoln in 1619, asked by magistrates whether she was dreaming when she saw her spirit, was adamant that she was awake.[57] Descriptions of compression and paralysis accord with lucid dream-states where sleepers are conscious of both the dream and the muscular lock dreaming induces. At Salem, Bernard Peach described how, as he lay in bed, Susanna Martin 'drew up his body into a heape & Lay upon him about an hour & halfe or 2: hours in all w'ch taim this deponent coold not stir nor speake'. He also described classic symptoms of struggling out of dream-sleep, until 'feelling himself begining to be loosined or Lightned', like the Suffolk minister, he grabbed the witch's hand and bit it.[58] Likewise, Richard Coman deposed that Bridget Bishop lay upon his chest 'and soe oppressed him that he could not speake nor stur noe not soe much as to awake his wife althow he Endeavered much soe to do itt'.[59] Whether such experiences were psychosexual in origin it is hard to say; but all correspond to the literal meaning of a nightmare – being helplessly ridden by a female spirit or hag while asleep – and accord with culturally established 'nocturnal assault traditions'.[60]

In the courtroom, as in popular belief, exactly how victims perceived their tormentors was not necessarily important. It is not recorded that Sarah Osborne was pressed about the Indian (presumably the slave Tituba) by her examiner, John Hathorne, who asked what she had *seen* in the loosest sense.[61] It was possible for real and imaginary realms to be defined differently in the seventeenth century, forming two halves of a whole, between which the traffic of words and images was unimpeded by the demands of empirical truth as we might understand it. For many witnesses, this was an unconscious process of cognition; but it also happened to be an effective means of legal storytelling by which to articulate fear and apportion blame. Depositions suggest that there was a way to tell a good dream, just as there may have been a way to tell a good ghost story.[62]

Like spirits, miracles were too engrained in popular understandings of God to be banished, even though the age of miracles had officially passed. Just two have been chosen for discussion: the processes of illness and recovery, and the outcomes of unofficial ordeals. Of course, what are here termed 'miracles' would have been seen by godly contemporaries simply as God's opposition to maleficence, quite unlike the gross thaumaturgical spectacles they reviled in England's Catholic past. Miraculousness for our purposes, however, consists less in the intrinsic nature of the phenomena, than the fact that they allowed witnesses to articulate their beliefs in a formal setting. Again, miracles tended to formalize suspicions rather than provide hard evidence, but were none the less useful for that. In 1664 Elizabeth Style of Somerset was prosecuted by Richard Hill, whose daughter had suffered alarming fits – possibly natural, possibly fraudulent – and, like a medieval saint, stigmatic, or Christ *in extremis*, had displayed 'holes made in her hand, wrist, face, neck and other parts of her body which the informant and others that saw them conceived to be with thorns, for they saw thorns in her flesh, and some they hooked out'. According to testimony made by, among others, the parish rector, these holes opened up before their very eyes, corroborating Style's confession that she stuck thorns into wax images.[63] Tales of miraculous recoveries were common. In the 1640s when a Yorkshire suspect asked forgiveness of a woman whose son lay sick, the woman claimed that she pricked the suspect's face and the child recovered at once.[64] According to her mother, a sick girl at Tynmouth (Northumberland) in 1660 recovered just enough after similar counter-magic to prove bewitchment, but not so much that there would then have been no case to answer.[65] Control tests underlined the significance of recoveries, regardless of how unobjective they seem. Testimony against one witch told of how a sick girl anointed with a potion from the *suspect's* bowl, experienced distress; when from her *mother's spoon*, relief.[66]

Stories of ordeals seem similarly contrived, especially demonstrations of the belief, backed by learned (but not biblical) authority, that corpses bled if touched by the murderer.[67] Witnesses against a Lancashire witch in 1612, deposed that she, 'coming to touch the dead corpse, it bled fresh blood presently in the presence of all that were there present', a point the judge emphasized in his instruction to the jury not to expect hard evidence, adding that 'unless it please Almighty God to raise witnesses to accuse them, who is able to condemn them?'[68] In the 1650s the physician Thomas Ady noted the anomaly that some who opposed the water ordeal because it was without scriptural foundation, took cruentation for granted. Among these he counted assize judges who, in his opinion, 'may be too presumptious in condemning a man upon any such evidence as that is'.[69] As it happens, swimming suspected witches was also ritualized: buoyancy was regulated by means of a rope, and thus the swimming test was not a test at all.[70] By the later seventeenth century, things were changing, albeit slowly. In the same month as the Salem courts were busy interrogating witches, one Kent village was swimming its suspects, but in deference to the advancing empiricism of the age paid a man 5s. to be swum as a control experiment.[71] Ordeals were rituals, and stories about them symbolic and representational; but in a social environment where emotions rather than rules underpinned truth, such symbols and representations could be a powerful means of articulating community convictions.[72]

The fourth motif were stock-dramas: role-plays foisted upon suspects to steer accusations.[73] These were orchestrated in the community, or fabricated in testimony, to link cause and effect in tight narrative sequences, especially the witch's actions and subsequent bewitchment. Some witnesses describe freezing at the sight of witches. John Louder 'had no power to set one foot forward' in the presence of Bridget Bishop; and an Englishman 'was always forcibly stayed' each time he tried to scratch a witch's face.[74] Descriptions of symptoms were more effective still. Alice Wade of Stretham (Isle of Ely) deposed in 1647 that after Dorothy Ellis stroked her baby's cheek, one of its eyes began to stream. After dark, Alice 'did light a candle and look upon her child and did find the side that Dorothy Ellis touched all swelled, and one of her child's eyes out'.[75] Even the most innocuous gestures could be seen as sinister. A Yorkshire suspect, who told a man at a Christmas hog-roast that 'she loved him and all at his house very well, and gave him a little clap with her hand on his knee', had her goodwill turned against her after the man's knee swelled up.[76] Physical marks gave substance to the ethereality of witchcraft. In Jacobean Buckinghamshire, when the body of a supposed witchcraft victim was laid out, it was said to be covered in bruises.[77] A Londoner, grabbed by a suspect as he tried to swim her in the Thames in 1704, experienced 'a strange pain on his arm, and looking on it found the exact mark of her hand and fingers as black as a coal'. She may well have bruised him, but the precision of the marks in his testimony was surely a significant embellishment.[78]

Material evidence dovetailed with suspicions in other ways and helped to develop them. After Bernard Peach claimed to have bitten Susannah Martin's fingers, 'the Rumer went that the s'd martin had a broken hand at that time'.[79] At Northampton in 1612, a woman who had led a search on a suspected witch found her washing 'all bespotted with the pictures of toads, snakes and other ugly creatures'; and the following year, the laundry of a Kent woman troubled by witchcraft was sprinkled with what she described as 'perfect red blood'.[80] As we have seen, other accusations relied on physical descriptions, especially clothing, as when Edward Dynham described two witches down to the colour of the man's stockings. Similarly, Richard Hill testified that during her fits his daughter, 'usually tells what clothes Elizabeth Style hath on at the time, which the informer and others have seen and found true'.[81] Even though this is unremarkable when one considers that suspects' wardrobes were unlikely to have been extensive, even stating the obvious could strike a chord in a stage-managed theatre of accusation, just as in a morality play or pantomime.

Legal miracles display the effectiveness of expressing one's convictions by orthodox means rather than by illegal countermeasures. The witch who, in a pamphlet of 1612, feared that 'the power of the law would be stronger than the power of her art', was, in effect, promoting this idea to a reading public. In the 1589 case of the witches of Warboys, no sooner had the Samuel family been hanged, but their victims' fits subsided;[82] once the woman accused of bewitching Sara Rodes had been searched, the girl's fits ceased;[83] and in 1664 a woman who had been on crutches for years was reported to have walked unaided the moment the jury returned a guilty verdict.[84] At the examination of George Burroughs at Salem, Susannah Sheldon testified that his two former wives appeared, crying that he had murdered them. As depositions against him were read out, the witnesses fell into fits.[85] Even imprisonment might torment a witch, or at least neutralize his or her powers. A Newcastle woman who in the 1660s claimed that Ann Mennin had made her children ill, noted that when she was imprisoned for another crime, her children 'grew better and mended pretty well, but since the said Mennin was set at liberty they have been very sore troubled and tormented as aforesaid'.[86] Unsurprisingly, informal custody, unsanctioned by God and the state, did not have the same potency as that imposed by a magistrate.[87]

Victims were best placed to direct their own dramas. A Yorkshire suspect, persuaded to beg forgiveness of Lady Mallory's daughter, sensed danger as the sick girl recovered and retracted her plea. However, the girl said: 'if she denied it I shall be ill again, and presently begun with her ill fits as formerly', adding that she would never be well until the witch was taken before a JP.[88] Suspects could scarcely win. At Ashford (Kent) in 1651, a cunning man, Anthony Harlott, predicted that if Sarah Harris was bewitched the witch would arrive in poor health. When a sick-looking Wilman Worsiter appeared, Harlott asked her how she was. 'Lord, am I brought hither to be a wondering-stock to all the company', she replied, falling to her knees and begging: 'good sir, show mercy on me and do not accuse me.' According to Harlott, she touched the child and said: 'I pray God bless thee, God send thee well to do,' and the child recovered. In fact, the source of Harlott's suspicion was Sarah Harris herself, prompting him to send for her to fulfil his prophecy.[89] Hence attempts by suspects to extricate themselves often made things worse.[90] This explains why some suspects broke down, such as the woman in Elizabethan Oxfordshire who admitted the charges against her in the hope of being shown mercy, or the Yorkshirewoman who said she 'did confesse unto them what they required in hope to be freed from further blowes'.[91]

Because deathbed scenes had high evidentiary status, last words were reported in an overblown fashion. The jury at the trial of the 'Witch of Edmonton' in 1621 were persuaded by a victim's dying oath, 'namely, that if she died at that time, she the said Elizabeth Sawyer was the cause of her death, and maliciously did by her witchery procure the same'.[92] In 1665 a Lancashire woman testified that a figure pulling down her chimney had vanished as her husband ran towards it. Subsequently, he sickened and declared that if he seemed likely to die, he would swear that witchcraft was the cause.[93] Also focused on the bedchamber were the rituals of possession and exorcism, both of which conformed to the cultural expectations of participants.[94] Testimony made by juries of matrons (searching for the witch's mark) was dramatized too, and their verdicts can be seen as 'simply expressions of local sentiment concerning the innocence or guilt of the accused'.[95] A witness against Ellen Garrison of Upwell (Isle of Ely) said 'she discerned but two teats near to her fundament and that upon her second search the day after she saw three much bigger than they were the day before'. According to Anne Clarke, they were 'such as she never sawe before and that (by her experience being a midwife) she verily believes them not to be natural'.[96] The subjective nature of such examinations is underlined by the fact that the existence of diabolic teats was often used *against* a suspect, but their absence rarely used as a defence.[97] Ironically, the best examples where it was come from Salem.[98]

III

So what do witchcraft depositions tell us about truth in the early modern world? How can one explain the currency of legal stories more likely to make a modern jury laugh than elicit its sympathy? Did witnesses sincerely believe the things they said? If not, how did they expect their testimony to be convincing? Assuming for a moment that they did believe their own testimony, we are left with a more difficult question: how could they really have experienced extraordinary phenomena such as bleeding wounds or encounters with spirits? Here the search for answers is less relevant than finding the right questions. Sincerity is usually impossible to determine, and, in any case, we have no reason to doubt it in most instances. We know that sane people hallucinate, and that eyewitnesses are unreliable, becoming confident about a certain version of events which crystalizes from repeated retelling.[99] Instead, we should concentrate on patterns of historically-specific social communication because these can be demonstrated, and help us to understand mentalities.

We have seen that pre-trial procedure was crucial for prosecutions, for here local beliefs and desires were translated into action. Performance was key. Ordeals were not objective experiments where truth was uncovered, but occasions when existing convictions were voiced graphically and memorably for an audience. Regarding testimony, witnesses colluded with neighbours or participated in a less-conscious process of gossip and discussion. What is certain is that they had to persuade, and for us to dismiss stylized testimony as perjury presupposes mentalities too like our own, and disregards the framework of values within which witchcraft accusations were made. That such actions might have been acceptable, even necessary, to rid the community of a perceived threat, makes them seem not only understandable but logical. The precedence of communal over individual loyalties meant witnesses could say with utter conviction, and without disingenuousness, things we would consider untrue, observing a 'third-truth value' – that is, neither true nor untrue by *our* epistemological standards.[100] Even today, truth varies according to the contexts in which it originates and is expressed, but the modern western world has become less sensitive to this fact, and less willing to admit to 'the essentially provisional nature of cognitive judgements'.[101]

Witchcraft confessions should also be taken seriously, both in form and content, and we need to suppress assumptions that, *de facto*, they stem from insanity or torture. Witchcraft was more than an ideological weapon: it was a fantasy for dispossessed people, which they not only understood, but described in particular ways.[102] Tituba's confession is a classic example. 'The black dog said serve me but I said I am a fraid,' she related, 'he said if I did not he would doe worse to me.' The black dog then became a man who promised her 'pretty things'.[103] Similar tales originate in England. In 1645, Suffolk folk confessed that the devil, appearing in various shapes, offered money and vengeance if they would sign a covenant. The Somerset witch Elizabeth Style confessed that 'the Devil appeared to her in the shape of a black Dog; that he promised her money, and that she should live gallantly, and have the pleasure of the world for twelve years if she would with her blood sign his paper'. At one meeting she feasted on wine, cakes and roast meat, danced, and was merry.[104] The content of Deliverance Hobbs's confession at Salem was almost identical.[105] In this way, witches dreamily encompassed their social elevation, in one case literally. Mercy Lewis claimed that George Burroughs's spectre carried her 'up to an exceeding high mountain and shewed me all the kingdoms of the earth and tould me that he would give them all to me if I would writ in his book'.[106] Other women were resigned to becoming witches. Ellen Baron deposed that before Elizabeth Foote was searched by women at Stretham (Isle of Ely), Foote bemoaned her incriminating bodily marks, lamenting: 'woe woe was the tyme that ever I was borne of such [an] accursed mother'.[107]

More commonly, however, becoming a witch raised hopes of blessed release from anxiety, suffering, and powerlessness. At Salem, Lydia Nichols deposed that Abigail Hobbs said that 'she was not a fraid of any thing for She told me She had Sold her selfe boddy & Soull to the old boy'.[108] Witchcraft even offered an alternative to Christian worship. Susanna Sheldon said she met Phillip English with a black man in a high-crowned hat whom English introduced as his God, who would relieve her discomfort;[109] and a monkey with claws and a man's face told John Louder: 'I am a Messenger sent to you for I understand you are trobled in mind, and if you will be Ruled by mee you shall want for Nothing in this world.' He resisted, however, striking at the beast and crying: 'the whole amor of god be between mee and you.'[110] Less resilient was Adam Sabie of Haddenham (Isle of Ely) who confessed that a spirit appeared to him 'in a flame of fire' and, like Abraham's vision in *Genesis*, inveighed: 'fear not Sabie for I am thy God'. The initiate was then dispatched to Lady Sandys house, where he was told to expect £20.[111] Witchcraft, in this sense, was not just a social and religious reality for the accuser but for the accused as well. Moreover, confessed witches adhered to universally recognized conventions about how to tell a good story, and thus seem very like the witnesses who spoke against them. In Jacobean Warminster (Wiltshire), Margaret Pilton spoke of trading souls for longer lives, and claimed to see apparitions whereby 'she brought the people in great admiration to admire at her'. A woman in Oxford even imagined that by saying certain words, she had transported herself into her sister's bedchamber to bewitch her child, only to find it 'armed with the prayers of the parents'. In this statement, she recognized the supremacy of providence.[112]

If witches and witnesses tailored their testimony for the benefit of magistrates, what does this tell us about élite beliefs? As one might expect, some JPs were credulous, some sceptical, the latter becoming more numerous after 1680. Many believed in the possibility of witchcraft, but were dubious of the proof used at law, and even came to doubt that conclusive proof existed at all. Yet much of this is as speculative as searching for the sincerity of witnesses. In recent years, social anthropologists and historians of mentalities have suggested that the importance of what people thought and believed lies less in what they said and wrote, but in what they *did* – the way they behaved in concrete social contexts.[113] And what JPs *did* above all else was apply the law. In England an Act declared witchcraft a felony, and the Marian statutes of bail and committal made JPs responsible for initiating prosecutions.[114] At one level, then, JPs were obliged to prosecute witchcraft, irrespective of private belief. In practice, of course, even diligent JPs needed persuading that it was not pointless to proceed, and required witnesses to justify their accusations. For this reason, the emotional power of testimony could be crucial to ensure that a case proceeded, although, ironically, to this end even sceptical JPs and judges may actually have helped witnesses to deliver effective evidence.[115]

Approaching witchcraft in this way shows mentalities in action rather than just as abstracts, producing not just a single synthesis of élite and popular attitudes and beliefs, but 'multiple orderings of reality'.[116] And yet it does something else as well. If pre-trial procedure helps to explain why witch trials occurred, it also explains why they declined. There were no convictions in New England after 1692, and after 1697 no prosecutions. In England, the last recorded execution, conviction, and trial occurred in 1685, 1712, and 1717 respectively.[117] Conversely, when the repeal of the Witchcraft Act did come in 1736, it had everything to do with religion and politics, and very little to do with the law.[118] Why trials should have ground to a halt much earlier is a complex matter, but an important factor is that witnesses' narrative strategies lost their persuasive power in the eyes of authority.

By 1680, standards of evidence closer to those expected in modern prosecutions were being observed in English courts.[119] Notwithstanding Dalton's advice on evidence, rates of conviction in witch trials had always been surprisingly low – 44 per cent at the Home Circuit assizes – and declined after 1600. Likewise, in New England the acquittal rate was high before the Salem trials, because a diabolical compact had normally to be proved; when evidentiary standards were reimposed, convictions for witchcraft once again became relatively rare.[120] Increasingly, successful prosecutions were those backed by physical evidence, but even this wore thin. The verdict against Joan Buts at the Surrey assizes in 1682 was met with 'the great amazement of some who thought the evidence sufficient to have found her guilty, yet others who consider the great difficulty in proving a witch, thought the jury could do no less than acquit her'.[121] In such a climate of opinion, witnesses were put on their mettle. At the trial of Jane Wenham in 1712, the clerk refused to frame an indictment for anything other than conversing with a familiar spirit in the shape of a cat, leading canny witnesses to exaggerate this aspect of the accusation rather than grievances which concerned them more, but which they realized were legally redundant.[122]

It is hard to say how influential spectral evidence had ever been once depositions had left the magistrate's parlour; the machinations of the courtroom are historically inscrutable. In 1604 in a case of alleged demonic possession, Anne Gunter of North Moreton (Berkshire), identified three familiars in a vision, evidence which was judged to be spectral as a consequence.[123] Spectral evidence was heard in courtrooms later in the century. At the Bury St Edmunds trials in 1662, Sir Matthew Hale admitted spectral evidence from witnesses who fell into fits as they testified.[124] The question which preoccupied English judges, however, was less whether spectral evidence was admissible, as whether it constituted proof upon which to base a conviction.[125] Apparitions did lead directly to convictions, most prolifically at Salem, where procedure 'inverted the proper relationship between spectral and "empirical" evidence',[126] even though the law of evidence remained vague until the mid-eighteenth century when truly adversarial procedure and evidential controls were formally established.[127] Yet from the early 1690s in England and New England alike, spectral evidence became firmly associated with injustice in witch trials, independent of the shifting balance between credulity and scepticism in educated circles.[128] In 1692 the Governor of Massachusetts, Sir William Phips (whose own wife was accused of witchcraft), followed the advice of the Chaplain to the King's Forces at New York, and others, in declaring that although witches undoubted existed as laid down in scripture, at Salem 'the devil had taken upon him several persons who were doubtless innocent'.[129]

A second factor is that in England at least, shared understandings between neighbours, and between witnesses and men in authority, declined as the cohesiveness of traditional communities waned. This is too large a development to describe fully.[130] Certainly, the vocalization of the cultural difference felt by England's local governors towards their social inferiors preceded universal and heartfelt contempt for their superstitious beliefs. In fact, as the case of Sir William Phips suggests, cautious credulity in witchcraft lingered among social élites despite escalating rates of acquittal at law. One London gentleman expressed a typical sentiment in 1697, saying that although he did not doubt the existence of witches, in Europe they were no longer tried because the courts found it 'impossible to distinguish possession from nature in disorder, and they choose rather to let the guilty escape than to punish the innocent'.[131] Simultaneously, we see signs of profound social and cultural fragmentation, especially with high levels of migration to the towns by the poor in need of work, and the rich – including absentee JPs – in search of diversion and luxury. Migration may have diffused some of the tensions behind witchcraft accusations; but it seems likely also to have diminished the common interests and social intimacy by which the authorities had, for generations, sustained political sensitivity to the demands of ordinary people.[132]

Depositions are crucial for reconstructing the social and legal contexts which show how witch trials were possible initially, and why, in the end, they became impossible. Storytelling strategies do not necessarily explain why certain people became suspected of witchcraft; but they do shed light on how they were pursued through the courts, and, more obliquely, on the thinking of witnesses when they dealt with men in authority. Nor is this just important for understanding witchcraft, the significance of which has almost certainly been exaggerated anyway. Far more pressing is the need for historians to listen carefully to the voices of the poorer sort, and for this purpose witchcraft boosts the signals emitted from the sources which have passed down to us. At the very least, we need to distance ourselves from the notion that our ancestors were weak-minded – a present-centred opinion 'based on a mixture of ignorance and dubious self-satisfaction'.[133] It is most fruitful to understand witchcraft not just from above or below (or even in the social spaces between), but, in keeping with the current concerns of cultural historians, from *within*. It has been the central contention of this chapter that this is how surviving documentary evidence – especially the testimony of witches and witnesses in depositions – can best be exploited historically.

Notes

1. J. S. Cockburn, 'Early Modern Assize Records as Historical Evidence', *Journal of the Society of Archivists*, 5 (1975), 216; Alan Macfarlane, *The Justice and the Mare's Ale: Law and Disorder in Seventeenth-Century England* (Cambridge, 1981), pp. 37–8.
2. On the value of depositions for the history of witchcraft, see Clive Holmes, 'Women: Witnesses and Witches', *Past and Present*, 140 (1993), 46–7; J. A. Sharpe, *Witchcraft in Seventeenth-Century Yorkshire: Accusations and Counter Measures* (York, 1992), p. 4.
3. For a discussion of problems and methodology, see Malcolm Gaskill, *Crime and Mentalities in Early Modern England* (Cambridge, 2000), ch. 1.
4. Cynthia B. Herrup, *The Common Peace: Participation and the Criminal Law in Seventeenth-Century England* (Cambridge, 1987), p. 160; T. A. Green, *Verdict According to Conscience: Perspectives on the English Trial Jury, 1200– 1800* (Chicago, IL, 1985), p. 137. In general, see John G. Bellamy, *Criminal Law and Society in Late Medieval and Tudor England* (Gloucester, 1984), chs 2–3; Thomas G. Barnes, 'Examination before a Justice in the Seventeenth Century', *Notes and Queries for Somerset and Dorset*, 27 (1955), 39–42.
5. For this view of magistrates, see Douglas Hay, 'Property, Authority and the Criminal law', in Douglas Hay et al. (eds), *Albion's Fatal Tree: Crime and Society in Eighteenth-Century England* (London, 1975), pp. 17–63, esp. 40, 51–2. Cf. James C. Scott, *Domination and the Arts of Resistance: Hidden Transcripts* (Yale, CT, 1990).
6. On these issues in general, see James Sharpe, 'The People and the Law', in Barry Reay (ed.), *Popular Culture in Seventeenth-Century England* (London, 1985), pp. 244–70; Adam Fox, 'Custom, Memory and the Authority of Writing', in Paul Griffiths, Adam Fox and Steve Hindle (eds), *The Experience of Authority in Early Modern England* (London, 1996), pp. 89–116; Roger Chartier, 'Texts, Printing, Readings', in Lynn Hunt (ed.), *The New Cultural History* (Berkeley, CA, 1989), pp. 154–75.
7. Miranda Chaytor, 'Husband(ry): Narratives of Rape in the Seventeenth Century', *Gender and History*, 7 (1995), 380. The interpretation of these aspects of testimony, however, remains highly tendentious, see Garthine Walker, 'Rereading Rape and Sexual Violence in Early Modern England', *Gender and History*, 10 (1998), 1–25

8. Clive Holmes, 'Popular Culture? Witches, Magistrates and Divines in Early Modern England', in Steven L. Kaplan (ed.), *Understanding Popular Culture* (Berlin, 1984), pp. 88–92, 94, 105. See, for example, the case of Sir Francis North at the Exeter assizes in 1682: Roger North,*The Lives of the Norths*, ed. Augustus Jessopp, 3 vols (London, 1890), vol. 1, pp. 166–9; vol. 3, pp. 130–1.

9. The classic account is Natalie Zemon Davis, *Fiction in the Archives: Pardon Tales and their Tellers in Sixteenth-Century France* (Stanford, CT, 1987). Cf. W. Lance Bennett and Martha S. Feldman, *Reconstructing Reality in the Courtroom* (London, 1981).

10. Gillian Bennett, 'Women's Personal Experience Stories of Encounters with the Supernatural', *ARV: Scandanavian Yearbook of Folklore*, 40 (1984), 87; W. Lance Bennett, 'Storytelling in Criminal Trials: A Model of Social Judgment', *Quarterly Journal of Speech*, 64 (1978), 1–22, quotation at p. 1. For a stimulating discussion of this in relation to witchcraft accusations, but taken in a slightly different direction, see Peter Rushton's contribution to this volume (Chapter 1).

11. Quoting Holmes, 'Women: Witnesses and Witches', p. 53.

12. Public Record Office, London (hereafter PRO), ASSI 45. A number are reproduced in J. Raine (ed.), *Depositions from the Castle of York Relating to Offences Committed in the Northern Counties in the Seventeenth Century*, Surtees Society, vol. 40 (1861).

13. Cambridge University Library (hereafter CUL), EDR E7–24 (assize files, 1615–65), especially EDR E12, 'Assize 1647 Michaelmas 1–51 Witchcraft'. For a selection, see *East Anglian Notes and Queries*, 13 (1909), 277–8; C. L'Estrange Ewen,*Witch Hunting and Witch Trials* (London, 1929), pp. 54–5; Enid Porter, *Cambridgeshire Customs and Folklore* (Cambridge, 1969), pp. 162–6, 174.

14. PRO, STAC 8. See C. L'Estrange Ewen, *Witchcraft in Star Chamber* (n. p., 1938).

15. Many contemporary pamphlets, tracts, and books reproduced depositions, the originals of which are now lost. There seems little reason to doubt their authenticity in most cases, especially those which conform closely to the style and form of manuscript testimonies.

16. Bengt Ankarloo and Gustav Henningsen (eds), *Early Modern European Witchcraft: Centres and Peripheries* (Oxford, 1990), pp. 1–2.

17. Classic studies include G. L. Kittredge, *Witchcraft in Old and New England* (Cambridge, MA, 1929); Paul Boyer and Stephen Nissenbaum, *Salem Possessed: the Social Origins of Witchcraft* (Cambridge, MA, 1974); John Demos, *Entertaining Satan: Witchcraft and the Culture of Early New England* (New York, 1982); Carol Karlson, *The Devil in the Shape of a Woman: Witchcraft in Colonial New England* (New York, 1987).

18. David Grayson Allen, *In English Ways: The Movement of Societies and their Transferal of English Local Law and Custom to Massachusetts Bay in the Seventeenth Century* (North Carolina, 1981); David Cressy, *Coming Over: Migration and Communication between England and New England in the*

History and Story in Witchcraft Trials

Seventeenth Century (Cambridge, 1987).

19. David D. Hall, *Worlds of Wonder, Days of Judgement: Popular Religious Belief in Early New England* (New York, 1989); Richard Godbeer, *The Devil's Dominion: Magic and Religion in Early New England* (Cambridge, 1992).

20. Richard Weisman, *Witchcraft, Magic, and Religion in Seventeenth-Century Massachusetts* (Amhurst, MA, 1984), pp. 13–16; Gail Sussman Marcus, '"Due Execution of the Generall Rules of Righteousness": Criminal Procedure in New Haven Town and Colony, 1638–1658', in David D. Hall, John M. Murrin and Thad W. Tate (eds), *Saints and Revolutionaries: Essays on Early American History* (New York, 1984), pp. 99–100, 102–5, 109.

21. Paul Boyer and Stephen Nissenbaum (eds), *The Salem Witchcraft Papers: Verbatim Transcripts of the Legal Documents of the Salem Witchcraft Outbreak of 1692*, 3 vols (New York, 1977), replaces W. Elliot Woodward (ed.), *Records of Salem Witchcraft Copied from the Original Documents*, 2 vols (Roxbury, MA, 1864–65; reprinted New York, 1969). For the longer perspective, see David D. Hall (ed.), *Witch-Hunting in Seventeenth-Century New England: A Documentary History, 1638–1692* (Boston, MA, 1991).

22. Quoting Weisman, *Witchcraft, Magic, and Religion*, p. 132.

23. James Sharpe, *Instruments of Darkness: Witchcraft in England, 1550–1750* (London, 1995), pp. 144–5; David Harley, 'Explaining Salem: Calvinist Psychology and the Diagnosis of Possession', *American Historical Review*, 101 (1996), 307–33; Bernard Rosenthal, *Salem Story: Reading the Witch Trials of 1692* (Cambridge, 1993), quotation at p. 9. On political myth-making about the Salem witch trials, see Philip Gould, 'New England Witch-Hunting and the Politics of Reason in the Early Republic', *New England Quarterly*, 68 (1995), 58–82.

24. As Jim Sharpe has observed of the East Anglian trials, few witch-panics outside England led to 200 prosecutions in six months: *Instruments of Darkness*, p. 130.

25. On this and other shifts in the recent historiography, see Alison Rowlands, 'Telling witchcraft stories: new perspectives on witchcraft and witches in the early modern period', *Gender & History*, 10 (1998), 294–302.

26. Cf. Malcolm Gaskill, 'Reporting murder: fiction in the archives in early modern England', *Social History*, 23 (1998), 1–30.

27. For a study which suggests that supernatural experiences offer a key to understanding basic mental functions in human beings, see Donald Ward, 'The Little Man who Wasn't There: Encounters with the Supranormal', *Fabula*, 18 (1977), 212–25.

28. Keith Thomas, *Religion and the Decline of Magic: Studies in Popular Beliefs in Sixteenth- and Seventeenth-Century England* (London, 1971), ch. 19; Gillian Bennett, *Traditions of Belief: Women and the Supernatural* (London, 1987), ch. 6; Nancy Caciola, 'Wraiths, Revenants and Ritual in Medieval Culture', *Past and Present*, 152 (1996), 3–45.

29. Centre for Kentish Studies (hereafter CKS), NR/JQp 1/30 ff. 1–6. For a full account of this case, see Malcolm Gaskill, 'The Devil in the Shape of a Man: Witchcraft, Conflict and Belief in Jacobean England', *Historical*

Research, 71 (1998), 142–71.

30. PRO, ASSI 45/5/1/87.
31. PRO, ASSI 45/6/1/166, 168–168A.
32. PRO, PL 27/1, testimony of John Nuttall, 1681.
33. PRO, STAC 8/207/21, m. 1. A household at Wakefield (Yorkshire) in 1656, fearing witchcraft, reported eerie noises, slamming doors, and 'several apparitions like black dogs and cats': PRO, ASSI 45/5/3/14.
34. British Library (hereafter BL), Sloane MS 972, ff. 7–7v.
35. BL, Add. MS 36674, ff. 189–92v; PRO, ASSI 45/6/1/168.
36. Boyer and Nissenbaum (eds), *Salem Witchcraft Papers*, vol. 1, pp. 94–5.
37. This was certainly the case with much of the testimony made against suspected secret murderers, see Gaskill, 'Reporting Murder', pp. 14–16.
38. Boyer and Nissenbaum (eds), *Salem Witchcraft Papers*, vol. 1, p. 102.
39. Ibid., vol. 2, p. 562. Samuel Wilkins described the apparition of John Willard as wearing 'a darke collored coot and a black hate very like that hate which I formerly saw': ibid., vol. 3, p. 843.
40. *Most Fearefull and strange Newes From the Bishoppricke of Durham* (London, 1641), pp. 5–6; PRO, ASSI 45/6/1/88. In another Newcastle case, a man and his wife made an apparition of a witch disappear by calling upon God: PRO, ASSI 45/7/1/7.
41. *Wonderfull News from the North. Or, a True relation of the Sad and Grievous Torments, Inflicted upon the Bodies of three Children of Mr. George Muschamp* (London, 1650), pp. 11–16. She described the angels as 'bodyed like Birds, as big as Turkies, and faces like Christians, but the sweetest creatures that ever eyes beheld': ibid., p. 12.
42. Boyer and Nissenbaum (eds), *Salem Witchcraft Papers*, vol. 3, pp. 839–40.
43. Ibid., vol. 2, p. 601.
44. See, for example, *The History of the Works of the Learned for the Year One Thousand Seven Hundred and Forty*, 2 vols (London, 1740), vol. 1, p. 901.
45. Michael Dalton, *The Countrey Justice* (London, 1618), p. 269; William Lambarde, *Eirenarcha, or of the Office of the Justices of Peace* (London, 1619), p. 212.
46. 1 Jac. I, c. 12 (1604); William H. Whitmore, *The Colonial Laws of Massachusetts*, 2 vols (Boston, MA, 1889), vol. 1, p. 55. Colonists reverted to English law after their charter was revoked in 1684; a new statute of 1692 followed the 1604 Act closely: Sanford J. Fox, *Science and Justice: The Massachusetts Witchcraft Trials* (Baltimore, MD, 1968), pp. 37, 41.
47. Dalton, *Countrey Justice*, p. 243.
48. Alan Gauld, *The Founders of Psychical Research* (London, 1968), pp. 207–9; Denys Parsons, 'Testimony and Truth', *Horizon*, 9 (1944), 393–401.
49. W. Dewi Rees, 'The Hallucinations of Widowhood', *British Medical Journal*, 4 (1971), 37–41; Sylivia H. Wright, 'Experiences of Spontaneous Psychokinesis after Bereavement', *Journal of the Society for Psychical Research*, 62 (1998), 385–95; Jean Wertheimer, 'Some Hypotheses about the Genesis of Visual Hallucinations in Dementia', in Cornelius Katona and Raymond Levy (eds), *Delusions and Hallucinations in Old Age* (London,

1992), pp. 201–8.
50. PRO, ASSI 45/6/1/69v.
51. John Brinley, *A Discovery of the Impostures of Witches and Astrologers* (London, 1680), p. 25. Earlier in the century, Richard Bernard warned that 'the strong imagination' of people who believed themselves bewitched led them to see apparitions and 'for feare' dream of suspects: *A Guide to Grand-Jury Men* (London, 1627; 1629 edn), pp. 195–6.
52. Historical Manuscripts Commission (hereafter HMC),*The Manuscripts of the Duke of Portland*, 10 vols (London, 1891–1931), vol. 1, p. 677; A. Rupert Hall and Marie Boas Hall (eds),*The Correspondence of Henry Oldenburg*, 12 vols (London, 1965–86), vol. 5, p. 15; Boyer and Nissenbaum (eds), *Salem Witchcraft Papers*, vol. 1, p. 94.
53. *The Poetical Works of Lord Byron*, ed. Humphrey Milford (Oxford, 1921), p. 90; Steven F. Kruger, *Dreaming in the Middle Ages* (Cambridge, 1992), ch. 6; Lucien Lévy-Bruhl, *Primitive Mentality* (London, 1923), ch. 3.
54. PRO, ASSI 45/3/2/129.
55. Boyer and Nissenbaum (eds), *Salem Witchcraft Papers*, vol. 1, p. 376.
56. Ibid., vol. 2, p. 611. My italic.
57. *The Wonderfull Discoverie of the Witchcrafts of Margaret and Phillip Flower ... Executed at Lincolne, March 11, 1618* (London, 1619), sig. E4.
58. Boyer and Nissenbaum (eds), *Salem Witchcraft Papers*, vol. 2, p. 562. For interesting comments about dreams, sleep paralysis and false memories, see Mark Pendegrast, *Victims of Memory: Incest Accusations and Shattered Lives* (London, 1996), pp. 116–20.
59. Boyer and Nissenbaum (eds), *Salem Witchcraft Papers*, vol. 1, p. 102. Cf. Sharpe, *Witchcraft in Seventeenth-Century Yorkshire*, p. 7.
60. David J. Hufford, *The Terror that Comes in the Night: An Experience-Centred Study of Nocturnal Assault Traditions* (Philadelphia, PA, 1982). For an example of a Scottish witch allegedly abducting a victim from her bed, see Paul Hair, *Before the Bawdy Court: Selections from Church Court and Other Records Relating to the Correction of Moral Offences in England, Scotland and New England, 1300–1800* (London, 1972), p. 227.
61. Boyer and Nissenbaum (eds), *Salem Witchcraft Papers*, vol. 2, p. 611.
62. On the use of 'story grammars' to relay information in different ways, see David C. Rubin, *Memory in Oral Traditions: The Cognitive Psychology of Epic, Ballads, and Counting-Out Rhymes* (Oxford, 1995), pp. 28–31.
63. Joseph Glanvill, *Sadducismus Triumphatus*, 4th edn (London, 1726), pp. 290–1. It is intriguing that a Somerset widow of the same name was tried at the assizes for witchcraft back in 1636, see J. S. Cockburn,*Western Circuit Assize Orders, 1629–1648: A Calendar*, Camden Society, 4th series (London, 1976), p. 99.
64. PRO, ASSI 45/4/1/131.
65. PRO, ASSI 45/5/7/95.
66. Glanvill, *Sadducismus Triumphatus*, p. 305.
67. Dalton, *Countrey Justice*, p. 243; James I, *Daemonologie* (London, 1603), p. 229; John Webster, *The Displaying of Supposed Witchcraft* (London, 1677),

pp. 305–10. For scepticism of this and other miracles, see Reginald Scot, *The Discoverie of Witchcraft* (London, 1584), pp. 171–2. See also Gaskill, 'Reporting Murder', pp. 8–13.

68. Thomas Potts, *The Wonderfull Discoverie of Witches in the Countie of Lancaster* (London, 1613), ed. J. Crossley, Chetham Society, vol. 6 (1845), sigs. Y3v, Z3.

69. Thomas Ady, *A Candle in the Dark* (London, 1655), p. 131. For examples from New England, see 'Ordeal of Touch in Colonial Virginia', *Virginia Historical Magazine*, 4 (1897), 185–97; Charles J. Hoadly, 'Some Early Post-Mortem Examinations in New England', *Proceedings of the Connecticut State Medical Society*, 69 (1892), 213.

70. BL, Add. MSS 36674, f. 148.

71. *Athenian Mercury* (28 Feb. 1693).

72. Cf. Max Gluckman,*The Judicial Process among the Barotse of Northern Rhodesia* (Manchester, 1955). On symbols in general, see C. R. Hallpike, *The Foundations of Primitive Thought* (Oxford, 1979), ch. 4; M. Lewis, 'Introduction', in Ioan Lewis (ed.), *Symbols and Sentiments: Cross-Cultural Studies in Symbolism* (London, 1977), pp. 1–24.

73. For a classic example in a pamphlet account, see Edmond Bower, *Doctor Lamb Revived, Or, Witchcraft condemn'd in Anne Bodenham A Servant of his, who was Arraigned and Executed the Lent Assizes last at Salisbury* (London, 1653).

74. Boyer and Nissenbaum (eds), *Salem Witchcraft Papers*, vol. 1, p. 100; C. L'Estrange Ewen, *Witchcraft and Demonianism* (London, 1933), p. 207.

75. CUL, EDR E12 1647/15.

76. PRO, ASSI 45/3/1/243. A boy who believed himself bewitched in 1658 denied that he had fallen out with the suspect, only that she had 'stroked him over the head and said he was a fine boy': PRO, ASSI 45/5/5/1.

77. PRO, STAC 8/270/1, m. 1.

78. *A Full and true Account Of the Discovery, Apprehending and taking of a Notorious Witch* (London, 1704).

79. Boyer and Nissenbaum (eds), *Salem Witchcraft Papers*, vol. 2, p. 563. This transcript says 'head', but the 'hand' in the earlier edition makes much more sense: Woodward (ed.), *Records of Salem Witchcraft*, vol. 1, p. 213.

80. CKS, NR/JQp 1/30 ff. 6–7; *The Witches of Northamptonshire ... Who were all executed at Northampton the 22 of July last, 1612* (London, 1612), reprinted in Barbara Rosen (ed.), *Witchcraft in England, 1558–1618* (Amherst, MA, 1991), pp. 350–1.

81. BL, Add. MS. 36674, f. 189–189v; Glanvill, *Sadducismus Triumphatus*, pp. 290–1.

82. *The Most Strange and Admirable Discoverie of the Three Witches of Warboys* (London, 1593), sig. O4.

83. PRO, ASSI 45/3/2/130.

84. *A Tryal of Witches, at the Assizes held at Bury St. Edmonds for the County of Suffolk on the Tenth day of March, 1664* (London, 1682), pp. 11–12.

85. Boyer and Nissenbaum (eds), *Salem Witchcraft Papers*, vol. 1, pp. 153–4.
86. PRO, ASSI 45/6/1/165.
87. James I, *Daemonologie*, p. 50.
88. PRO, ASSI 45/5/3/132, 133A.
89. CKS, Q/SB 2/12–12a. The grand jury found the bill, but no verdict was recorded: Q/SRc E4, ff. 78, 102. Cf. the manipulation of John Hutton of Sunderland: *Wonderfull News from the North*, p. 8. In a case from Littleport (Isle of Ely), a suspect appeared at the precise moment that a drink was offered to the horse she was supposed to have bewitched, a point quite deliberately stressed in testimony against her: CUL, EDR E12 1647/5.
90. When an Ely man defended his name against a neighbour 'raising such a crime upon him as to be a witch', the neighbour went lame: CUL, EDR E12 1647/12.
91. Georgiana Fullerton,*The Life of Lady Falkland, 1585–1639* (London, 1883), pp. 10–11; PRO, ASSI 45/1/5/38v–39.
92. Henry Goodcole, *The Wonderfull Discoverie of Elizabeth Sawyer a Witch, late of Edmonton, her Conviction and Condemnation and Death* (London, 1621), sig. B2v. In 1651 a woman allegedly said 'th[a]t if she were to dye at that Instant, she would take it upon her death yt Elizabeth Likeley had bewitched her': PRO, ASSI 45/4/1/111.
93. PRO, PL 27/1, testimony of Jane Gregory, 1665.
94. J. A. Sharpe, 'Disruption in the Well-Ordered Household: Age, Authority and Possessed Young People', in Griffiths, Fox and Hindle (eds), *Experience of Authority*, pp. 187–212; James Sharpe, *Instruments of Darkness*, ch. 8.
95. Quoting Holmes, 'Women: Witnesses and Witches', p. 74. On the subjectivity of female searchers in Massachusetts, see Fox, *Science and Justice*, ch. 7.
96. CUL, EDR E12 1647/1–2. Searchers who examined Ann Green at Littleport in 1646 and Elizabeth Foote of Stretham in 1647 gave very similar testimony: CUL, EDR E12 1647/4; EDR E12 1647/7.
97. Holmes, 'Women: Witnesses and Witches', pp. 73–5.
98. Rebecca Nurse's teat was judged to be 'only as a dry skin without sense', and on Elizabeth Proctor's body, the searchers said, 'not any thing appears, but only a proper procedeulia Ani': Boyer and Nissenbaum (eds), *Salem Witchcraft Papers*, vol. 1, p. 108.
99. Elizabeth F. Loftus, *Eyewitness Testimony* (Cambridge, 1979), esp. chs. 3–5. The classic study remains Frederic C. Bartlett, *Remembering: A Study in Experimental and Social Psychology* (Cambridge, 1932).
100. David E. Cooper, 'Alternative Logic in "Primitive Thought"', *Man*, new series 10 (1975), 238–56. The anthropologist Lucien Lévy-Bruhl spoke of people in 'primitive' societies believing 'two incompatibible certainties':*The Notebooks on Primitive Mentality* (Oxford, 1975), p. 6. On the compatibility of apparently contrasting intellectual traditions, see Brian Vickers, 'Introduction', in Brian Vickers (ed.), *Occult and Scientific Mentalities in the Renaissance* (Cambridge, 1984), pp. 1–55.

101. Quoting Steven Lukes, 'On the Social Determination of Truth', in Ruth Finnegan and Robin Horton (eds), *Modes of Thought: Essays on Thinking in Western and Non-Western Societies* (London, 1973), p. 248. Reality is constructed from symbolization, communication, and interpretation, and shifts easily: Bennett, 'Storytelling', p. 21.

102. Lyndal Roper, 'Witchcraft and Fantasy in Early Modern Germany', *History Workshop Journal*, 32 (1991), 19–43; Malcolm Gaskill, 'Witchcraft and Power in Early Modern England: The Case of Margaret Moore', in Jenny Kermode and Garthine Walker (eds),*Women, Crime and the Courts in Early Modern England* (London, 1994), pp. 125–45; Diane Purkiss, *The Witch in History: Early Modern and Twentieth-Century Representations* (London, 1996), ch. 6. Cf. Pendegrast, *Victims of Memory*, pp. 440–1.

103. Boyer and Nissenbaum (eds), *Salem Witchcraft Papers*, vol. 3, p. 748.

104. BL, Add. MS 27402, ff. 104–21; Glanvill, *Sadducismus Triumphatus*, p. 295–6.

105. Boyer and Nissenbaum (eds), *Salem Witchcraft Papers*, vol. 2, pp. 419–23.

106. Ibid., vol. 1, p. 169. Joseph Ring said a strange man showed him a book, 'to which he would have him sett his hand with p[ro]mise of any thing that he woold have & ther wear presented all delectable things p[er]sons and places Imaginabl': Ibid., vol. 2, p. 565.

107. CUL, EDR E12 1647/7.

108. Boyer and Nissenbaum (eds), *Salem Witchcraft Papers*, vol. 2, p. 413.

109. Ibid., vol. 1, p. 320.

110. Ibid., p. 100.

111. CUL, EDR E12 1647/17v; *Genesis*, xv:1.

112. HMC, *Report on Manuscripts in Various Collections*, 8 vols (London, 1901–13), vol. 1, pp. 86–7; Ewen, *Witchcraft and Demonianism*, p. 452. For the activity of witches in the dream-realm, see Carlo Ginzburg, *The Night Battles: Witchcraft and Agrarian Cults in the Sixteenth and Seventeenth Centuries* (Baltimore, MD, 1983).

113. See, for example, G. E. R. Lloyd, *Demystifying Mentalities* (Cambridge, 1990); Robert Darnton, *The Great Cat Massacre and Other Episodes in French Cultural History* (London, 1984); Pierre Bourdieu, *Outline of a Theory of Practice* (Cambridge, 1977).

114. 1&2 Ph. & M., c. 13 (1554); 2&3 Ph. & M., c. 10 (1555); John H. Langbein, *Prosecuting Crime in the Renaissance: England, Germany, France* (Harvard, CT, 1974), ch. 1.

115. On this and related legal matters, see C. R. Unsworth, 'Witchcraft Beliefs and Criminal Procedure in Early Modern England', in T. G. Watkin (ed.), *Legal Record and Historical Reality. Proceedings of the Eighth British Legal History Conference, Cardiff, 1987* (London, 1989), pp. 71–98.

116. Quoting S. J. Tambiah, *Magic, Science, Religion, and the Scope of Rationality* (New York, 1990), p. 97. On the diversity of religious positions regarding witchcraft, see John Teall, 'Witchcraft and Calvinism in Elizabethan England: Divine Power and Human Agency', *Journal of the History of Ideas*, 23 (1962), 21–36.

117. Thomas, *Religion and the Decline of Magic*, pp. 537–8; BL, Add. MS. 35838, f. 404. The last recorded trial on the Northern Circuit was in 1693, and on the Home Circuit 1701: PRO, ASSI 45/16/3/54–6; Ewen, *Witch Hunting*, pp. 264–5. In 1704 a woman was convicted at the Kent quarter sessions: CKS, Q/SB 27 (1702–4), ff. 1, 30–3, 33, 56.

118. For a full explanation, see Ian Bostridge, *Witchcraft and its Transformations, c.1650–c.1750* (Oxford, 1997), ch. 8.

119 Barbara J. Shapiro, *Probability and Certainty in Seventeenth-Century England* (Princeton, NJ, 1983), pp. 163–226; Sharpe, *Instruments of Darkness*, pp. 220–34.

120. Sharpe, *Instruments of Darkness*, pp. 111–13; Brian Levack, 'The English Law of Proof and the Salem Witchcraft Trials', unpublished paper.

121. *An Account of the Tryal and Examination of Joan Buts* (London, 1682).

122. [Henry Stebbing], *The Case of the Hertfordshire Witch Consider'd* (London, 1712), p. 26; Holmes, 'Women: Witnesses and Witches', p. 50.

123. PRO, STAC 8/4/10; Brian P. Levack, 'Possession, Witchcraft and the Law in Jacobean England', *Washington and Lee Law Review*, 52 (1996), 1618–19. For the broader ramifications of this fascinating case, see James Sharpe, *The Bewitching of Anne Gunter* (London, 1999).

124. *A Tryal of Witches, At the Assizes held at Bury St. Edmonds for the County of Suffolk* (London, 1682).

125. Levack, 'Possession, Witchcraft and the Law', p. 1619, n. 23.

126. Dennis E. Owen, 'Spectral Evidence: The Witchcraft Cosmology of Salem Village in 1692', in Mary Douglas (ed.), *Essays in the Sociology of Perception* (London, 1982), pp. 275–301, quotation at p. 277. See also Daniel G. Payne, 'Defending against the indefensible: spectral evidence at the Salem witchcraft trials', *Essex Institute Historical Collections*, 129 (1993), 62–83.

127. J. H. Langbein, 'The Criminal Trial Before the Lawyers', *University of Chicago Law Review*, 45 (1978), 300–6, 314–15; J. M. Beattie, *Crime and the Courts in England, 1660–1800* (Oxford, 1986), pp. 362–76.

128. Demos, *Entertaining Satan*, pp. 287–8, 392–4. For criticism of the evidence used at Salem, see Increase Mather, *Cases of Conscience Concerning Evil Spirits Personating Men* (Boston, MA, 1693); Robert Calef, *More Wonders of the Invisible World* (London, 1700).

129. *Calendar of State Papers, Colonial Series, America and West Indies, 1689–92* (London, 1901), p. 720; Boyer and Nissenbaum, *Salem Possessed*, p. 32; Owen Manning and William Bray, *The History and Antiquities of the County of Surrey*, 3 vols (London, 1804–14), vol. 2, pp. 714n–715n. In 1703, the Speaker of the Massachusetts Assembly considered banning spectral evidence: Payne, 'Defending against the Indefensible', p. 82.

130. In general, see Gaskill, *Crime and Mentalities*, ch. 3.

131. HMC, *The Manuscripts of the Duke of Roxburghe* (London, 1894), p. 132.

132. On shared social understandings, see John Walter and Keith Wrightson, 'Dearth and the Social Order in Early Modern England', *Past and Present*, 71 (1976), 22–42.

133. Quoting Briggs, *Witches and Neighbours*, pp. 408–9.

Chapter Four
Sounds of Silence: Fairies and Incest in Scottish Witchcraft Stories

Diane Purkiss

his chapter is about storytelling, about two stories told by two seventeenth-century Scottish women accused of witchcraft. The stories these women told are fairy stories, in every sense; stories that had been told before, stories that pass the time, stories that express cultural truths, stories that circulate in oral form and baffle those who wish to add them to the written lexicon, and above all, stories about fairies. I want to argue here that Scottish witches told stories about fairies not out of any straightforward belief in fairies, not out of any longing to satisfy their interrogators, but because the court setting allowed these women to talk about feelings, experiences, and desires that could never normally be given a hearing within their cultures. The women might have told the stories before, but here they were giving their stories to their entire world. The fairy stories I am going to be discussing are the sounds of silence in two senses. Firstly, they represent a moment when a normally silent group – women of the lower orders – makes an appearance as storytellers on the historical stage. Secondly, they represent the things those women could not ordinarily say.

Because the fairy stories I am going to be discussing are told in the context of witchcraft prosecutions, we have to begin by agreeing to abandon some of our preconceived notions about witchcraft in order to hear them. In particular, rather than seeing the interrogators and the justices as enemies to whom words had to be given, placatingly, obediently, we might see them as therapists, a class of persons who also have all the power, all the authority, but who might be the only attentive audience a woman has ever had *with* that power and authority. Even hostile power and authority do rub off on the storyteller; someone important is listening. We also have to remember that in Scotland confessions had to be repeated in court to be valid, so the stories represented in a confession as part of assize papers were stories told by the accused, or at least repeated by her, in a very public space. Some of the stories told by accused witches may have been stories which perhaps could not be told until released by the court procedure, stories that expressed a powerful mixture of memory and desire, stories that are paradoxically liberating, though told under terrible duress. Duress might even serve as a kind of alibi, allowing a woman to say what cannot be spoken. Fairies often represent that which cannot be said, because of the cross-cultural taboo on even saying the word 'fairy'.

Just to make it more difficult, we also have to contend with the many different kinds of document which make up the records of a Scottish witch case. The practice was broadly to gather information locally for a series of documents which amounted to a kind of indictment, which was used to argue for a trial. This was then sent up to the Justiciary Court, who would decide whether there was a basis for a trial. So we have that kind of documentation, evidence collected locally. Then all the evidence was often regathered, sometimes with a fresh confession, for an assize trial. The different circumstances in which confessions might be made meant that the stories about fairies told by the accused may have had different purposes. For instance, a story told in a person's own locality might have been told because an encounter with the fairies was the basis of the woman or man's claim to sorcerous powers, the story he or she told her clients or had told about him or her to explain the 'sight' or healing powers claimed. It might have been a story she told often; it might have been a story other people told about her; either way, it might have been part of her identity within her community. It might have been a story she could not afford not to tell, could not afford to disavow. In this case, duress might come not from the courts, but from a woman's own public identity, and even personal integrity. In other cases, in other documents, perhaps especially, though by no means exclusively, assize documents, some stories might have been told to satisfy a demanding interrogator, to stave off other questions: a woman might drag a folktale from her memory to make silence rather than to break it. If you are asked about what you do not know, you talk about what you do know, to show willing, to cooperate with the investigation. Folktales, of course, do not necessarily imply belief; some of the women who told these fairy stories might have been repeating stories they might tell on other occasions with no legal significance, adventure stories told for pleasure or entertainment that were fitted by the women, as well as the interrogators, into the rough mould of pact witchcraft.

In hearing about fairies, we have to bear in mind all the time that the essence of fairy beliefs is ambivalence, a play between belief and disbelief. The early modern populace did not 'believe' in fairies and they did not disbelieve. This ontological instability or oscillation is not an accident, and it is not a reflection of the demise of fairy beliefs. Just as the middle classes used to rise in every single historical period, so every historical period is marked by a terrible decline in 'real' fairy belief. Every folktale teller, from the Wife of Bath to the taletellers of Newfoundland in the 1980s, begins his or her fairy story with a disclaimer: 'this is what they used to believe a few years ago'. 'Our mother's maids used to fright us', says Reginald Scot. This repetition of half-belief is not a historical accident; it reflects the nature of fairies. Fairies both are and are not; they exceed the terms of what is likely or acceptable or sayable in the everyday. They are encountered on boundaries, either in space – between town and wilderness – or in time – at midday, at midnight, at the change of the year, on the eve of a feast, on Halloween or May Eve, in a festive space marked out from normal life, like Yule, or 'the reathes of the year', like Isobel Sinclair.[1] Yuletide was especially important for apparitions of various kinds, perhaps because it was the boundary of the year. They could also be encountered at moments of social or physical transition: birth, copulation, and death, adolescence, betrothal, defloration, and, of course, death and burial.

The ontological dubiety of fairies is precisely what makes them natural and even inevitable symbols for other things that cannot be said, or cannot be acknowledged, or cannot be believed. In shaping stories about fairies, the women I'm discussing here were also shaping memories, including memories of incest. In saying this, I'm not making any kind of claim about the truth of these women's memories. If we've learnt anything in the past few years, we've learnt that memory is not a simple reservoir, but a processual engagement with cultural materials, expressive, yes, but not simply so. For two Scotswomen to remember incest through fairies is not to argue that they did or did not experience incest; it is to argue that there is an intrinsic and logical connection between fairies and incest that both these women use in their story making. As Angela Bourke puts it, stories about fairies become ways of providing fictional characteristics for otherwise anomalous or unknowable places; this no-man's-land of the mind is therefore a place where what cannot normally be spoken can be represented, however obliquely.[2] The fairies are liminal in every possible way, and one form of that liminality is their position between heaven and hell. A Scottish folktale sees fairies as among the followers of the devil. They tried to get back into heaven when they saw hell, but found the gates barred against them. They settled in the mounds, between hell and heaven, and became fairies. Those who fell in the sea became seals. I tell this story not to claim that there was a general belief that fairies were devils, though of course there was often a perceived overlap in the eyes of the élite, but to point out the reason that such an overlap seemed likely; fairies, being liminal, boundary walkers, could overlap with devils easily, and could also end up situated on the boundary between different discourses. Similarly, fairies share many of the characteristics of the dead; in some stories they *are* the dead, or the dead are with them, in others it is difficult for teller and reader alike to tell the difference between a ghost or revenant and a fairy.[3] Such overlaps also made it easy for people, interrogators and accused, to see fairies and lost souls or devils as interchangeable, or at least related. But the link between fairies and the returned dead is not a confusion; like the dead who come back to feast in their homes, the dead for whom many Scottish families put out food at key times of the year, the fairies are both a society separate from human society and crucially intertwined with it. Both foreign and familiar, like the dead they can develop social relations of gift exchange and dependency with the living; like the dead, they can be angered. Like the dead, they are both present and absent, constantly on the borders of being.

Boundaries – personal, social, bodily, discursive – are on display in the first of the two cases I would like to discuss, the story of Elspeth Reoch, who was charged with witchcraft on 12 March 1616, in Kirkwall, Orkney. I'm going to focus on two specific moments in Elspeth's story: her first encounter with the fairies and its sequel, and her incestuous and necrophilic relations with a dead kinsman who has become a fairy.[4] Elspeth confessed that when she was a young girl of twelve, she was staying with her aunt who lived in a loch when one day, having been out of the loch in the countryside and waiting at the lochside for a boat, she had a strange encounter. The setting could hardly be more significant. Elspeth is on a visit within the family, but outside the parental home; she is also outside this foster or substitute home, outside the loch, but also on the side of the loch, on its margins, suspended between home and the strange world, just as her adolescence suspends her between her birth family and the family she will enter at marriage. In both Scotland and Ireland, fairy legends are always linked to features of the known landscape, especially to dangerous, marginal or conspicuous places within it; Elspeth's encounter by a loch is evidently part of the Scottish idea of the otherworld. Lochs are inhabited by water-spirits, spirits who drag the unwary down to their abode; the Loch Ness monster is a last trace of these kelpies. This belief has an obvious social function; it is a way of saying that lochs – any water – can be death to the unwary. But lochs are also often property boundaries, and sometimes clan and hence identity boundaries, spaces between one name and another. Women, who remain outsiders in their husbands' clans, even in their fathers', are metaphorically on the lochside all their lives. Spaces like the one in which Elspeth has her first fairy encounter are not women's spaces, in the sense that (say) the kitchen or the birthing room are. They are rather spaces of femininity, spaces whose status mirrors that of women. As Angela Bourke has shown in a remarkable series of studies of folklore, such fairy places may be metaphors for areas of silence and circumvention in the social life of the communities around them: places out of place, times out of time.[5]

Two men come to Elspeth at the lochside. One is clad in black, and the other has a green tartan plaid. The fairies of Scotland often wear green, and also wear plaids.[6] The man with the plaid pays her a compliment, one with mild overtones of courtship: he says she is a 'pretty'. Their interaction is sexualized by this overture. He then offers her a courtship gift, 'he wald lerne her to ken and sie ony thing she wald desyre'. The other man is not enthusiastic, claiming that Elspeth will not keep the source of her knowledge to herself. It is basic to fairy folklore in all cultures that the source of a fairy gift has to remain a secret, or else it is lost. But the man in green presses on, and here Elspeth asks an eager question, 'being desyrous to knaw said how could she ken that'. His advice is also about boundaries and changing states:

And he said Tak ane eg and rost it And take the sweit of it thre Sondayis And with onwashin handis wash her eyes quhairby she sould sie and knaw ony thing she desyrit.

An egg is a common ingredient in fairy magic and counter-magic; it symbolizes birth, hidden life, the pregnant belly, food. It is also about renunciation; Elspeth is not to eat the egg, but only its sweat, the moisture of its boiling, just as folktales warn against eating the fairy food, a particularly hard prohibition for a hungry islander for whom eggs may have been a luxury. The refusal of commensality with the fairies is always a test, a test of greed and self-control. Elspeth must close some parts of herself in order to open others. The egg remains untouched, unbroken; it is what it exudes, the sweat or steam of its boiling, which Elspeth must take and use. This becomes the fairy ointment, a staple of folktales, which confers magic sight on the eyes on which it is rubbed. There are English cases involving the fairy ointment; it confers the ability to see not only the fairies, but stolen and lost goods and buried treasure; in other words, it is the foundation of a cunning woman's business credentials.[7] Elspeth must also renounce a piece of acculturation: she must not wash her hands before touching the ointment. Such gestures mark a renunciation of a place within human society for a place outside it. To refuse food, or water for washing, is to refuse the household that offers them, Elspeth's family household.

What kind of knowledge does Elspeth want? The man in green sends her to her family, where she uncovers a secret. Elspeth goes to another aunt's house, where there is a widow, perhaps a lodger, that has with her a granddaughter, perhaps visiting her relative as Elspeth is visiting her aunt. This girl is an image of Elspeth in age and circumstances. But this girl is pregnant, pregnant with a child whose father is the husband of another woman. No-one in the family knows this yet, but the man in green tells Elspeth, and tells her to announce the fact. She 'sould luik in hir face', a shaming, challenging gesture, and tell her 'she is with bairne to ane uther wyfes husband'. This suggests that Elspeth knows about the interior of the female body, about secrets, about the family's secrets, sexual secrets. To be cunning is to know. Perhaps this is an older woman recalling the unbelievable oddity of adult sexuality as seen by a maturing child. But it is also about the specific discovery that sex can be the ruin of women and their reputations. More deeply it is about the discovery that not all babies are wanted, that not all babies are part of kinship structures that are authorized, that make sense. Like women in Scotland, the baby is always already marginal to kinship groups. The baby and the girl who carries it are silences, silences Elspeth has breached.

At first the girl denies Elspeth's words. But soon she realises that Elspeth is a source of knowledge. This girl has been shamed; her pregnancy and its origins have been revealed. It is as if Elspeth has brought the infant to birth. And this premature birth suggests the idea of abortion. She asks Elspeth if she can give 'sum cure at hir that she micht part with bairne'. The baby can be silenced in death, returned to the unspeakable. Elspeth urges the girl to consult someone else, Allan McKeldow, who refuses to procure an abortion for the girl. And what is the result? Thereafter: 'within two years she [Elspeth] bore her first bairne quhilk wes gottin be ane James Mitchaell at the kirk of Murthilie upoun Spey within Balveny.' This too is a child born outside marriage. Elspeth has learnt her lesson well. The result of sexual and familial knowledge is that Elspeth has more truly become the mirror of the disgraced granddaughter. One outsider begets another. Or – to put it another way – Elspeth's story of the pregnant girl who is desperate to get rid of her baby is a displaced self-portrait. Unwanted babies in early modern Scotland were occasionally left 'for the fairies', a euphemism for child abandonment. The frustratingly elliptical record of the case of Jonet Drever shows this:

> the said Jonet Drever ... To be convict and giltie of the fostering of ane bairne in the hill of Westray to the fary folk callit of hir our guid nichbouris.[8]

Where other neighbours shun the mother of a bastard, the fairies can be good neighbours indeed.[9]

Elspeth's story is one of emergence into an unruly womanhood, not sanctioned but no doubt exploited by her society. But her story does not end there. Elspeth's encounters with the fairies occur at the two most common life moments for such encounters: the threshold of womanhood and the aftermath of childbirth. The moments in life when a fairy encounter is most likely are infancy, puberty, and childbirth for women. Elspeth follows her adolescent encounter with another even more extraordinary meeting with the fairy after childbirth. She has her baby in her sister's house, within the bosom of her birth family. And yet the house proves to be as liminal as the lakeside by virtue of her own parturient presence in it, for she sees again

the blak man ... that first came to hir at Lochquhaber And callit him selff
ane farie man quha wes sumtyme her kinsman callit Johne Stewart quha
wes slane be McKy at the doun going of the soone And therfor nather deid
nor leiving bot wald ever go betuix the heaven and the earth.

He 'deals with' Elspeth for two nights, and he is relentless. He will
never let her sleep 'persuading hir to let him ly with hir':

And upoun the thrid nycht that he com to hir she being asleip and laid his
hand upoun hir breist and woke her. And thairefter semeit to ly with her.

Such childbed encounters with apparitions of many kinds are
reasonably common in Scottish, and even English witchcraft cases,
though no other confession that I know of mentions sex.[10]
Sex from the dead? This makes sense in the system of Scottish
ancestry, where everyone descended from a single heroic ancestor.[11]
Identity is imparted to the clan by the dead through sex and
reproduction. But Elspeth is a woman, and she seems to get her identity
from the dead in another, more indirect fantasy, a fantasy about birth
and the birth process. The many fairy legends which tell of women in
childbirth being swept through the air are vivid metaphors for the birth
process; passage is rite of passage, reflecting the dangers of childbirth.
In folklore there are many stories of women who have pins put in their
knees by the fairies, and with agony and turmoil the pins are found
and removed. Until they are removed the women cannot speak. Angela
Bourke remarks of these stories that the pins and their removal are
metaphors for pregnancy following first sex.[12] In Elspeth's story the
tactful metaphors disappear, and the narrative runs suddenly
backwards. The baby is born, and the pain brings a fairy kinsman to
have sex with her, sex that is trebly illicit: after childbirth, with a
kinsman, with the dead.
    Scottish élite views of witchcraft created a unique opportunity for
these fairy stories to be told. Just as English belief in familiars and
witchmarks prompted tales of hobs and brownies, so Scottish belief in
compact witchcraft as the basis for a trial created an odd, unintended
fit between that belief and a common story in folk culture. This gives
us an insight into one of the commonest Scottish witch stories, a
narrative that recurs in dozens of cases. The following is just one version
of it:

the second tyme the devill appeired to hir at the foot of her owen yaird about fyve yeiris efter in the licknes of ane man in grein cloathes, and that he desyrit her to becoem his servant ... and that she promeisit to become his servant. Quherupone he desyrit her to renunce hir baptisme and Jesus Chryst, quhilk she did ... bot cannot presentlie remember quhither he had carnall dealings with hir at that tyme or not, bot rememberis perfytlie that efterward he did ly with hir.[13]

In all these cases, and there are dozens, a woman meets a man, who may be wearing black or green, or may have a specific name. He asks her to be his servant, or he offers her something. She may refuse at first, but eventually agrees. He then has sex with her, and the woman then often confesses to renouncing baptism at his request, or to receiving a mark from him. I'm not suggesting that all these cases are really stories about fairies, though I don't think I can rule out the possibility either at this stage. However, fairy stories give us some insight into the way this story works and what it means and why women tell it. Whatever the nature of the being involved, the point is the same because he is always otherworldly. The experience is the same: it's the experience of a change of identity mediated through sexual congress, a specifically female experience, socially very common. Sex in both kinds of story is a way of saying something, confirming something; it is itself a magical act, creating a specific relationship of dependency and bondage. This story is about transformation, about moving from one state to another, from one role to another.

Women come back from the fairies damaged. In Elspeth's case the price for the opening of her body is the closing of her mouth:

And to be dum for haveing teacheit hir to sie and ken only thing she desyrit He said that gif she spak gentlemen wald trouble hir and gar hir give reassounes for hir doings Quhairupoun she mycht be challengeit and hurt ... And upoun the morow she haid na power of hir toung nor could nocht speik quhairthrow hir brother danghir with ane branks quhill she bled becaus she wald nocht speik and pat ane bow string about hir head to gar her speik And thairefter tuik her three severall tymes Sondayis to the kirk and prayit for hir Fra the quhilk tyme she still continewit dumb going about and deceaveing the people Synding telling and foir shawing thame quhat they had done and quhat they sould do.

Here the boundaries of the body are crucial; breached by birth and by the fairy man, the only boundary left to Elspeth is her mouth. Her silence seals her upper body; it mirrors her restraint with the egg, her mouth closed against the temptation of food, from which her 'sight' comes. Yet her silence is not her own; it is a sign of her fairy lover's care for her, but also his power over her. He has sealed her body against others. Yet in breaking his seal, breaking silence, Elspeth appears to take control, but in reality simply puts herself under the control of yet another set of men. Talking about fairies is an unusual opportunity, then, because usually fairies are something to be silent about. Talking about them is clearly Elspeth's way of saying something about herself, something about herself so important that she would rather die than stop saying it. And yet to talk is to lose everything, including her one protector. For in fairy legends those who talk about the fairies incur their wrath. Interrogator and fairy man are united in wishing to punish Elspeth for what she says.

Elspeth's story is linked by the theme of incest to the less sensational, and evidentially much more problematic, story of Janet Weir. Janet Weir is the sister of Major Weir, a noted pro-Cromwellian and covenanter whose enemies, political and religious, finally cornered him with a series of charges of sexual deviance, notably bestiality and incest. Janet Weir is the sister with whom he is said to have had the incestuous relationship, but she was also charged with sorcery and, moreover, seems to have claimed Weir himself was a sorcerer. Here is the material witness's account of her incest:

> Margaret Weir, the wife of Alexander Weir, Bookseller in Edinburgh, testify'd, that when she was of the Age of 27 yeers, or thereabouts, she found the Major her brother and her sister Jane, lying together in the Barn at Wickes-shaw, and that they were both naked in the bed together, and that she was above him, and that the Bed did shake, and that she heard some scandalous Language between them in particular, that her sister said, she was confident she should prove with Child.[14]

As described, Janet's behaviour is sexually transgressive; she is on top, and she is talking eagerly about producing a child who will be the offspring of incest. This may have led her accusers to ask her about witchcraft, and hence to have elicited the story she tells, but that story is so greatly at variance with what they probably expected and hoped to hear that I want to consider its relation to incest at greater length. What I want to ask is this: why do two women, Elspeth and Janet, talk about incest and fairies in the same breath? Why do fairy stories seem relevant to stories about incest? I do not know if these women really are incest survivors. My point is rather that these women *talk about* incest and fairies in the same breath, and that there's a series of interesting discursive and psychic relations between them.

First, incest puts you outside the law and gives you magical powers. If you survive this huge apocalyptic transgression and the house doesn't fall on you, then you are magical. Hence it is a symbol of magic – as in Elspeth's confession – as well as the reason for it. Writing about modern incest survivors, Judith Herman remarks reluctantly that some women embraced their identity as sinners with defiance and pride. As initiates into forbidden sexual knowledge, they felt they possessed almost magical powers. One woman described herself as a 'bad witch' and expressed the fear that she could cause others to sicken with her thoughts.[15] Though undeniably in an abject position of self-loathing, this woman has turned self-loathing to some account. Such stories also hint at the possibility, unthinkable till recently, that incest might be a self-aggrandizing fantasy for some women. Through incest, the subject is outside the law, outside society, perhaps even outside language. This outsider status can be desolation, or it can become a source of ambivalent empowerment. From outside, the wounded subject can strike at the healthy. Having survived the transgression of this, perhaps still the greatest of all taboos, what can she fear? She is invulnerable. To talk of incest is therefore to talk of surviving outside the normal. Perhaps that is what Janet and Elspeth are talking about. Women are outsiders in the Scottish kin system anyway, which may have given them unstable identities. If they divest themselves of their position within that kin system, a position defined as a receptacle for male identity, male seed, what other kind of identity can they have? Or rather, what kind of identity can women have at all that is not Other? Fairies, of course, are a kind of ultimate symbol of otherness, and perhaps also an alternative, unauthorized kinship structure; if you are outside human kin relations, perhaps you can be inside something else, something more glamourous.

Another point of connection between incest and fairies: incest is analogous to death, because it places you outside the community's laws. Fairies are associated with the dead, sometimes are the dead, or are captives of the dead. Elspeth's black man is dead. Bessie Dunlop's fairy guide was also dead: 'Thome Reid, quha deit at Pinkye, as he himselff affirmit; what wald tell hir, quhen evir sche askit.'[16] Like Elspeth's fairy helper, Thom Reid has died young, by violence. To gain knowledge and identity from the dead is to gain it from ancestors. But what if that knowledge is somehow of the wrong kind, as it is in Elspeth's case? What if it places you not inside the clan or kinship structure, but outside it? Incest is about kinship bonds. Compact witchcraft, which as far as the judiciary and the Kirk are concerned includes compacts with fairies and which, as far as the deponents are concerned, involves overlap between fairies and demons, or at any rate blurriness, involves a change of kinship, with or without an explicit disavowal of previous ties. Sex with a person is a way of compact with them, a means of becoming someone different. For women, this is most aptly symbolized in marriage. Yet marriage is never inclusive in Scotland; kinship is agnatic rather than cognatic, which means that married women remain marginal to their husband's clan; that is why Scottish women keep their maiden names after marriage. We can see the fairies are a kind of clan, and similarly, women can join them without being included. The symbolic outsider status of the incest victim symbolizes this fragility of identity. Covenanting, which as everyone knows has to do with Scottish notions of kinship, is a religious kinship structure in which women could be included. This is especially relevant to Janet Weir. Weir died accusing the men and women who saw her die of breaking faith with the Protestant covenant.[17] The charge of incest of which she was accused mirrored their lack of fidelity.

We also have to remember something much more basic: the pleasure of making up or confessing to crimes one has not committed is analogous to the pleasures of the kind of supernatural Munchausen's syndrome involved in claiming to be fairy-taken. Both cast the woman as a culpable victim, someone who falls into evil and does not try hard enough to escape. Perhaps something really spectacular had to happen to women to allow them to be seen, and to see themselves, as suffering victims. There is also the pleasure of invention. Inventing horrors leads to invented displacement from those horrors, a double displacement, as this testimony from an alleged Satanic abuse survivor and multiple personality disorder victim shows:

> It started to get into ritual abuse memories, I've had memories of being in a cage with wild, hungry cats and snakes, naked and cold and hungry and terrified. They poked something real hot, like a red-hot poker, in the cage. Then when I was five, I was tied upside down and lowered over a fire until it started to singe my hair.[18]

Now, Jasmine, one of Angela's alters, takes over the story:

> I have a red light to keep me safe, like blood, when I go to the woods ... I go to the Blue Land, where the wind blows a lot, and bells make sounds, and people teach you things without saying a word.[19]

Angela has created a truly dramatic trauma, one which places her outside the law, and she has also created her own refuge from this trauma, the Blue Land, an infantile space with affinities not with early modern Scottish fairies, but with post-romantic fairies, little jingly thingies representing ideal childhood. Like Angela, Janet Weir invests both in trauma and in its recuperation through supernatural refuge, though the refuges are very different. Janet's equivalent of the Blue Land was a story about spinning, which is told in several different ways in different reports on her trial:

> That when she keeped a school at Dalkeith, and teached childering, ane tall woman came to the declarant's hous when the childering were there; and that she had, as appeared to her, ane chyld upon her back, and on or two at her foot; and that the said woman desyred that the declarant should imploy her to spick for her to the Queen of Farie, and strik and battle in her behalf with the said queen (which was her own words); and that the next day ane little woman came to the declarant, and did give her a piece of a tree, or the root of some herb or tree, as she thought, and told her that as long as she had the samen, she wold be albe to doe what she should desyre; and thent the said woman did lay ane cloth upon the floor near the door, and caused the declarant set her foot upon the samen, and her hand upon the crown of her own head, and caused the declarant repeit these words thrice, viz. 'All my cross and trubles goe to the door with the' which accordinglie she did; and that she gave the woman all the silver she hade, being some few turners, and some meall; and that after the said woman went away, the declarant did spin a verie short tyme, and that she did find more yearne upon her pirne, and good yearne, nor she thought could be spun in so short a tyme; which did so affright the declarant, that she did set by her wheile, and did shut the door, and did stay within her house for the space of twentie dayes or thereby, and was exceedinglie trubled, and weeped becaus she thought what she had don in manner forsaid was in effect the renuncing of her baptisme.[20]

Another account is tonally very different, having far less to say about the cause of Janet's miraculous spinning:

> But for her selfe, she said, she never received any other benefit by her Commerce with the Devil, then a constant supply of an extraordinary quantity of yarn, which she was sure (she said) to find ready for her upon the Spindle, what ever business she had been about.[21]

What we have here is a very common transcultural folktale motif applied to a situation in which it looks out of place. A woman is accused of incest and of abetting her brother's sorcery, and she at once comes out with a long rigmarole about a fairy lady and spinning. Why spinning? I think it just might be about three things: first, names. The Scottish folktale 'Whuppity Stoorie' is a version of *Rumplestiltskin*, but in Scotland it is a woman who helps another, mortal woman with her spinning; the woman must either find her name or be 'taken' herself, or give her her child.[22] Giving up your baby in exchange for security is the ultimate crime in agnatic kinship. Finding someone else's name is a way to keep your own. The name is also honour or reputation. Hence the entire story may be a screen, an attempt at self-exculpation of the loss of name and kinship structure implied in the charge of incest. The second idea is that the central motif in Janet's story is the same as that in the folktales: being able to spin with help from the fairies is about gaining an undeserved reputation for industry when you are actually a lazy girl. It is about deceit, pretending to be someone other than who you are. Third, the woman who facilitates Janet's spinning may have a deeper meaning. Very often in fairy stories, the fairies are the only allies a woman has. The case of Janet Rendell makes this painfully clear. Janet is a beggar who is refused alms, and she is rescued by a grey-bearded figure called Walliman:

> Twentie yeiris since and mair ye being above the hill of Rendall having soucht charitie and could not have it the devill appeirit to you, Quhom ye called Walliman, claid in quhyt cloathis with ane quhyt heid and ane grey beard, And said to you He sould learne yow to win almssbe healling of folk and quhasoever sould geve yow almiss sould be the better ather be land or sea. And these yt gave yow not almiss sould not be healled and ye haveing trustit in him and entering in pactioun with him, He promiseit to yow that quhasoever sould refus yow almiss and quhatever ye craved to befall thame sould befall thame, and thairefter went away in the air from you.[23]

A fairy may be someone who will take your side when everyone else has abandoned you. Children commonly fantasize a rescuing hero when in difficulty – even quite everyday difficulty – at school or at home. Abused children engage in what is called Positive Projective Anticipation, the belief that a future friend or spouse will some day help undo the effects of the current situation.[24] So, of course, do children who are not abused; such fantasies surface in folktales like *Cinderella*, where inadequate parental care is supplemented by the care of a dead mother who sometimes returns as herself, sometimes as a fairy.[25] For Janet Weir, positive projective anticipation might have ceased to take the form of orthodox Christianity and come to take the form of an imaginary fairy facilitator who gained her a reputation for spinning and industry, perhaps even offered to gain her a few extra pennies. She knows this is a rebellion, an alliance with someone outside the Kirk, which is why she feels so miserable, so guilty.

The intertwining of memory and desire, speech and silence in these stories mimics uncannily the dilemmas of our own day, our own anxieties about recovered memories and whether they can be deemed a syndrome. As Janice Haaken observes, both sides in the current recovered memory debate seem eager to argue that violent sexuality and violent desire always comes from outside the woman; from the perpetrator, from the therapist.[26] But in these cases, violent desires seem intrinsic to the stories these women are telling, stories which are not part of the usual script of pact witchcraft, though they can be forced roughly into its shape. These stories not only undo our assumption that fairies are small gauzy-wingy thingies; they also undo the assumptions about the true nature of femininity which tend to accompany the gauzy-wingy beings. And that is only one part of their supreme relevance to our own preoccupations. In these witchcraft cases, we can actually witness the process by which story turns into memory. What happens here is that cultural materials in general circulation are appropriated by individuals. We think of memory as individual, but one of the commonest forms of forgetting is what is termed source amnesia, forgetting the source of acquired information. A story originally heard as about another can slowly come to feel as if it is our own story. In describing two Scottish women's telling of fairy stories, we may be dealing with just such a phenomenon. If so, we need to ask what it was about the standard stories of fairy encounter that made it possible for Elspeth Reoch and Janet Weir to claim those stories for themselves, to make them their own. It may be that these stories in circulation always did represent a specific world of female desires and anxieties, that they were always a way of saying the unsayable. If so, they could easily become what Janice Haaken calls 'transformative memories', memories, whether authentic or not, that make sense of a life, that turn its disorder and fragmentation into meaning.[27] If so, they may also be transformative of us in looking at the complex, tangled otherness of the past.

Notes

1. Margaret Dicksone (8 June 1649) meets her man in green at midday: *Register of the Privy Council of Scotland*, 2nd series, ed. David Masson, 8 vols (Edinburgh, 1899–1908), vol. 8, p. 191, hereafter *RPC*. Katherine Jonesdochter, spouse of Thomas Kirknes in Stenhous, 2 October 1616, is especially vulnerable to fairy sexuality at Halloween and Holy Crosday. She also sees the trowis at Yule: *Court Book of Shetland*, ed. Gordon Donaldson (Lerwick, 1991), pp. 38–9. Katherine Carey, 1616: at 'the doun going of the sun, ane great number of fairie men mett her', among them a 'maister man', *Records of the Sherriff Court of Orkney*, f. 94, reprinted in part in J. G. Dalyell, *The Darker Superstitions of Scotland* (Edinburgh, 1835), p. 536. See also and more briefly, G. F. Black, *Examples of Printed Folklore Concerning the Orkney and Shetland Islands*, Folklore Society, vol. 3 (London, 1903), p. 55. Though common throughout Europe, the Yuletide links of the fairies may point to Icelandic influence in the Orkneys in particular. There is a strong Icelandic tradition of mischief-making spirits (*jolarsveinar*) coming to the farm over the 12 days of Christmas and making rather hearty mischief: taking bites out of the sausages and hilariously pulling away the stool when one is about to sit down. They are attracted by the merrymaking and feasting, but they go away on Twelfth Night, St Thorlak's day (he is the patron saint of Iceland). I am deeply indebted to Carolyne Larrington for information about Icelandic trowis (personal communication). On the other hand, all this could apply equally well to the Greek Yuletide demons, the *kallikhantzaroi*.
2. Angela Bourke, 'Reading a Woman's Death: Colonial Texts and Oral Tradition in Nineteenth-Century Ireland', *Feminist Studies*, 21 (1995).
3. There are numerous examples: see for instance Black, *Folklore*, vol. 3, pp. 23–4; Barbara Rieti, *Strange Terrain: The Fairy World in Newfoundland*, St John's, Newfoundland, no. 45, 1991, p. 21. Rieti's work is relevant because Newfoundland was a principal site of Highland emigration. In other stories, trowis are not the dead, but the keepers of the dead: see Alan Bruford, 'Trolls, Hillfolk, Finns and Picts: The Identity of the Good Neighbours in Orkney', in Peter Narvaez (ed.), *The Good People: New Fairylore Essays* (New York, 1991), pp. 116–41. 'Katherein for art and part of witchcraft and sorcery in hanting and seing the trowis ryse out of the kirkyeard of Hildiswick and Holiecrosse Kirk of Eschenes and that she saw thame on the hill callit Greinfaill at monie sindrie tymes and that

they come to ony hous quhair thair wes feasting or great mirrines, and specillie at Yule': *Court Book of Shetland*, pp. 38–9.
4. There are two printed transcriptions of Elspeth's story: *Maitland Miscellany*, vol. 2, pt 1 (1840), pp. 187–91; and Black, *Folklore*, pp. 111–15. The original is in *Records of the Sherriff Court of Orkney*, f. 63. I am very grateful to Miranda Chaytor for first telling me the story of Elspeth.
5. Bourke, 'Reading a Woman's Death', p. 568.
6. Margaret Bennet, 'Balquhidder Revisited: Fairylore in the Scottish Highlands, 1690–1990', in Peter Narvaez (ed.), *The Good People*, p. 107. Robert Kirk, *The Secret Commonwealth of Elves and Fairies*, ed. Stuart Sanderson (Cambridge, 1976), p. 73: 'so are they seen to wear Plaids and variegated garments in the Highlands of Scotland'.
7. The fairy ointment is also a staple of folklore. For an actual case of a cunning woman who claimed to have used it, see the case of the Somerset woman Joan Tyrrie, Wells Diocesan Records, Somerset Record Office, D/D/CA Act Books 21–22.
8. Jonet Drever and Katherine Bigland alias Grewik, 7 June 1615, Kirkwall: *Spalding Club Miscellany*, ed. John Stuart, vol. 1 (Aberdeen, 1841), pp. 167–8, also transcribed in Black, *Folklore*, pp. 72–4.
9. Again, this function is cross-cultural; unmarried mothers in the Greek islands leave their babies 'for the nymphs'. See my *Into the Dark: Fairies and Others* (Penguin, forthcoming), ch. 1.
10. The best-known case is Bessie Dunlop: 'Remembering hir, quhen sche was lyand in chyld-bed-lair, with ane of hir laiddis, that ane stout woman com in to hir, and sat doun on the forme besyde hir, and askit ane drink at hir, and sche gaif hir; quha alsua tauld hir, that hat barne wald de, and that hir husband suld mend of his seiknes. The said Bessie ansuerit, that sche remembrit wele thairof; and thom said, That was the Quene of Elfame his maistres, quha had commandit him to wait upoun hir, and to do hir gude': *Ancient Criminal Trials in Scotland*, ed. Robert Pitcairn, 3 vols (Edinburgh, 1833), vol. 1, pt 2, p. 53.
11. On Scottish ancestry and kinship, see Jenny Wormald, *Court, Kirk and Community: Scotland, 1470–1625* (Edinburgh, 1981).
12. Angela Bourke, 'Fairies and Anorexia: Nuala Ni Dhomhnaill's "Amazing Grass"', *Proceedings of the Harvard Celtic Colloquium*, 13 (1993), pp. 32–5.
13. Agnes Hunter, 8 June 1649, *RPC*, pp. 190–1. Other cases include Margaret Dicksone, who first meets a man in black, and then a man in green who lies with her; Isobel Brown, who also meets a man, *RPC*, p. 195; Katherine Jonesdochter, 2 October 1616: 'Katherine Jonesdochter for converversing [sic] lying, keiping companie and societie witht the deill, quhom she callit the bowman of Hiliswick and Bechenes, quha come to hir quhen she wes in hir motheris hous, being ane young lass, at quhilk tyme he lay with hir, mair nor 40 yeiris syne and yeirlie and ilk yeir sensyne and speciallie at Hallowevin and holy Crosday, and that the last time he lay with hir he gave hir ane mark (*Court Book of Shetland*, pp. 38–9); Jonet Morison, 19 January 1662, Rothesay: *Highland Papers*, ed. J. R. M. MacPhail, Scottish

History Society, 2nd series, vol. 20, pp. 23–4, 27.
14. George Hickes, *Ravillac redivivus*, 1678, pp. 64–5. This case is recounted many times in different places, from many different points of view, due to Weir's political importance: John Lamont, *Diary*, ed. G. R. Kinloch (Edinburgh, 1830), pp. 271–2; G. Sinclair, *Satans Invisible World Discovered* (Edinburgh, 1789), pp. 152–3; Robert Law, *Memorialls*, ed. C. K. Sharpe (Edinburgh, 1818), p. 27; Scottish Record Office, Justiciary Court MS JC2/13; *Records of the Proceedings of the Justiciary Court* (Edinburgh, 1661–78), vol. 2, pp. 10–15; *The Trial, Indictments, and Sentence of Major Thomas Weir ... also his sister Joan Weir* (n.d.).
15. Judith Herman, *Father-Daughter Incest* (Cambridge, MA, 1981), pp. 97, 98. This is the book at the centre of the controversy about recovered memory.
16. A marginal note says: 'Confessit by hirself and fylit be the Assiis thairof'. Bessie's trial, one of the best-known Scottish witch cases involving fairies, is transcribed in full in *Criminal Trials in Scotland*, vol. 1, pt 2, pp. 49–58, 8 November 1576. For other instances of fairies as the dead or as guardians of the dead, see note 3; and also Lewis Spence, *The Fairy Tradition in Britain* (London, 1948).
17. 'I see a great crowd of People come hither to-day to behold a poor old miserable Creatures Death, but I trow there be few among you, who are weeping and mourning for the broken Covenant', Hickes, *Ravillac*, p. 72.
18. 'Angela', in Mark Pendergrast, *Victims of Memory: Incest, Accusations, and Shattered Lives* (London and New York, 1997), p. 289. It should be noted that Pendergrast is entirely sceptical about Angela's utterances.
19. 'Jasmine', Angela's 'alter', in ibid., p. 290.
20. Scottish Record Office, Justiciary Court MS JC2/13, reproduced in Law, *Memorialls*, note on p. 24. Another account, in which far more emphasis is placed on Janet Weir's iteration of a magical formula, is given in *Records of the ... Justiciary Court*, vol. 2, pp. 10–15; the chapbook, *The Trial, Indictments, and Sentence*, stresses not the spinning, but the healing power Janet gained from the magical rod.
21. Hickes, *Ravillac*, p. 67.
22. 'Whuppity Stoorie', in *The Penguin Book of Scottish Folktales*, ed. Neil Philip (London and New York, 1995), pp. 3–7, from a transcription made about 1784. In this version the green woman helps with other rural tasks, but in other versions spinning is the task involved.
23. Black, *Folklore*, pp. 106–8; *Abbotsford Club Miscellany*, vol 1, pp. 181–5.
24. Julie Osborn, *Psychological Effects of Child Sex Abuse on Women*, Social Work Monographs (Norwich, 1990), app. 3, p. 38.
25. On Cinderella and the mother, see Marina Warner, *From the Beast to the Blonde: On Fairytales and their Tellers* (London, 1994), pp. 201–17.
26. Janice Haaken, *Pillar of Salt: Gender, Memory and the Perils of Looking Back* (London, 1998), pp. 2–5.
27. Ibid., pp. 14–15; 251–5.

Part Two

Contexts of Witchcraft

Chapter Five
Towards a Politics of Witchcraft in Early Modern England

Peter Elmer

ollowing the publication of Stuart Clark's groundbreaking study of demonology in 1997,[1] it is probably no exaggeration to state that historians of witchcraft are better placed than ever before to understand how early modern Europeans conceived of witchcraft, and how it informed every aspect of their thought and culture. Largely concerned with the theoretical base of witchcraft, Clark has little, however, to say about the practical consequences of witchcraft belief, particularly the relationship between thought and action which culminated in the actual prosecution of men and women for the crime of witchcraft. In this chapter, I would like to suggest a number of ways in which it might be possible to utilize aspects of his research to generate a better understanding of one element of this process, namely the problematic nature of the uneven geographical and temporal pattern of witch trials. My initial interest in this subject was prompted by a desire to explore more fully the problem of the decline of élite belief in witchcraft in seventeenth-century England. It soon became apparent that the normal explanations for this phenomenon carried little conviction. As many observers, including Keith Thomas, have noted, the arguments adopted by the so-called 'sceptics' at the end of this period were no different in kind from those put forward by men like Reginald Scot a century earlier.[2] In addition, the admittedly incomplete record of witchcraft trials pointed to a growing reluctance on the part of 'educated' grand jurymen to indict and condemn accused witches from a very early date.

In order to arrive at a more convincing explanation for the demise of belief in witchcraft among early modern English élites, two issues required further exploration. Firstly, it was necessary to adopt a much broader chronological framework beginning with the legislative and judicial initiatives of the early years of the reign of Elizabeth I. And secondly, it was imperative not just that the incidence of the witch trials was understood within the context of local and national concerns, but also that these should be related to the various idioms (themselves prone to change over time) in which it made sense for educated Englishmen to talk of witches and witchcraft.

The conclusions reached here are highly speculative, reflecting the embryonic stage of the current study. None the less, it is possible, I think, to suggest some broad outcomes and possible avenues of future research. In the first half of this essay, I would like to focus on a number of basic principles which inform my approach to the subject. In the second half, I shall attempt to provide a brief account of how, in practice, these might illuminate our understanding of the incidence of witch trials and the question of their relation to contemporary thinking on the subject. Far too often, historians of witchcraft have tended to fall into one of two well-defined camps: those interested in exploring the dynamics of witch-hunting, and those concerned with the ideas and beliefs which made such trials possible. Typically, there seems to be little common ground between the two, *despite* the fact, frequently acknowledged, that those who wrote demonologies were more often than not prompted to do so because of their *actual* experience and observation of witch trials. The result of this two-pronged approach has been to minimize the extent to which historians have been able to substantiate a meaningful relationship between the two fields of enquiry. Here, an alternative approach is adopted. Throughout, my preoccupation is with the way in which the mental world of the demonologists intersected with the day-to-day actions and concerns of the men and women who were participants in the drama of witch trials.

One of the unresolved mysteries of English witchcraft is the seemingly random geographical and temporal distribution of witch trials. Though our knowledge of such patterns is inevitably skewed by the uneven survival of legal records, it is none the less clear that there were marked peaks and troughs in the prosecution of English witches which are further complicated by pronounced regional variations in the occurrence of trials. Our knowledge of the social and psychological genesis of witchcraft accusations, which has been exhaustively studied in the last 30 years, provides minimal help in explaining this particular phenomenon. The tensions which produced the accusations were, after all, omnipresent in English society at this time and continued to shape interpersonal relations long after the repeal of the witchcraft statutes in the eighteenth century. Witch trials, on the other hand, were a relatively rare occurrence.

To explain why this was so clearly demands a new approach to the surviving evidence. For accusations to reach the courts, powerful figures had to be convinced of both the genuine nature of such claims and the threat which they implied to the moral and physical welfare of their particular communities. The attitudes of men of influence and authority, the ruling élites in villages and towns, as well as local JPs and ministers, were inevitably crucial to this process. Unfortunately, however, we know very little about the processes whereby such men, most of whom possessed a minimal education, formed their judgements. What criteria, for example, did they bring to bear in evaluating the evidence of those who accused their neighbours of witchcraft and similar practices? And why, on certain occasions, were they willing to promote legal action against suspected witches, and on others, to suspend their judgement?

One possible line of enquiry which I would like to develop here focuses on what I term the 'politics of witchcraft'. This involves an appreciation of the way in which élite preconceptions about witchcraft were moulded by the broader political climate which prevailed at a particular time and place. Moreover, it demands a sensitivity on the part of the historian not just to local circumstances – the precise political and religious context in which the accusation of witchcraft had arisen – but also to national events, and the wider political arena in which local ruling élites performed their allotted role. This in turn requires close reading of the ideological significance of witchcraft in early modern thought. From the point of view of this study, the most significant aspect of Clark's work is the importance which he attaches to those conventions of early modern thought which stressed that social, political, and natural order in the world were dependent upon the harmonizing of contraries or opposites. Depicted by Clark as 'a cosmological and cognitive paradigm of universal application', recourse to the language of binary opposition is clearly fundamental to our understanding of how demonology functioned in practice in this period. Put simply, in describing and attesting to the feats of witches and demons, demonologists were in the same breath seeking to reinforce the faith of their fellow Christians in God and the Church, the existence of the former logically proven by that of the latter, and vice versa.[3]

Realistically, one might expect that those learned in such ideas would be far more likely to believe accounts of actual demonic behaviour if their sense of religious and political order was currently under threat. Equally, it would seem logical to assume that the greater the degree of actual polarization and strife in the community, the greater the likelihood that witchcraft accusations would be taken seriously by those in authority. Conversely, one might expect fewer cases of witchcraft to receive official sanction in times of political and religious calm. Whatever the case, one might reasonably expect to find more interest in witchcraft, be it theoretical or practical, at those times and in those places where it was commonly felt that the religious and political consensus had broken down, or was in the process of doing so.[4]

Clark's work is also suggestive in one further respect. In comparing the inversionary nature of popular festive culture with that of learned demonology, he refers to the debate among historians of popular culture who contend that festive culture functioned in one of two ways. On the one hand, some have argued that it characteristically acted as an *integrative* force in the community, the brief periods of licensed misrule acting ultimately to reinforce normative behaviour and the political *status quo*. On the other, it is suggested that it could just as easily perform a *subversive* role, particularly, in Clark's words, 'when circumstances rendered the structures of authority unstable and vulnerable to challenge'.[5] The ambiguity inherent in festive behaviour in early modern culture is, I believe, directly comparable to the function performed by witchcraft trials at this time, for they too seem to have operated in one of two seemingly contradictory ways. The punishment of witches, for example, could on occasion promote cohesion and unity in a community, reinforcing in the process the dominant political values of the ruling group. But equally, it might serve as a vehicle for criticism and complaint, thus providing a valuable opportunity for malcontents to vent their dissatisfaction with, and opposition to, the ruling élite. In the case of the former, the authority of those in power was strengthened by the purge of such disorderly members of the body politic. With respect to the latter, the presence of witchcraft in the community was seen as symptomatic of a wider moral and political failure on the part of those in authority. In both cases, the witch constitutes a sign of divine disapproval, though how this sign is to be construed ultimately depends on a variety of factors which have little to do with the authenticity of the particular accusation levelled against the witch.

If this analysis is correct, then witchcraft represented a highly flexible and seemingly contradictory body of ideas for early modern Europeans to draw upon. On certain occasions, it seemed provident to downplay the threat posed to society by witches. At other times, it made perfect sense to prosecute such evildoers. Whatever the case, such a 'political' analysis of the genesis of witch trials strongly underlines the point that it would be erroneous to correlate 'scepticism' or 'credulity' with any one religious or political grouping in early modern England. Belief in witchcraft was not, as some have inferred, the special preserve of a 'Puritan' minority. Nor was 'scepticism' associated exclusively with their Anglican opponents. Putting to one side the debate surrounding the usefulness of such labels, it is evident that no single religious or political movement monopolized belief in witchcraft and the subsequent persecution of witches in early modern England. Moreover, as a corollary to this approach, I would strongly argue against the prevailing convention in witchcraft studies which segregates participants in witch trials and debates into two clearly defined camps, that of 'sceptics' and 'believers'. The assumption that élites were predisposed by virtue of their learning to one or other of these two positions is, I believe, untenable. The surviving evidence suggests not simply that educated early modern Englishmen judged accusations of witchcraft by reference to the respective merits of such cases (the objective criteria which we, in our innocence, assume must have informed the debates of grand jurors, JPs, clerics, and the like), but rather that their view of probable guilt or innocence was largely determined by a range of factors related to the broader political climate of the day.

Recent case studies of individual witch trials have strongly hinted at the importance of the local political culture in the genesis of such events.[6] If, however, we are to make sense of national patterns of witch trials, it is equally important to acknowledge the role of demonology in the wider world of political thought and action, which, in turn, must have helped to shape opinion at the local level. Again, the work of Clark in this respect is invaluable, in particular his assertion that to prosecute witches was to invoke the fear of disorder which lay at the heart of early modern political discourse. Accordingly, the ability to counter such a threat presupposed divine sanction of the godly ruler, regardless of the precise way in which that authority was wielded. Under such circumstances, we might infer two further deductions about the general incidence of witchcraft trials. Firstly, that the manifestation of the power inherent in the godly magistrate to counter the threat of the witch was more likely to be invoked at moments of acute crisis such as the establishment of political order *ab initio*. And secondly, that it was correspondingly less likely to be cited in the case of well-established regimes where the mere suggestion of diabolical infiltration of the body politic might be construed as a challenge to the *status quo*. Either way, belief in witchcraft represented a vital test of political legitimation, so much so that the distribution of witch trials frequently provides the historian with a valuable barometer of the prevailing religious and political climate, both at local and national level.

Can such a model be applied to England between the mid-sixteenth and early eighteenth centuries? The answer necessarily lies in the examination of a wide range of case studies, but in general terms, it is possible, I believe, to advance a broad correlation between witch-hunting and politics. Thus, it is no surprise that the peak of prosecutions for witchcraft in England coincided with the early years of the reign of Elizabeth I. The need to create a new political and religious consensus in the wake of the mid-Tudor crisis created a natural environment for the promotion of witch-hunting. During these years, there seems to have been little internal debate in the ranks of the ruling élites as to the reality of witchcraft. Privy councillors and bishops were as likely to promote witch-hating, and on occasions witch-hunting, as those lesser members of the ruling orders who made up the political nation. It was also during this period that anti-Catholicism emerged as one of the central themes of English witchcraft discourse.[7] At all levels of society, discussion of witchcraft and the prosecution of witches accompanied a wider commitment to moral, religious, and political renewal. Society was cleansed of its Catholic past not so much by an attack on Catholics as witches, but rather through the elaboration in pamphlets, sermons, and charges to grand juries of the inherently diabolical and superstitious nature of the old faith.

In this early stage then, witchcraft clearly functioned as a vehicle for consensus and as a positive test of the new regime's right to rule. By the 1580s, however, as consensus gave way to growing divisions within the upper echelons of government (mostly religious in origin) so, for the first time, it is possible to detect signs that belief in witchcraft and the punishment of witches was beginning to prove problematic and potentially divisive. Indeed, there is some evidence to suggest that one of the most radical assaults on the reality of witches, Reginald Scot's *Discoverie of Witchcraft* (1584), may have been prompted in part by fears in Scot's native Kent of a Puritan assault on the Elizabethan church settlement. Scot, who prior to the 1580s seems to have supported the work of militant Protestant evangelists in Kent, performed a dramatic *volte face* in 1582 when he played a prominent role in the anti-Puritan backlash in that county. The timing of the publication of his anti-witchcraft treatise, and the inclusion in it of a number of cases of deceit perpetrated by Puritan ministers and their supporters in Kent, hints at an underlying political motive for the work.[8]

As the religious divisions deepened in the 1580s and 1590s, it would appear that a confessional divide was beginning to emerge with respect to witchcraft, witch-hunting, and diabolical possession. Now, more often than not, it was the Puritan wing of English Protestantism which appeared most eager to promote the prosecution of witches against the seemingly 'sceptical' opposition of their conformist Anglican brethren.[9] This fits neatly with what one might expect of a group within the Anglican church committed to a programme of further religious reform which interpreted the presence of witchcraft as a sign of the failure of those in power to regenerate the nation. On the other hand, it should not lead us to equate support for Puritanism *per se* with witch-hating and witch-hunting. Numerous examples from this period and much later can be cited to disprove this particular fallacy. For example, in godly Maldon in Essex, there is evidence to suggest that the 'scepticism' of the Presbyterian lecturer, George Gifford, may have been shaped by accusations of witchcraft levelled at some of his supporters in the borough.[10] Similarly, in Jacobean Northamptonshire, the Puritan leadership of the county seems to have encouraged a highly 'sceptical' approach to witchcraft both before and after the celebrated trials of 1612. John Cotta, the well-connected Puritan physician of Northampton, may have been giving vent to such attitudes in the subsequent treatises which he wrote on the subject in 1616. In the process, he was almost certainly echoing the views of leading Puritan gentlemen in the county, such as Sir Richard Knightley who, in 1608, following the examination of suspected witches in the county, declared that he had known one of the accused for a long time and could find no ground for suspicion of witchcraft.[11] The crucial factor here is that both the borough of Maldon and county of Northamptonshire were under firm Puritan control, despite attempts to subvert that authority. Perceived by their rulers as model, godly communities, it seemed incongruent to give credence to claims of witchcraft which, by their very nature, tended to undermine this image. The example of that godly 'city on a hill', Dorchester, provides yet further evidence for such a view. During the 40 years of Puritan hegemony in the city in the early seventeenth century, only two cases of suspected witchcraft came before the town's Puritan JPs. Both were rejected, one, almost certainly, because it emanated from sources hostile to the Puritan governors of the borough.[12]

At the level of central government, similar forces may have been at work. Though belief in the potential of the devil and his minions to perpetrate harm on English men and women remained widespread, there was clearly a reluctance on the part of those in authority to attest to *actual* diabolical incursions upon the stage of the English body politic. James I's so-called 'scepticism', and that of his son Charles I, may well have reflected the latent ambiguity which lay at the heart of contemporary belief in witchcraft. On the one hand, it was necessary to pay lip service to the theoretical presence of the devil's servants, witches, in Jacobean and Caroline England. On the other, it was a testament to the charismatic influence and power which such divinely sanctioned rulers wielded that, in practice, witchcraft was perceived as a largely non-existent threat to the kingdom.[13]

The onset of civil war and widespread political and religious disorder in the 1640s ushered in a new phase in the history of English witchcraft. Though large-scale witch-hunting was relatively scarce outside of East Anglia, there is little doubt that the language of witchcraft animated much of the religious and political discourse of this period. Pamphlets, sermons, newsletters, and private correspondence testify to the renewed interest of the political nation in the language of learned demonology. It was during this period, for example, that royalist preachers began to invoke texts such as 1 Samuel 15:23 ['For Rebellion is as the Sin of Witchcraft …'] in order to stigmatize their opponents as agents of a diabolical pact against Church and State. Not surprisingly, the latter replied in kind by calling for a radical dispossession of the body politic, which they claimed had been corrupted by the political innovations and crypto-Catholic policies of Charles I's government.[14] Such references permeate the vitriolic religious and political debates of this period, both locally and nationally. In the process, they almost certainly helped to shape the series of trials which took place in East Anglia in the mid-1640s and led to the execution of several hundred witches.

These trials have been routinely dismissed as an aberration in the annals of English witchcraft. More often than not, the episode has been ascribed to the malign influence of a single figure, the self-styled 'Witchfinder General', Matthew Hopkins, or, alternatively, explained away as the product of the general breakdown of the normal processes of law and order in East Anglia as a result of the exigencies of civil war. However, careful study of local conditions, and their interaction with national events and concerns, suggests a different picture.[15] Hopkins himself was undoubtedly a significant figure, his messianic and charismatic personality influential in acting as a catalyst for witch-hunting in the region. But far more important than Hopkins was the receptive state of those communities which he visited, and which had been primed for witch-hating by earlier events. Close study of the towns and villages which produced witches in the mid-1640s reveals that the vast majority had undergone intense religious and political polarization in the years immediately prior to the trials. They were consequently fertile ground for witch-cleansing as a prelude to the re-creation of a new godly order in the region, based on evangelical Puritan reform.

Particularly noteworthy is the fact that the greatest support for Hopkins emanated from Suffolk, and not Essex, where Hopkins had begun his crusade. During the late 1630s, Suffolk, a traditional hotbed of Puritanism, was subjected to violent religious upheaval in the wake of the appointment of the militant Arminian, Matthew Wren, to the bishopric of Norwich in 1636. Many of those communities subsequently visited by Hopkins in 1645 had been the object of Wren's anti-Puritan campaign of reform. Few were left untouched by his assiduous attention. Not surprisingly, when civil war provided the opportunity for a Puritan backlash, all signs of Laudian innovation and ceremonialism were rapidly expunged. Recently appointed supporters of Wren and Laud were deprived of their livings, and the Parliamentary Covenant was enthusiastically adopted in most parishes. To add to the sense of apocalyptic renewal, many of these same parishes were subjected in 1643 and 1644 to the iconoclasm of William Dowsing, whose appointment by Parliament gave added credence to the view at the local level that root and branch reform of the Church was now sanctioned by the national leadership of the Puritan movement. Consequently, when Hopkins arrived in Suffolk in 1645 he encountered communities primed for witch-cleansing as a final act in the moral redemption of the godly commonwealth.[16]

Micro-studies of those involved in the identification and punishment of witches at this time suggests that many had been active, either as victims or protagonists, in the dramatic events of the preceding decade. The vast majority were clearly associated with the Puritan élites which now governed these communities. Many had suffered personally at the hands of Bishop Wren and his agents. Some actively assisted Dowsing in his campaign of licensed destruction, while others witnessed against those malignant and scandalous ministers who had supported Wren's campaign of 'thorough'. In the case of Edward Parsley, a bricklayer of Manningtree, Essex, the connection between popular puritanism, opposition to Wren, and support for Hopkins is transparent. In 1636 Parsley played a key role in the religious rioting which accompanied the visit of the new bishop, Matthew Wren, to Ipswich. Armed with a long staff, he demanded to know of one of Wren's clerical commissioners:

> by what authoritie they came thither, and whether they had brought the great seale of England with them, and publiquely reviled the said Com[missione]rs and said they had oppressed many good men and that they would have all his Ma[jes]ties Subiects to be the Queenes subiects. And … seditiously then publiquely affirmed that his Ma[jes]ties proclamacons were of no force without a parliam[en]t for that his Ma[jes]tie could do nothing.[17]

Other details gleaned from the official examination of Parsley reveal a degree of political and religious sophistication which it is not easy to equate with a poor, starving bricklayer. Asked, for example, by Dr Goad, one of Wren's commissioners, by what authority he addressed him so, Parsley replied that he was 'sent unto you from god & I am full of the spirit of God'. He was also eager to dispute with Goad 'that there ought to be noe altars since Arons preists' and that 'the Saboth was Morall'. Parsley ultimately escaped punishment in the courts through the collusion of the Puritan magistrates of Ipswich, who were charged by Wren himself with bringing him to justice. No more is heard of him until nine years later when he appeared as a witness, alongside Hopkins and Stearne, to the witchcraft of Elizabeth and Ellen Clarke who, like Parsley, were inhabitants of Manningtree. Though many who testified in the trials of the mid-1640s may well have done so out of malice or ignorance, the case of Edward Parsley, and others like him, suggests that the genesis of the accusations owed more to the political and religious world views of ordinary parishioners than has hitherto been recognized.[18]

The expression of moral and godly reformation through witch-hunting can also be found in other communities and regions of England in the aftermath of the Civil War. Newcastle in 1649 and Kent in the early 1650s seem to have undergone a similar process. In both cases, the urge to punish witches with the full force of the law was largely orchestrated by newly established godly factions within these communities.[19] The 1650s, moreover, continued to witness to the popularity of the language of witchcraft and demonism in religious and political debate. Now, the emphasis of supporters of the Cromwellian regime was not so much on the demonization of vanquished royalists, but rather the demonization of religious extremists and radical sectaries. It is perhaps not too much of an exaggeration to describe this war of words (which sometimes spilled over into actual accusations of witchcraft against religious dissidents like the Quakers) as something of a demonological free-for-all in which everyone, regardless of religious or political affiliation, seemed eager to appropriate the language of witchcraft in order to make sense of the confused and disorderly state of the nation.[20]

Herein lies the core of the solution, I believe, to the problem of witchcraft's decline as a coherent body of ideas and its failure to generate widespread communal assent. In an increasingly divided society, educated men slowly withdrew from holding or publicizing such beliefs, not because they now saw through the logical inconsistencies or contradictions inherent in witchcraft, but rather because of the exposure of such ideas to the fierce heat of ideological division and debate. As Ian Bostridge has shown, the process was slow, with witchcraft continuing to exert a purchase on the minds of England's élite well into the eighteenth century.[21] But from the 1660s onwards, and largely as a result of the permanent divisions inflicted upon the body politic by the conflicts of the Civil War, witchcraft, both in theory and practice, was subject to a process of politicization which increasingly prevented a consensual approach to the subject.

It is impossible in the brief space here to do justice to the mass of evidence to support this claim. However, by focusing on the last significant attempt to resurrect witchcraft as a normative set of beliefs after the Restoration, I hope to demonstrate the validity of a politically informed approach to this subject. This period, interestingly, also seems to have witnessed the last peak in actual prosecutions and trials for witchcraft, after which the witchcraft statutes became largely redundant. During the course of the 1660s, élite preoccupation with witchcraft once again rose to significant levels. This was true especially for two well-defined groups: the latitudinarians and Nonconformists. The two, of course, had much in common. For 'latitudinarian' conformists, the desire to create a broader and more comprehensive church settlement, which would have included large numbers of moderate dissenters, formed the core of their ecclesiological position.[22] This aim was in large part shared by their Nonconformist brethren, many of whom were equally committed to the restoration of a single, unified church, and were equally hostile to the claims of radical sectaries and Catholics for inclusion in such a settlement. The desire of both groups to see the body politic exorcized of its civil-war excesses and restored to health was overwhelming and found expression, amongst other things, in the revival of interest in witchcraft in the 1660s.

For many Nonconformists, in particular, in this period, witchcraft was a powerful explanatory device which enabled those who suffered official persecution to make sense of their plight. The process is exemplified in the actions of men like Thomas Spatchet, a leading dissenter in the Suffolk town of Dunwich, whose witchcraft-induced fits in the 1660s closely mirrored the ups and downs of religious policy in those years. The providential nature of his misfortunes is unmistakeable. As a leading member of the borough corporation, Spatchet was miraculously struck dumb by a local witch just weeks before he was due to take his oath to the restored regime. And as a lay minister in the 1650s, there was more than a touch of good fortune in the fact that he became completely immobilized at the moment the Five Mile Act became law. Equally marvellous were his recoveries, which unfailingly coincided with the issue of royal indulgences or discussion of imminent religious comprehension. For many Nonconformists and their 'latitudinarian' sympathizers in the restored Church, Spatchet's contorted and bewitched body represented a powerful metaphor for the general ills of the nation. It also suggested a radical cure for those ailments in the form of symbolic dispossession of the body politic.[23]

Similar sentiments, I believe, informed the endeavours of another charismatic Restoration figure, the celebrated miracle healer, Valentine Greatrakes. Greatrakes is an intriguing figure, not least because so little attention has been paid by historians to the explanations which he offered for his cures, in particular, his tendency to liken them to exorcisms. Prior to his arrival in England in January 1666, Greatrakes had in fact played a major role in one of the few cases of Irish witchcraft for which substantial depositions exist.[24] He was, it seems, a self-confessed expert in demonology and psychic phenomena, who delighted in regaling his English friends and acquaintances with stories of witches and demons. But more to the point, his own religious and political background, and that of those who proved to be his staunchest supporters, fits the pattern suggested above. Greatrakes himself was clearly sympathetic to the plight of Nonconformists, amongst whom he numbered some of his closest friends. At the same time, the core of his following in England was provided by some of the most eminent advocates of religious moderation within the Anglican church.

A further clue as to why witchcraft should have appealed in particular to 'latitudinarians' and Nonconformists in the early years of the Restoration is provided by the profiles of Greatrakes's patients and supporters. For regardless of their precise religious or political affiliation, they were characteristically men who had either performed some service for the Cromwellian regime or begun their careers in the 1650s. That is, they were all tainted, potentially at least, by their past allegiance to a discredited regime, and now sought reintegration into the restored body politic of the 1660s which many saw as their natural birthright. A prime example is provided by Greatrakes's leading Irish patron, Roger Boyle, the Earl of Orrery. Despite an illustrious career as a leading agent of Cromwellian government in Scotland and Ireland, he survived the Restoration to occupy a leading role in the government of the province of Munster. On the surface, his was one of the success stories of the period. But this was not Orrery's perception. He never quite came to terms with his earlier disloyalty to the crown, nor could he accept the harsh terms of the Clarendon Code which excluded, in his eyes, many pious and loyal subjects of the restored monarchy. Consequently, he spent much of the Restoration acting as a go-between with men like Richard Baxter, who, despite numerous periods of imprisonment, never faltered in his pursuit of a revised and more comprehensive church settlement. What is particularly significant about the two men's collaboration from the point of view of this study, however, is the fact that both shared a passionate and lifelong interest in witch trials, many of Orrery's personal experiences of psychic phenomena finding their way into Baxter's published demonology of 1692.

This combination of concerns – witchcraft and religious comprehension – also seems to have infiltrated the thinking of important figures in the judiciary, whose response to accusations of witchcraft was pivotal in determining the fate of suspects. A good example is the celebrated judge, Sir Matthew Hale, who made his name in the service of Cromwell, but survived the purge of 1660. Thereafter, Hale, a close friend of many leading Nonconformists, including Richard Baxter, tirelessly used his formidable powers as a circuit judge to protect dissenters from the full vigour of the Clarendon Code. At the same time, he subscribed to the reality of witchcraft, frequently presiding over cases of witchcraft in the 1660s which led to guilty verdicts. In one particularly well-publicized case (published in 1676 from trial papers held by Hale), the chief victims of the witches' *maleficium* were the daughters of a Suffolk gentleman and prominent Nonconformist, Samuel Pacey of Lowestoft. Hale's intervention in this instance almost certainly sealed the fate of the two accused witches. To what extent Hale's familiarity with the victims' father affected his judgement in this case is impossible to state with certainty. What is clear, however, is that those who shared his distaste for the new laws against dissenters do seem to have been noticeably more willing to pursue those enemies of Christ, witches, than they were to subject innocent, god-fearing Christians to the full rigour of the new penal laws against dissent.[25]

But why should Nonconformists and latitudinarians have shared this preoccupation with witchcraft at this particular juncture? It has already been suggested that accounts of witchcraft were more likely to have been taken seriously at moments of acute religious and political anxiety such as the 1660s. Moreover, for those Nonconformists like Spatchet and Pacey who claimed to be the victims of witches, the idea of a demonic conspiracy provided a logical explanation for their particular misfortunes as well as the plight of their co-religionists. What is less clear is why 'latitudinarian' sympathizers should be so eager to authenticate and publicize such accounts. One explanation is suggested by the urgent need in the post-Restoration period to redefine the effective boundaries of the restored Christian commonwealth. In refocusing élite attention on the threat posed to church and state by the witch, and reascribing the latter to her rightful place in the moral and political universe, the vision of the unitary state was reaffirmed. To paraphrase the latitudinarian position, it was far better to prosecute those *real* enemies of God, the witches, whose every action was antithetical to good government, than to punish men whose only crime was to differ on the non-essentials of religious faith and opinion. Thus Thomas Barlow in 1660, in the course of arguing for a broad church with limited toleration, argued that the civil magistrate should only discipline citizens for '*matters of fact* such as sorcery or sacrilege', and refrain from punishing people for matters of opinion such as religious belief.[26] Witch-hunting, then, was not simply consonant with religious moderation, but may have been, within the particular religious and political circumstances prevalent at this time, a necessary adjunct of the latitudinarian position. To modern sensibilities, such a combination of interests appears wildly incongruent. For contemporaries, however, it clearly possessed a powerful appeal. In order to underline the point, we might note the reaction of hard-line Anglicans to witchcraft at this time. This is particularly significant with respect to those who implemented the judicial system and were responsible for policing Restoration communities. In the case of the Lowestoft witches, for example, it is worth noting that the single voice of opposition to the proceedings against the accused witches came from Judge John Keeling, a man with a reputation for extreme harshness in his dealings with Nonconformists. Several Justices of the Peace in Lancashire and Yorkshire seem to have shared Keeling's hatred for dissent and leniency towards accused witches, clearly influenced on occasions by their knowledge of the political context in which accusations of witchcraft arose. One is left to speculate just how common was the attitude of one Suffolk gentleman, who remarked in the case of Thomas Spatchet and Samuel Manning (a fellow nonconformist preacher) that if the witch 'bewitched none but [them], and such as they are, she should never be Hanged by him'.[27]

By the second half of the seventeenth century, the fate of witchcraft, both as a body of ideas and as a crime, was inextricably bound up with the demands of contemporary religious and political debate. The overt politicization of witchcraft undoubtedly played a part in its demise as a crime, but this should not lead us to overlook its continuing appeal to members of the élite anxious to understand and explore its relevance to the wider controversies of the period. Thus, at moments of acute political confrontation, such as the Exclusion Crisis, it was frequently invoked by both sides in the conflict in order to legitimate their respective positions. But it was never the property of a single faction or party. Tory sympathizers, who downplayed the threat of witchcraft before 1679, were as likely to promote its reality in the changed circumstances of the late seventeenth and early eighteenth centuries. Indeed, it was the remarkable flexibility of witchcraft, a product of its inherent ambiguity, which made it such a powerful addition to the arsenal of early modern political discourse and accounts, in part, for its longevity. To acknowledge the existence of witches in a given community or to invoke the language of demonology in political debate was necessarily to raise the spectre of disorder which lay at the heart of early modern political behaviour and thought. The ability to counter such a threat presupposed the divine legitimation of the ruler, be they monarch, bishop, magistrate, or corporation, and was more likely to be implemented in cases of new and insecure regimes. Conversely, instances of witchcraft tended to be dismissed by those secure in their authority, where the mere suggestion of diabolical infiltration of the body politic might be considered by the powers-that-be as a challenge to their legitimate claim on power. In either case, the occurrence of witchcraft represented, in Clark's memorable phrase, 'a critical test of political legitimacy', with witch trials and demonological debate representing an invaluable instrument for measuring religious and political conflict in early modern communities.[28]

Notes

1. S. Clark, *Thinking with Demons: The Idea of Witchcraft in Early Modern Europe* (Oxford, 1997).
2. K. V. Thomas, *Religion and the Decline of Magic* (London, 1978), p. 684; cf. H. R. Trevor-Roper, 'The European Witch-Craze of the Sixteenth and Seventeenth Centuries', in Trevor-Roper, *Religion, the Reformation and Social Change* (London, 1967), p. 169.
3. Clark, *Thinking with Demons*, p. 36 and chs 3–5, *passim*.
4. Cf. G. R. Quaife, *Godly Zeal and Furious Rage: The Witch in Early Modern Europe* (London and Sydney, 1987), pp. 120–1. I share Quaife's strictures on the functionalist model of witchcraft as state-building. For general discussion of this, and its limited application to the early modern period, see B. P. Levack, 'State-Building and Witch Hunting in Early Modern Europe', in J. Barry, M. Hester and G. Roberts (eds), *Witchcraft in Early Modern Europe: Studies in Culture and Belief* (Cambridge, 1996), pp. 96–115.
5. Clark, *Thinking with Demons*, p. 25.
6. See, for example, A. Gregory, 'Witchcraft, Politics and "Good Neighbourhood" in Early Seventeenth-Century Rye,' *Past and Present*, 133 (1991), 31–66; A. R. DeWindt, 'Witchcraft and Conflicting Visions of the Ideal Village Community', *Journal of British Studies*, 34 (1995), 427–63.
7. N. Jones, 'Defining Superstitions: Treasonous Catholics and the Act against Witchcraft of 1563', in C. Carlton et al. (eds), *State, Sovereigns and Society in Early Modern England* (Stroud, 1998), pp. 187–203.
8. For an alternative account of the origin of Scot's scepticism in his covert support for the principles of the radical sect, the Family of Love, see Chapter 6 by David Wootton in this volume.
9. This is most evident, of course, in the debate surrounding the Puritan exorcist, John Darrell, and the case of Mary Glover in London; see D. P.

Walker, *Unclean Spirits: Possession and Exorcism in France and England in the Late Sixteenth and Early Seventeenth Centuries* (London, 1981); M. MacDonald (ed.), *Witchcraft and Hysteria in Elizabethan London: Edward Jorden and the Mary Glover Case* (London and New York, 1991).

10. A. Macfarlane, 'A Tudor Anthropologist: George Gifford's *Discourse* and *Dialogue*' in S. Anglo (ed.), *The Damned Art: Essays in the Literature of Witchcraft* (London, 1977), pp. 141–2, 154 n. 21.

11. Northamptonshire Record Office, P[eterborough] D[iocesan] R[ecords], CB40, f. 276v. I discuss Cotta's Puritanism in the forthcoming article in the *New DNB*.

12. D. Underdown, *Fire from Heaven: Life in an English Town in the Seventeenth Century* (London, 1992), pp. 78–9, 165.

13. In the case of Charles I, there are some interesting parallels with his attitude to touching for the king's evil, an attribute of early modern monarchy analogous to notions of magisterial inviolability from witchcraft. During the 1630s, when Charles accounted himself 'the happiest king in Christendom', he consistently disappointed his subjects by failing to conduct regular healing sessions. After 1640, however, and the subsequent breakdown of political order, Charles rediscovered his therapeutic powers, in much the same way as his supporters now gave full vent to their belief in a demonic conspiracy. See Clark, *Thinking with Demons*, chs 38–43, esp. pp. 655–7; J. Richards, '"His Nowe Majestie" and the English Monarchy: The Kingship of Charles I before 1640', *Past and Present*, 113 (1986), 88–93.

14. I sketch the beginnings of this process in my '"Saints or sorcerers": Quakerism, Demonology and the Decline of Witchcraft in Seventeenth-Century England', in Barry, Hester and Roberts (eds), *Witchcraft in Early Modern Europe*, pp. 163–6.

15. For a recent reinterpretation of the Hopkins' trials which suggests the advantages of such an approach, see J. Sharpe, *Instruments of Darkness: Witchcraft in England, 1550–1750* (London, 1996), pp. 128–47. I am currently engaged in a major study of this episode in which I lay particular emphasis upon the interaction of local and national concerns in the origin and progress of the trials. For a recent attempt to underline the importance of such an approach in the case of the Stour Valley riots of 1642, see J. Walter, *Understanding Popular Violence in the English Revolution: The Colchester Plunderers* (Cambridge, 1999).

16. The itinerary of Dowsing's campaign of iconoclastic destruction in East Anglia in 1643–44 bears close parallel with the route taken by Hopkins a year later. For a recent study of Dowsing, which positions his iconoclasm within the context of his well-informed and highly individual analysis of contemporary events, see J. Morrill, 'William Dowsing, the Bureaucratic Puritan', in J. Morrill, P. Slack and D. Woolf (eds), *Public Duty and Private Conscience in Seventeenth-Century England: Essays Presented to G. E. Aylmer* (Oxford, 1993), pp. 173–203. Idolatry and witchcraft were, of course, frequently linked in the popular imagination. The Jacobean preacher, Peter Hay, for example, described the sin of witchcraft as 'Idolatry in the

Superlative degree'; P. Hay, *A Vision of Balaams Asse* (London, 1616), p. 32.

17. East Suffolk Record Office, C2/18/1, p. 2.

18. Ibid., pp. 12–13; C. L'Estrange Ewen (ed.), *Witch Hunting and Witch Trials* (London, 1929), pp. 223–4, 227.

19. For Newcastle, see R. Howell, *Newcastle-upon-Tyne and the Puritan Revolution* (Oxford, 1967), pp. 232–3. The rash of prosecutions in Kent in 1652 still awaits detailed study.

20. See esp. my '"Saints or Sorcerers"', pp. 145–63.

21. I. Bostridge, *Witchcraft and Its Transformations, c.1650–c.1750* (Oxford, 1997).

22. There is much debate over the use of the term 'latitudinarianism'. While sympathetic to John Spurr's strictures on the historical attempt to locate and define a 'latitudinarian' party in the Restoration church, I remain convinced of the existence in this period of a mood or ethos among influential members of the established church who were temperamentally opposed to theological dogmatism and the politics of religious coercion. See J. Spurr, '"Latitudinarianism" and the Restoration Church', *The Historical Journal*, 31 (1988), 61–82.

23. S. Petto, *A Faithful Narrative of the Wonderful and Extraordinary Fits which Mr Tho Spatchet ... was under by Witchcraft* (London, 1693); Elmer, '"Saints and Sorcerers"', p. 175 n. 87.

24. P. Elmer, *Valentine Greatrakes, the Body Politic and the Politics of the Body in Restoration England* (forthcoming). In this full-length study, I seek to demonstrate how Greatrakes's religious and political background informed the reception of his cures, with particular reference to the demonological debate in Restoration Ireland and England.

25. For a recent study of the Lowestoft witches which struggles to accommodate the religious moderation of Hale and Sir Thomas Browne with their advocacy of witchcraft, see G. Geis and I. Bunn, *A Trial of Witches: A Seventeenth-Century Witchcraft Prosecution* (London and New York, 1997).

26. S. Shapin and S. Schaffer, *Leviathan and the Air Pump: Hobbes, Boyle and the Experimental Life* (Princeton, NJ, 1985), p. 303; [T. Barlow], *Several Miscellaneous and Weighty Cases of Conscience* (London, 1692), vol. 1, p. 45 [first written in manuscript in 1660].

27. Elmer, '"Saints or Sorcerers"', p. 178 n. 95; Petto, p. 19. For the 'scepticism' of the Lancashire JP and ardent royalist, Sir Roger Bradshaigh, combined with his hatred of nonconformity, see *CSPD, 1665–6*, p. 225. John Webster's sceptical treatise, *The Displaying of Supposed Witchcraft* (1677) was dedicated to five Tory Yorkshire JPs who were especially active in the war against dissent.

28. Clark, p. 552. For just one example of the way in which disputes over witchcraft were inextricably bound up with religious and political tensions, both at the local and national level, see J. Westaway and R. D Harrison, '"The Surey Demoniack": Defining Protestantism in 1690s Lancashire', in R. N. Swanson (ed.), *Unity and Diversity in the Church* (Oxford, 1996), pp 263–82.

Chapter Six
Reginald Scot / Abraham
Fleming / The Family of Love*

David Wootton

y title's eccentric punctuation reflects the problematic character of my subject, which is the last book of Reginald Scot, *Discoverie of Witchcraft* (1584), 'A Discourse upon divels and spirits': a discourse that is relatively inaccessible, and consequently rarely read.[1] The views expressed in that book are very odd, but are strikingly reminiscent of those of Scot's collaborator, Abraham Fleming, who is best known as the editor of the posthumous edition of Holinshed's *Chronicles* (1587) (often referred to as 'Shakespeare's Holinshed'), but who is primarily of interest here as the author of *The Diamond of Devotion* (1581). My argument is that the religion of Scot (1538?–1599) and Fleming (1552?–1607) is that of the Family of Love, a cult founded by Hendrick Niclaes (1502?–1580?).

Some readers will find my argument surprising, and at various points they may feel that it stretches the bounds of belief. Fleming himself reports in the *Chronicles* that Mark Scaliot, an Elizabethan blacksmith, had forged fetters so fine that they could be used to tether a flea, a fact

*   This paper is a revised version of 'The Serpent in the Garden: Reginald Scot and Abraham Fleming', cited in Stuart Clark, *Thinking with Demons* (Oxford: Clarendon Press, 1997), p. 544. Earlier versions of this paper were given to Michael Hunter and Lyndal Roper's seminar at the Institute of Historical Research and to the 'Reading Witchcraft' conference. I am also grateful to Stuart Clark, Christopher Marsh, Annabel Patterson, and Nicholas Tyacke for their comments.

that he would have found incredible had he not seen it with his own eyes.[2] Here Fleming's sense of the difficulty of believing what he reports is precisely what renders him a credible witness. The links I seek to forge are made out of clues, inferences, and textual correspondences, not metal beaten gossamer-fine, so I can offer no eyewitness testimony. But texts, juxtaposed, can tell a story which is clear and unambiguous, and readers can see the evidence with their own eyes. If the evidence appears surprising, it is because we are too quick to assume we already know how the Elizabethans pictured their world.

Reginald Scot

Reginald Scot's *Discoverie of Witchcraft* has not received the attention it deserves.[3] Scot's purpose in the *Discoverie* is straightforward: it is to argue that devils do not enter into pacts with individuals, that spells can have no effect, and that consequently witchcraft is an impossible crime. There may be those who want to use spells to harm others; but nobody can, in fact, employ other-than-natural powers for any purpose. Scot's systematic scepticism makes him an isolated figure, for his arguments are much more radical than those of mitigated sceptics such as Weyer (1563) or Montaigne (1588). The very existence of the *Discoverie* should provoke puzzlement, as should its considerable influence on the writers of Scot's own day.[4] Later critics of belief in witchcraft (the next was to be Thomas Ady in 1655) always referred back to it, so that the *Discoverie* remained a living text into the eighteenth century. Indeed, more recently it has acquired new life: the Thomas/Macfarlane account of English witch trials, which are portrayed as arising out of conflicts between neighbours, owes much to Scot's account and to the accounts of those (such as George Gifford, 1593) who were heavily influenced by him.[5] The 'modernity' of Scot's analysis of social relations in the English village cries out for explanation.

Unfortunately modern literary and historical scholars have not served Scot well. Even the best scholars use editions of the *Discoverie* which omit the crucial 'Discourse upon divels and spirits', and only Annabel Patterson has recognized the importance of Scot's own contribution to Fleming's Holinshed.[6] But two scholars have offered contrasting accounts of Scot's views as expressed in the Discourse. In Sydney Anglo's view, Scot is a Sadducee: he does not really believe in spirits, but sees them merely as metaphors of good and evil.[7] His disbelief goes so far that he is best thought of as a proto-deist rather than a Christian, for many of his arguments against witchcraft tell equally against Christ's miracles. This interpretation accords with the views of James I, but is directly at odds with Scot's own insistence that he is not a Sadducee.[8] Leland Estes, by contrast, thinks that Scot is sincere in his claim to believe in the miracles of Christ and in the Resurrection, and wishes to classify his rationalist religion as Erasmian.[9] More recently, James Sharpe has largely accepted Anglo's interpretation: 'In effect (and despite his disavowals), the logic of Scot's arguments led to a denial of the reality of the spirit world as surely as it led to a denial of the reality of witchcraft.'[10] In Stuart Clark's account: 'Scot's most telling argument was his reduction … of all demonic agents to a non-corporeal condition, thus removing them from physical nature altogether.' This 'destroyed at one blow the very essence of magic and witchcraft'. But Clark carefully avoids claiming that Scot denied the reality of the demonic or the possibility of miracles, for Scot's 'most subversive arguments stemmed … from a radically unorthodox theology, not from an alternative natural philosophy'.[11]

We need to pause over this theology. Scot was certainly conscious of disagreeing with orthodox theologians over how to read the Bible:

> For whatsoever is proposed in scripture to us by parable, or spoken figurativelie or significativelie, or framed to our grosse capacities, etc.: is by them so considered and expounded, as though the bare letter [i.e., the literal meaning], or rather their grosse imaginations thereupon were to be pre-ferred before the true [i.e., the figurative] sense and meaning of the word.[12]

He interprets the Bible not as a historical text, but as a series of stories suited to the capacities of the uneducated. Thus the story of the fall of Lucifer should not be read as implying that there really was an angel who fell from heaven; Lucifer is simply a personification of the morning star and thus an emblem of pride, and the story of the fall of Lucifer foreshadows an actual event, the fall of Nebuchadnezzar.[13] The true significance of the story is that it is a warning to all who read it of the dangers of pride.

Similarly there was no devil who entered into the serpent and seduced Eve. This is merely a dramatic story:

How those words are to be considered may appeare, in that it is of purpose
so spoken, as our weake capacities may thereby best conceive the substance,
tenor, and true meaning of the word, which is there set downe in the manner of a tragedie, in such humane and sensible forme, as wonderfullie
informeth our understanding; though it seem contrarie to the spirituall course
of spirits and divels, and also to the nature and divinitie of God himselfe;
who is infinite, and whome no man ever sawe with corporall eies, and lived.[14]

Genesis 3 reports that God condemned the serpent to creep on his belly:
'But although I abhor that lewd interpretation of the familie of love,
and such other heretikes, as would reduce the whole Bible into
allegories: yet (me thinkes) the creeping there is rather metaphoricallie
or significativelie spoken, than literallie' (a paradoxical sentence, in
which the views of the Family of Love are simultaneously condemned
and adopted).[15] Indeed, whenever spirits and devils are mentioned in
the Bible, it would seem that they are to be interpreted metaphorically:

Such as search with the spirit of wisedome and understanding, shall find,
that spirits, as well good as bad, are in the scriptures diverslie taken: yea
they shall well perceive, that the divell is no horned beast. For sometimes in
the scriptures, spirits and divels are taken for infirmities of the bodie; sometimes for the vices of the mind; sometimes also for the gifts of either of them.[16]

Naturally, when the New Testament speaks of Christ casting out
devils, it is speaking metaphorically, not literally. The seven devils cast
out of Mary Magdalene were 'a great multitude, and an uncerteine
number of vices'. This was a true miracle, for it is 'as difficult a matter,
with a touch to make a good Christian of a vicious person; as with a
word to cure the ague, or any other disease of a sicke bodie'. [17]

I denie not therefore that there are spirits and divels, of such substance as it
hath pleased GOD to create them. But in what place soever it be found or
read in the scriptures, a spirit or divell is to be understood spirituallie, and
is neither a corporall nor a visible thing. Where it is written, that God sent
an evill spirit betweene *Abimelech*, and the men of *Sichem*, we are to understand that he sent the spirit of hatred, and not a bulbegger ... spirits are
spoken of in scripture, as of things spirituall; though for the helpe of our
capacities they are there sometimes more grosselie and corporallie expressed,
either in parables or by metaphors, than indeed they are.[18]

'Despite his disavowals', Scot thus opens himself up to the interpretation proposed by Anglo and to the charge of Sadducism, for it is easy to read him as holding that spirits 'are onelie imaginations in the mind of man' or that 'spirits and divels are onlie motions and affections.'[19] But, if it is hard to make sense of his claim to believe that devils and spirits 'are living creatures', it seems he does believe in 'the spirit of the devil' and 'the spirit of God', the Holy Ghost: that is, in active immaterial forces for good and evil:[20] 'In summe, this word [Spirit] dooth signifie a secret force and power, wherewith our minds are mooved and directed; if unto holy things, then it is the motion of the holie spirit, of the spirit of Christ and of God: if unto evill things, then it is the suggestion of the wicked spirit, of the divell, and of satan.'[21] It might seem that there is a sense in which the devil is only another name for ourselves, or at least our fallen natures: 'in truth we never have so much cause to be afraid of the divell, as when he flatteringlie insinuateth himselfe into our harts, to satisifie, please, and serve *our* humours, entising us to prosecute *our own* appetits and pleasures, without any of these externall terrors.'[22] And it might seem that the Holy Spirit is simply a way of talking about God in us.

This last position Scot is at some pains to refute, defending belief in the Trinity against those he calls the Pneumatomachi, who hold that 'by the name of holie spirit is ment a certaine divine force, wherewith our minds are mooved' – a view which appears identical to his own definition of spirit as 'a secret force and power' just two pages before. But, just as it is hard to make sense of his claim that spirits and devils are both purely spiritual and have 'substance' or are 'living creatures', so his defence of the Trinity appears to undercut itself, for he assures us that 'Against these shamelesse enimies of the holie spirit, I will not use materiall weapons, but syllogistical charmes.' In a book dedicated to showing that charms are inefficacious, this is puzzling. There then follows a debate for and against belief in the Holy Spirit as a member of the Trinity, in which ten strong arguments against belief are met with ten 'syllogistical' responses. A careful reader might well wonder which side was winning the argument, especially when Scot writes: 'I must needs exhort all to whom the reading hereof shall come ... that they so ponder places to and fro, as that they reserve unto the holie spirit the glorious title of divinitie, which by nature is to him appropriate', and proceeds to praise the heathen philosophers who had believed in an *Anima mundi*, which was truly divine, but yet: 'they separated the soule of the world (which they also call the begotten mind) from the most sovereigne and unbegotten God, and imagined certeine differences of degrees, and (as *Cyrill* saith) did Arrianize in the trinitie.' The claim is that anti-Trinitarianism is a pestilent opinion, 'the poison whereof though to them that be resolved in the truth it can doo little hurt, yet to such as stand upon a wavering point it can doo no great good': which is to say that it is harmless.[23]

Scot's notion of a person is thus radically different both from that of orthodox Christian theologians of his day and from ours. The orthodox believed that individuals were tempted by passions within them and devils outside them. Scot believed in the reality of the devil and the Holy Ghost, but located them entirely inside the self, which thus becomes multiple and internally conflicted. One might compare Scot's wicked and good spirits to Freud's Thanatos and Eros, two conflicting drives always at work, but difficult to perceive. To deny the materiality and multiplicity of the demonic was not to deny its reality:[24] Scot's demons have the same ontological status as Freud's unconscious wishes.

Scot takes his argument a step further, for he believes that good can triumph here and now over evil. Those who received the Holy Spirit can be, like Mary Magdalene, perfected: 'For it doth purifie and cleanse the whole man from top to toe, it doth burne out the soile and drosse of sinnes, and setteth him all in a flaming and hot burning zeale to preferre and further Gods glorie.'[25] When Christ cured Mary Magdalene of sin, the miracle was that he did it instantaneously, for in time a preacher can bring about the same cure, just as doctors can in time cure disease. And when Christ cast out devils, his injunction was simple: 'Go your waies and sinne no more.'[26] Scot thus believes that some sort of Fall has taken place which has given the demonic entry into ourselves; but this fall is remediable, and we can take on a new, divine, and unconflicted nature.

Here we have 'a radically unorthodox theology' which destroys 'the very essence of magic and witchcraft'. And at the heart of this theology is a belief in the perfectibility of human nature.

Abraham Fleming

Between 1576 and 1588, between Cambridge and ordination, Fleming worked as a jack-of-all-trades in publishing: a learned corrector or editor, a translator, an indexer, an author.[27] His varied and insignificant productions make him an easy target for gentle ridicule. Annabel Patterson sees his characteristic contribution to Holinshed as being a 'constant emphasis on political obedience' which 'is possibly consistent with his rather drab career as a minor literateur, moralist, and journalist, who published translations of Virgil and Musaeus, pamphlets on English dogs, blazing stars, and "A Paradoxe, proving by reason and example that baldnesse is much better than bushie haire." After he dedicated his *Bucoliks ... and Georgiks* of Virgil to Whitgift in 1589 his clerical career advanced ...'[28] But this leaves her with an editor who is more contradictory and puzzling than she cares to admit. For all his emphasis on obedience, Fleming's accounts of the execution of Catholic plotters seem, as Patterson realizes, intent on provoking sympathy, not hostility. Fleming indulges in what seems to be a deliberately 'disproportionate emphasis on state violence', and this implicit radicalism is complemented by his identification with the needs and aspirations of the common people, his admiration for their 'inter-communitie of life', a word invented by Fleming to describe an egalitarian ideal.[29] Fleming thus becomes enigmatic, apparently deferential to authority, but always verging on subversion.

Patterson rightly sees links between Fleming's 'anthropological' interest in the common people and his association with Reginald Scot.[30] Fleming worked closely with Scot: Scot contributed a very long account of the rebuilding of Dover harbour to Fleming's *Chronicles*. Later he wrote a work that has since been lost: a biography of his kinsman, Sir Thomas Scot, for a planned second edition of Fleming's *Chronicles* which never appeared.[31] And Scot worked closely with Fleming: throughout the *Discoverie* we find Latin poems 'Englished by Abraham Fleming', and in the list of 'authors used in this Booke', we find 'Gnimelf Maharba', or Abraham Fleming.

It is natural then for us to ask what it was that these two authors had in common, and our first suspicion must be that they shared a common religious commitment. But where to look for Fleming's religious beliefs? Not, I would suggest, in *The Conduit of Comfort*. A copy of the fifth impression (1624), on which Fleming's name appears, survives, and a few leaves, but not the title page, of a 1579 edition which is attributed to Fleming in the Stationers' Register.[32] This is a work of perfectly orthodox Puritan piety, entirely in line with conventional accounts of Fleming in the secondary literature, which stress his anti-Catholicism. Not here, because when we turn to Fleming's *A Memoriall of the Famous Monuments and Almesdeedes of W.*

Lambe esquire (1580) we learn that Lamb, who had built a conduit to bring fresh water into London, had fallen under suspicion of being a Catholic. To establish his orthodoxy he began to spend long hours in public view, listening to sermons at St Paul's Cross. But he obviously felt the need for a more explicit statement of his faith, and published a work entitled *Lamb's Conduit of Comfort*, which he gave free to the poor. We must presume that Fleming had ghostwritten the book for Lamb, and that after Lamb's death, he had felt free to reissue it under his own name. From it we learn not what Fleming believed in 1579, but what Lamb wanted people to think Lamb believed, and what Fleming, by now a respectable clergyman, claimed to believe in later years.

We might profitably turn elsewhere. To Fleming's translation of Savonarola's commentary on the 31st and 51st Psalms (1578), a mystical work in which Savonarola stresses that the lover and the thing that is loved are of one nature (thus the Christian is of one nature with God), and portrays men as caught between two forces, hope and heaviness. Hope is the voice of God, though it is often impossible to distinguish God's voice from our own thoughts, while heaviness is the voice of the devil. Here we seem to be in the spiritual world portrayed by Scot in the 'Discourse'.

Or we might turn to a work that appeared in 1581 as *De vera christianae hominis fide*, attributed to the otherwise unknown Jacobus Wittewronghelus, and accompanied by a prayer by Fleming. This was translated by Arthur Golding, a prolific translator, as *Concerning the True Beleefe of a Christian Man*, now attributed to an equally unknown 'S.C.', and accompanied by a preface, a prayer, and marginal comments by Fleming. Our unknown author is a vehement Protestant, but one who rejects the view which he acknowledges is 'commonly', even 'universally', taught, that 'Gods commandements are unpossible to be obayed.'[33] Faith alone is insufficient for salvation, for we can fulfil 'the righteousness of the law' if Christ's spirit is in us, and we are 'saved by obaying'.[34] Through faith and obedience, we will be transformed. We will learn to become enemies to ourselves, for the self is bound up with the flesh and with self-love, and we must divorce our flesh and become instead embodiments of the Spirit.[35] We will put on the nature of Christ, and 'repayre the image wherafter we were created'.[36] Through faith, believers have the power to work miracles: 'not bodily myracles, which were appoynted to the first trayning of the Church unto faith', but spiritual miracles. 'For, to cast out divels, is to cast out the vices of lecherie, covetousnes, wrathfulnes, and such other. Also to speake with new tongs, is to speake with fyre and burning speach, such as no man can withstande.'[37] Faith 'maketh a man partaker of the nature of God, and causeth all things to be possible to him'.[38] Here again we seem to be in Scot's world, where literal interpretation gives way to metaphorical, but this author is willing to go so far as to suggest that perhaps 'men ought not to be put to death for religion' and that 'the goods of Christians ought to be common among them.'[39]

Or we might turn to the *Monomachie of Motives in the Mind of Man* (1582). This is an adaptation of a work often attributed to St Augustine, a dialogue between vice and virtue. But where in pseudo-Augustine virtue gets by far the longest speeches and the best lines, in Fleming's adaptation vice and virtue are placed on an equal footing, the soul delicately balanced between their conflicting promptings. Here, too, we find the idea, often repeated, that we can be made perfect through faith: 'by the fire of afflictions thou triest thy children like silver, and finest them, that they may be made fit and woorthie coine to receive the stampe of their Creator and King.' Thus we can be remade in God's image: 'We knowe this for a truth, that except we resemble thee in qualitie, according to thy sonne our Saviours admonition, exhorting us to be perfect and holie, as thou our father art perfect and holie; there is no hope that we shall attaine to that incorruptible fruit of our heavenlie calling.'[40] And here we find a peculiar attitude to authority, both submissive and highly critical:

> Thou hast said, and expresslie charged, that we should be subject to the higher powers, yea, even to the Scribes and Pharisies sitting in Moses chaire, whom thou commandest us to heare, and to doo according to their persuasion and counsell: but not to make their course of life and trade of dealing, a patterne for us to followe and imitate.[41]

Three very different texts, yet with common themes. But translations and adaptations are slippery and inconclusive. The text on which my argument must rely is Fleming's *Diamond of Devotion*, a lengthy work of 1581, which is in part a reprint of a work Fleming had published earlier in the same year, the *Footpath of Faith*. Here too we learn that Christ's commandments can and must be obeyed, even if it means giving all we have to the poor. Thus, like Noah and Abraham, we can become just and upright, we can be 'perfect'.[42] We will learn 'that Jesus Christ is ours, and all that he hath done, that we are grafted into his bodie, and made one with him, and therefore fellow heires with him of everlasting life'.[43]

Much more remarkable is the fact that the prayers in the *Diamond* seem to be intended for a specific group of people all of whom expect to be saved, and yet who at the same time insist that they are not sectaries. They are 'a peculiar and chosen people ... ordained to salvation, whereas contrariwise, a great number are appointed to condemnation'.[44] They are certain of their election, called into 'this glorious estate of grace ... not in suspense or doubtful', bound together 'one with another in Christ our head'.[45] They are 'a peculiar people unto thee, zealous of good workes, and addicted unto the devout service of thee', sequestered 'from the number of the pagan people, who are altogether ignorant of thee, and thy divine worship', a people visited by the Holy Spirit, a people in which 'the old leaven of maliciousnes' has been 'quite cleansed away'; they have been 'changed into new dowe, to serve thee in holines and righteousnes'.[46]

As they pray, they recognize themselves to be, like Noah and his family, like Lot and his kindred, in imminent danger, surrounded by enemies. These enemies appear to act in the name of the Church or the State:

> Enter thou with me, O Lord, when I am cited to appeare before the Sathanicall synagogue, which presumptuouslie call the professours of thy Gospell to a reckoning of their religion: O be thou mine assistant!
>   Make them ashamed of their malicious imaginations, and in their owne snares let them be intangled, overwhelme them in the pit which they have prepared for others, so shall I magnifie thy heavenlie power.[47]

In 1581 such language would not necessarily be surprising if it came from Catholics or separatists; but these men and women are hostile to both groups, insisting they are neither 'superstitious Papists' nor 'cavilling Schismatics'.

There are two further puzzling features. The first is that this persecuted group appear to be confident that they are in the process of defeating their enemies, that the tide of battle has already turned:

> We give the glorie due unto thy most blessed Name, for saving the ship of thy Church shaken with the tempests of tyrannous and tempestuous seas: for protecting it from the malice of spiteful pirats, who with the gunshot of their bloudthirstines, seeke to sink this ship thy little vessell, and to overwhelm it in the waves, that the remnant of thy beloved may be rooted out,

and utterlie destroyed.

 Praise and thanks be ascribed unto thee, for rescuing thy sellie sheepe from the chops of ravening wolves, whome it hath pleased thee, whiles they have attempted the ruine and undoing of thy little household, to overthrowe, and to cast the shame of their owne envious devises in their owne faces, confounding thy foes, who bragged of triumph, by making flesh their arme: and crowning thy souldiers with garlands of victorie, contrarie to hope and expectation. Beseeching thee to continue this thy care and kindness to thy congregation, cooped up in narrowe and streight corners of the world, and trenched about with thousands of enimies, who watch a due time to mingle our bloud with own owne sacrifices.[48]

Second, they have a very peculiar conception of history, for Fleming and his co-religionists believe the true religion has come only recently to England, and has yet to be accepted there:

It is now twentie and odde yeares, since we have had among us the jewell of Gods word, than the which nothing is more precious, unto the which anie thing compared appeareth mere mucke, by the which anie thing tried, is found lighter than vanitie. This word ... is contemned, neglected, and de-spised, the preachers of the same derided, the prophaners thereof preferred, the professers of it abused, the suppressers thereof maintained ...[49]

If we count back 20 years from 1581, we come to the year in which the teachings of Hendrick Niclaes, writing as H.N., were first proclaimed in England.[50]

The Family of Love

In 1561 an Arrianizing mechanic preacher called Christopher Vittels became the first English missionary of the Family of Love. He gathered around himself a group of fellow believers who shared Niclaes's conviction that both the Old and the New Testaments are to be read as metaphor not history; that we must kill off our fleshly selves and be reborn as Christ (we can all be Marys, they said, in that Christ can be made flesh in us); and that this death and rebirth represent the true Last Judgement and the authentic life after death. Where orthodox Christians believed in an historical crucifixion and redemption, Niclaes believed in an internal, spiritual crucifixion and redemption, and constantly urged his followers to look inwards, not outwards: 'The whole outward Worlde, is very-great and unmeasurable : and how great and unmeasurable soever the same is, yet is notwithstanding the inward World without comparison; much greater, inwardlie in us.'[51]

During 1574 and 1575, 18 of H.N.'s works were translated into English, published in Cologne, and smuggled into England. In 1575 a group of Familists were forced to recant at Paul's Cross, and in 1578 and 1579 three Puritan authors (John Rogers, John Knewstub, William Wilkinson) published sustained attacks on the Family of Love – attacks to which members of the Family were bold enough to reply. One calling himself E.R., for example, defended freedom of conscience: 'It is not Christian like, that one man should envie, belie, and persecute an other, for any cause touching conscience. William Tindale compareth them to Antichrists disciples, that do breake up into the consciences of men.'[52]

In 1580 the sustained campaign against the Familists reached fruition. A royal proclamation was issued against them, and significant numbers were arrested and interrogated. Some seem to have spoken their minds freely. Thus Anthony Randall, a Devon vicar deprived of his living on suspicion of Familism in 1581, insisted that the book of Genesis was allegorical, not historical.

> He saith he hath taught openly, and will teach during his life, (being not forbidden by the Prince,) that as many as receive Jesus Christ and his doc-trine do fulfil, keep, and do al the moral law, given by God to Moses: and so to live clean and clear without sinning, or the act of sin. And moreover, that every one that preacheth any doctrin contrary to this, neither knoweth God or his Christ; not yet the power and strength of the Holy Spirit.[53]

The same year Parliament debated a bill against them. And yet the Familists fought back, confident in the fact that they were well-connected, for there were numerous Familists at court: the Keeper of the Royal Armoury at East Greenwich, one or both of the Yeomen of the Jewel House, one of the Gentlemen Pensioners, and five of the Yeomen of the Guard are those who happened to come to the attention of the authorities. One of their number published *An Apology for the Service of Love* to persuade members of parliament that Familism should not be outlawed. Similarly, when James I came to the throne in 1604, his hostile comments regarding the family in *Basilikon Doron* were met with a new defence, *A Supplication of the Family of Love*.

The Familists were difficult to persecute because they were communicating members of the Church of England who were prepared to swear to any declaration of religious orthodoxy – they advocated Nicodemism, or hypocrisy in the cause of self-protection. They insisted they were no threat to the political order because they taught unquestioning obedience to established authorities. But this alone does not explain their survival – it is clear that they had protectors in high places, and it has been suggested that the Queen herself was sympathetic to them.[54] The 1581 bill was quashed by members of the Privy Council, and the proclamation against them became a dead letter. Known Familists won further promotion at court. Familist communities survived unmolested into the seventeenth century, communities in which great stress was laid on love between friends, on the ideal of 'communialitie', and on the need to give to the poor.[55]

The story I have told, of religion transformed from miracle into metaphor, and of persecution successfully resisted, may seem incredible; but it is fully documented in Christopher Marsh's *The Family of Love in English Society, 1550–1630*.[56]

Testing the Links

I trust it will now be apparent that there are striking similarities between the beliefs of the Family of Love and those of Scot, of Fleming, and of the author of *Concerning the True Beleefe of a Christian Man*, all three of whom openly teach 'that as many as receive Jesus Christ and his doctrine do fulfil, keep, and do al the moral law'. At precisely the moment that Fleming was writing prayers for a group of believers facing persecution, and determined to resist their enemies, the Family of Love was struggling with the aftermath of the royal proclamation. When Fleming writes 'It is now twentie and odde yeares, since we have had among us the jewell of Gods word', he can only be thinking of the teachings of Hendrick Niclaes as preached by Christopher Vittels. What appear to be the puzzles of Fleming's Holinshed, as read by Patterson, immediately disappear. Why does Fleming celebrate 'intercommunitie'? Because the value of communal friendship was central to Familism. Why does he both insist that authority must be revered and yet make the persecution of religious belief by the authorities appear despicable? Because this tension lay at the heart of Familist teaching.

Likewise the puzzles and paradoxes of Scot's *Discoverie* are dissolved. Why does he offer metaphorical readings of the Bible? Because this was orthodox Familism. Why does he insist that devils and spirits are purely spiritual? Because this was Familist teaching. Indeed, the Familists believed that 'There is no devill but suche as the painters make' and 'That the witch, which raysed up the devill in the lykeness of Samuell, was no witch, but the wisedome of God, and the spirit she raysed up was Samuell himselfe'.[57] Why does he present arguments against belief in the Trinity to such telling effect? Because the Familists were anti-Trinitarian.[58]

It has always been a central puzzle of the history of Familism in England that where, on the Continent, major intellectual figures were associated with Niclaes or his renegade disciple Hiel (figures such as Plantin, Lipsius, Ortelius, Montano), in England Familists appear to have been obscure and intellectually insignificant. This contrast now needs to be reconsidered. Fleming's Holinshed and Scot's *Discoverie* gave currency to Familist sentiments, and Fleming appears to have been engaged in a veritable industry of Familist publication during the key years of persecution.

But does the evidence justify so radical a revision of our understanding of Elizabethan intellectual life? Would the links I have forged restrain even a flea? I offer a few final scraps of evidence. I do not pretend they are conclusive; indeed, I am sure they are not. But it is precisely the accumulation of detail, an intellectual microhistory to complement the social microhistory of Marsh's work on wills and landholding, which can alone make this story convincing.

First, Familists held that 'all things are ruled by nature', which was indistinguishable from God's decree, and thus that it was superstitious to say 'God save you', as if God could be deflected from his purposes.[59] So, too, in the closing pages of the *Discoverie*, Scot singles out this apparently harmless phrase for reprobation:

> [Y]ou shall not heare a butcher or horssecourser cheapen a bullocke or a jade, but if he buie him not, he saith, God save him; if he doo forget it, and the horsse or bullocke chance to die, the fault is imputed to the chapman. Certeinlie the sentence is godlie, if it doo proceed from a faithfull and a godlie mind: but if it be spoken as a superstitious charme, by those words and syllables to compound with the fascination and misadventure of infortunate words, the phrase is wicked and superstitious, though there were farre greater shew of godlinesse than appeereth therein.[60]

Second, the Familists are supposed to have believed that Niclaes kept a register of his followers, a literal book of life. At first sight this appears to tell directly against my argument, for Scot writes: 'I thinke none so grosse, as to suppose, that the wicked are the children of snakes, according to the letter: no more than we are to thinke and gather, that God keepeth a booke of life, written with penne and inke upon paper; as citizens record their free men.'[61] But if we go back to the story of the Familist book of life, we find it originates with the 'confession' of Leonard Romsye in 1580, a confession which Marsh describes as containing 'much that was sensational, fabricated or plagiarised'. Indeed Romsye may have been a paid *agent provocateur*. When his target, John Bourne, confessed to believing in such a book he did so under duress. We should not be surprised, therefore, to find a Familist author pausing to mock this fabrication.[62]

Third, if Scot is a Familist, we should find within his work some evidence of Nicodemism. We find it when Scot discusses why those accused of witchcraft confess. His subject is: 'What the feare of death and feeling of torments may force one to doo, and that it is no marvell though witches condemne themselves by their own confessions so tyrannicallie extorted.' But the bulk of the chapter is in fact about how 'Peter the apostle renounced, curssed, and forsware his maister and our Saviour Jesus Christ, for feare of a wenches manaces.' It is important to Scot to stress: 'Christ did cleerelie remit *Peter*.'[63] It is hard to read this passage as anything other than a defence of Nicodemism.

A reference to Peter also appears in 'The defense of the mynisters of Kent'.[64] This text, a Puritan reply to a lost text in which Scot attacked Puritanism, quotes Scot.[65] The substance of Scot's attack is simple: the Puritans are undermining authority and bringing conflict to the Church. He, for his part, insists on the need to maintain 'the quiet of the Church', and he argues that the Puritans are presumptuous: 'thei rashly promise to give their lives for the Q., wherin thei presume upon their owne power and shew their ignorance in Christs precepts, and I believe thei woulde in time of neede denie her fower times before the Cockes should crowe once ...' As Scot's adversary points out, he has 'rapped his owne knockles', for the rash promise made by the Puritan ministers is one made by everyone under the Act of Supremacy. Scot's interpretation of Christ's precepts appears to have been Nicodemist.

Fourth, it no longer seems that an extraordinary sociological insight was necessary to enable Scot to explain witchcraft accusations in terms of a breakdown in charity between neighbours, for he would have been alerted to such conflicts by the constant Familist insistence on what Fleming termed 'the knot of unitie and concord,' a tie knit fast by mutual charity.[66]

Thus the details can be accumulated. Suddenly the most puzzling, but also the most insignificant details become part of a larger pattern. Why does the *Discoverie* end with a Latin poem about love? Why is it sent from a loving friend to his loving friends?[67] Why does the word 'familie' appear, as if out of place, thrust into the last few lines of Fleming's Holinshed? Why did Scot's *Discoverie* soon appear (somewhat abbreviated) in Dutch, published by a Familist printer, Thomas Basson?[68] These now appear as telltale, unobtrusive indicators of Familist membership.

Similarly, phrases and tropes recur. Niclaes, Fleming, and Scot all think of the Bible as a looking glass.[69] Fleming fears the 'satanical synagogue', while Niclaes fears 'a Devels Synagogue'.[70] Particularly striking is the theme of travel. Both Scot and Fleming insist that those eager to learn the truth have always been prepared to travel abroad, to go down to the sea in ships in order to learn esoteric wisdom, 'which', in Scot's phrase, 'when a man hath he seemeth to be separated from mortalitie'. Fleming breaks off an account of Drake's voyages in order to insist that sea travel is 'a thing ordeined of God, and time out of mind used amongst men, as may appeere by the words of the prophet David, They that go downe to the sea in ships, and occupie their businesse in great waters: these men see the works of the Lord, and his wonders in the deepe.' It is the traveller, not the stay-at-home who feels secure only when he can see the smoke rising from his chimney, who discovers true religion:

> Plato, after he had been well instructed by Socrates, sought out the Magies and wise men of Egypt, by whose means he saw the books of Moses: then he went into Italie, to heare Architas Tarentinus, the most renowmed philosopher of that countrie. Appollonius, who matched in learning all the philosophers of his time, travelled over all the three parts of the world, to see and conferre with all the skilfull men of his age: and being returned into his countrie, inriched with wonderfull knowledge, he distributed all his goods (whereof he had great abundance) amongst his brethren, and to the poore: and withdrawing himselfe into the field, he lived with bread and water onelie, that he might have his mind free for the contemplation of heavenlie things ...[71]

Here there is not only a veiled reference to journeys to Holland to sit at the feet of H.N., but also a pun on 'travel' or 'travail', which can refer both to painstaking labour and to the labour of birth, for each Familist sought to give birth to Christ within himself. Scot begins the *Discoverie* by claiming that 'time bewraieth old errors, and discovereth new matters of truth', and a few years later the proverb 'Truth is the daughter of time' appears as the title of a Familist tract.[72] The final words of *Temporis filia veritas* echo these interlocking themes: 'Behold even through such a great Trouble and travell aforesayd, will gentle Ladye Tyme, bring forth her most bewtifull Daughter Trueth: now in these last dangerous dayes, to the glory of God, the preservation of Princes, and to an everlasting Peace among all People.'[73]

Of course, any new theory must also face and overcome difficulties. Thus Scot's patron, Sir Thomas Scot, to whom the *Discoverie* is dedicated, is held by one scholar to have been a Puritan opponent of the Family of Love because he was a member of the Parliamentary committee charged with introducing a bill against them: though as the committee was divided and failed to ensure passage of the bill, this evidence is at best ambiguous.[74]

There remains one final problem. Scot had access to a fine library, and though poor, published an expensive and unauthorized book. His book was dedicated to Sir Roger Manwood, Baron of the Exchequer, to Sir Thomas Scot, to the Dean of Rochester, and the Archdeacon of Canterbury. Fleming's *Diamond* and *Monomachie* were dedicated to Sir George Carey, Marshall of the Queen's Household. The *True Beleefe of a Christian Man* was dedicated (by Fleming) to the Bishop of London. Marsh has proved that the Familists had friends in high places. Nevertheless, the idea the Familists had so many prominent accomplices is hard to believe; yet it is equally implausible that all these dedicatees were unwitting dupes. The simple truth is that little short of royal patronage can explain the freedom that English Familists had to publish, and, indeed, one Familist tract, *Temporis filia veritas* of 1589, is dedicated to the Queen herself. Mysteries remain, but I believe I have shown the links between Scot, Fleming, and Familism are genuine and robust.

Notes

1. Reginald Scot, 'A Discourse upon divels and spirits', in *The Discoverie of*

Witchcraft, ed. Brinsley Nicholson (1886), (repr. Totowa, NJ and Menston, 1973), pp. 411–70. Other modern editions omit this crucial Discourse: Montague Summers (ed.), (London, 1930; repr. New York, 1972); Hugh Ross Williamson (ed.), (Carbondale, IL and Arundel, 1964). Fortunately, there is also a facsimile reprint of the 1584 edition (Da Capo Press, New York, 1971). As this and the Nicholson edition reproduce the page numbering of the 1584 edition, it is this which I give henceforth.

2. *Holinshed's Chronicles*, ed. Henry Ellis, 6 vols (London, 1807–08), vol. 4, p. 406.

3. There is one book on Scot: Robert H. West, *Reginald Scot and Renaissance Writings on Witchcraft* (Boston, MA, 1984).

4. For two examples of Scot's influence, see Michael MacDonald's introduction to *Witchcraft and Hysteria in Elizabethan London* (London, 1991), pp. xlii–xliii; and Stephen Greenblatt, *Shakespearean Negotiations* (Oxford, 1988), p. 100.

5. Keith Thomas, *Religion and the Decline of Magic* (London, 1971); Alan Macfarlane, *Witchcraft in Tudor and Stuart England* (London, 1970). On Gifford, see Macfarlane, 'A Tudor Anthropologist: George Gifford's *Discourse* and *Dialogue*,' in Sydney Anglo (ed.), *The Damned Art: Essays in the Literature of Witchcraft* (London, 1977), pp. 140–55.

6. Two recent examples of scholars who appear not to have read the 'Discourse' are James Sharpe, *Instruments of Darkness: Witchcraft in England, 1550–1750* (London, 1996), who uses the defective Summers edition; and Annabel Patterson, *Reading Holinshed's Chronicles* (Chicago, IL, 1994), who uses the defective Williamson edition. But Patterson throws important new light on Scot in her discussion of his contribution to Holinshed, pp. 95–8, 210–11. For what is in likelihood a further contribution by Scot to Holinshed, see 'the note of RS esquire' on violent tempests in Kent, *Holinshed's Chronicles*, vol. 4, pp. 926–7.

7. Sydney Anglo, 'Reginald Scot's *Discoverie of Witchcraft*: Scepticism and Sadduceeism', in Anglo (ed.), *The Damned Art*, pp. 106–39.

8. James VI and I, *Daemonologie* (Edinburgh, 1597), Preface; Scot, *Discoverie*, pp. 491, 492, 540, 549.

9. Leland Estes, 'Reginald Scot and his *Discoverie of Witchcraft*: Religion and Science in the Opposition to the European Witch Craze,' *Church History*, 52 (1983), 444–56.

10. Sharpe, *Instruments of Darkness*, p. 55.

11. Clark, *Thinking with Demons*, pp. 211–2, 242.

12. Scot, *Discoverie*, p. 509. See also p. 507.

13. Ibid., pp. 501–2.

14. Ibid., p. 536.

15. Ibid., p. 539.

16. Ibid., p. 509.

17. Ibid., p. 511.

18. Ibid., pp. 510, 514.

19. Ibid., pp. 492, 540.

20. Ibid., p. 540.
21. Ibid., p. 547.
22. Ibid., p. 507 (italics mine).
23. Ibid., pp. 548–60.
24. Ibid., p. 515.
25. Ibid., p. 545.
26. Ibid., p. 511.
27. Elizabeth Story Donno, 'Abraham Fleming: A Learned Corrector in 1586–87' *Studies in Bibliography*, 42 (1989), 200–11.
28. Patterson, *Reading Holinshed*, p. 26.
29. Ibid., pp. 70, 259–60; see also 212.
30. Ibid., pp. 188, 212.
31. Ibid., p. 233.
32. Donno, 'Abraham Fleming, Corrector', p. 204.
33. *Concerning the True Beleefe of a Christian Man*, B1v; B2r. An interesting comparison may be made with [Hiel], *A Spiritual Journey of a Young Man* (London, 1659).
34. *True Beleefe* (London, 1582?), B1r; D4v.
35. Ibid., E1v; E2r; E8v. See also Fleming's 'Prayer', G2r. Compare *A Monomachie of Motives in the Mind of Man*, trans. Abraham Fleming (London, 1582), p. 60.
36. *True Beleefe*, F3r.
37. Ibid., C6v, C7r
38. Ibid., C7v
39. Ibid., D3v; D4r; D3r.
40. *Monomachie*, pp. 121, 199. Compare *True Beleefe*, 'Epistle Nuncupatorie'.
41. *Monomachie*, p. 47.
42. Abraham Fleming, *The Diamond of Devotion* (London, 1581), pp. 2, 11, 59, 187.
43. Ibid., p. 110.
44. Ibid., p. 163.
45. Ibid., p. 164.
46. Ibid., pp. 170–1.
47. Ibid., p. 266.
48. Ibid., pp. 178–9.
49. Ibid., pp. 67–8. The section entitled 'A Guide to Godlines', by contrast, appears to approve the magisterial reformation: pp. 90–1, 103.
50. Christopher Marsh, *The Family of Love in English Society, 1550–1630* (Cambridge, 1994), p. 67.
51. Quoted in Marsh, *Family*, p. 20.
52. Quoted in ibid., p. 43.
53. Quoted in ibid., p. 36.
54. Ibid., pp. 119–22.
55. On giving to the poor, ibid., pp. 182–7; on 'communialitie', J. W. Martin, *Religious Radicals in Tudor England* (London, 1989), pp. 187, 189.
56. See also Christopher Marsh, 'Piety and Persuasion in Elizabethan England:

the Church of England Meets the Family of Love', in Nicholas Tyacke (ed.), *England's Long Reformation, 1500–1800* (London, 1998), pp. 141–65.

57. William Wilkinson, *A Confutation of Certaine Articles Delivered Unto the Family of Love* (1579) (Amsterdam, 1970), pp. 66–7.

58. Jean Dietz Moss, *'Godded with God': Hendrik Niclaes and His Family of Love* (Philadelphia, PA, 1981), p. 72.

59. Ibid., p. 71.

60. Scot, *Discoverie*, pp. 484–5.

61. Ibid., p. 538.

62. Moss, *'Godded with God'*, pp. 76, 80; Marsh, *Family*, p. 82. But was it metaphor or literal truth that Fleming had in mind when he expresses his fear that his name might be 'scraped out of the register booke of everlasting life'? (*Monomachie*, p. 109).

63. Scot, *Discoverie*, pp. 37–9.

64. Albert Peel (ed.), *The Second Part of a Register*, 2 vols (Cambridge, 1915), vol. 1, pp. 230–41, esp. 233–4.

65. Peter Clark was the first to recognize this: *English Provincial Society from the Reformation to the Revolution: Religion, Politics, and Society in Kent, 1500–1640* (Hassocks, 1977).

66. *Monomachie*, p. 207.

67. On 'loving friends', see Marsh, *Family*, pp. 91, 167.

68. On Basson, see ibid., p. 169.

69. Scot, *Discoverie*, p. 86; Fleming, *Diamond*, p. 21; H.N., *An Introduction to the Holy Understanding of the Glasse of Righteousnesse* (c.1575).

70. Fleming, *Diamond*, p. 266; Marsh, *Family*, p. 26.

71. Scot, *Discoverie*, A2rv; A7v; *Holinshed's Chronicles*, vol. 4, pp. 907–8. Scot's familiarity with the Low Countries is apparent from his *A Perfite Platforme of a Hoppe Garden* (1574).

72. Scot, *Discoverie*, A7r; B3rv; p. 131.

73. *Temporis filia veritas* (1589), ed. F. P. Wilson (Oxford, 1957), B4v.

74. Mark Konnert, 'The Family of Love and the Church of England', *Renaissance and Reformation*, 15 (1991), 139–72, at 161.

Chapter Seven
Hell upon Earth or the Language of the Playhouse

Jonathan Barry

n 1719 the Reverend Arthur Bedford, rector of Newton St Loe in Somerset, published a book running to 400 pages, entitled, *A Serious Remonstrance in Behalf of the Christian Religion, against the Horrid Blasphemies and Impieties which are still Used in the English Playhouses, to the Great Dishonour of Almighty God and in Contempt of the Statutes of this Realm. Shewing their Plain Tendency to Overthrow all Piety, and Advance the Interest and Honour of the Devil in the World; from almost Seven Thousand Instances, Taken out of the Plays of the Present Century, and especially of the Last Five Years, in Defiance of all Methods hitherto Used for their Reformation.*[1] As the title suggests, this offered an exhaustive analysis of the language used in the texts of the plays recently performed and published, intended to demonstrate that such language amounted to a conspiracy to invert the religious order of England, replacing the authorized language of the Bible and Protestant Christianity with diabolic and pagan language, such that participation in the theatre was, in effect, the worship of the devil.

Stuart Clark's work has recently reminded us not only of the general importance of reading demonologies in their appropriate intellectual and linguistic context, but of the specific need to consider the full range of writings of demonologists and, equally, the demonological content of many writings of the early modern period that were not, formally speaking, demonologies.[2] This chapter offers such a reading of the demonological ideas contained in the anti-theatrical writings of Arthur Bedford, seen in the context of his publications as a whole and his participation in various movements. His writings, in turn, offer us a distinctive reading of the use of demonological and witchcraft imagery in the plays of the early eighteenth century. The word 'reading' is doubly significant here, because Bedford's study of these plays was entirely based on the written texts of the plays concerned, since his religious views prevented him from attending any plays in person, as to do so would have been to engage in devil-worship.

The Reverend Arthur Bedford is not, it must be admitted, a name to be conjured with in the history of literary criticism or cultural analysis. He figures as a footnote in the debate over the stage led by Jeremy Collier around 1700. He is given rather more attention by William Weber as a pioneer of the ancient music movement. Weber recognizes the ideological dimensions of this and offers the best sketch in print of Bedford's thought.[3] As a demonologist, Bedford has been ignored until very recently, when Ian Bostridge briefly noted his attacks on the stage.[4] My own work on Bristol has highlighted Bedford's place in the local campaigns for the reformation of manners, during his time as vicar of Temple parish between 1689 and 1713.[5]

During his Bristol years, Bedford was already in close contact with various London organizations such as the Society for the Promotion of Christian Knowledge and the Society for Propagating the Gospel, as well as the Society for the Reformation of Manners, and by the 1720s he became an important figure in these and related bodies from his base at Hoxton in north London, where he was chaplain to the Haberdasher's Hospital founded by Aske, an almshouse and charity school. During his career (he was born in 1668 and died in 1745), Bedford was successively chaplain to the second Duke of Bedford and Frederick Prince of Wales, but he never achieved church promotion. He died an embittered man who felt that his services and intellectual achievements had not been properly recognized.[6]

Bedford's lack of preferment, despite impeccable Whig credentials and excellent connections, may suggest that he was seen, even by his friends and allies, as rather an obsessive and unreliable personality, although Thomas Hearne's dismissal of him as 'looked upon as a crazed man' may say more about his Jacobite distaste for Bedford's politics (and the supposed Presbyterianism of Bedford's younger brother, an Oxford tradesman) than about Bedford's personality.[7] Hearne's comments came in connection with Bedford's publications attacking Newton's version of scripture chronology.[8] Though it is tempting now to see an attack on Newton as proof of insanity, we should recall that

Bedford was, in his eyes and those of many, perhaps most, contemporaries, upholding Anglican orthodoxy against the dangerous radicalism of Newton's theology. The central thread of Bedford's whole career, indeed, could be said to be the restatement of Trinitarian orthodoxy in the face of various new movements of thought, be they Arianism, Hutchinsonianism, or Wesley's new doctrine of assurance.[9] Underlying this was a conviction that this Anglican orthodoxy represented the doctrine and practice of the Bible and of primitive Christianity, as found in the Church Fathers. To Bedford the mission of the Church of England was to bring about the conversion of the world through making available the original texts of primitive Christianity (such as the translation of the Psalter and New Testament into Arabic, which he oversaw), which in turn would prove the true Christianity of the Church of England.[10]

In supporting this mission, Bedford was a tireless promoter of good causes within the penumbra of voluntary societies which emerged to forward the aims of the Church of England after 1689. Since Gary Bennett's pioneering analysis, there has been a great revival of interest in these societies and what they reveal about post-Revolutionary England.[11] Bedford's case fully substantiates recent accounts which stress the centrality of a providentialist vision of the Church and state of England as a God-given bastion against Popery, divinely rescued in 1688 in order to fulfil a world-mission, which was endangered by the sins and divisions that had flourished in England since 1688, which might lead God to punish the nation, not least by judging them unworthy of their missionary role. Bedford's thought, including his demonology, must be seen in the context of the godly state. It reinforces the case for emphasizing this context for the nourishing of demonological views, as argued by Stuart Clark for intellectual history and Christina Larner, and others, explaining witch-hunting. Clark, however, identifies the pursuit of the godly state solely with the tradition of Bodinian absolutism, while Larner regards the ideology of the godly state, in Scotland at least, as largely defunct by 1700.[12] Bedford's case illustrates the longevity and flexibility of the godly state, and how firmly it could be applied into the eighteenth century by a strongly Whig defender of the Glorious Revolution and parliamentary monarchy. This accords with recent work by Peter Elmer and Ian Bostridge on English demonology between the Civil War and the mid-eighteenth century, but even Bostridge implies that, by 1712 at least, in England (unlike Scotland) demonology was a Tory ideology.[13] Yet in

1719 Bedford's *Serious Remonstrance*, the culmination of his publications, appeared, and in 1729 he was still repeating the same case in another sermon attacking the stage in London.

How then can we understand a prominent Whig clergyman publishing such a work in 1719? The simple explanation for this has been to regard Bedford as a man born in the wrong age, marginal, and aberrant, even mad. This was the response of the two literary critics who have examined his works on the stage. J. W. Krutch regards Bedford as 'a curious example of fanaticism', an 'industrious pedant ... completely out of touch with the world', and his works as 'foolish', 'appalling', 'ponderous and unreadable'. Bedford's providentialism is so alien to Krutch that he cannot understand why Bedford should find the attribution of power to chance more reprehensible than mere profanity, although he stumbles near to the truth when he observes: 'Bedford had simply pushed other-worldliness to a point where any phrase not saturated with an immediate sense of the presence of the Hebraic God must be ranked as blasphemous.' Only to a non-providentialist, of course, is this attitude 'otherworldly', though Bedford might have rejoiced in the attribution of 'unworldliness'. Krutch is left baffled by the evident fact that 'Bedford was not recognized as a fool by his contemporaries. Defoe read him with approval', falling back on the cliché that 'Bedford represented merely the extreme of the spirit generally widespread – the spirit of the once dominant Puritan.'[14] Even less sympathetic is Jonah Barish, who wrongly assumes Bedford to be a 'dissenting parson', presumably because as 'a hard-shelled fundamentalist, he reverts with crashing emphasis to the old Puritan charge of idolatry', displaying 'a truly horrendous grimness and humourlessness'.[15]

The use of the term Puritan here, in good seventeenth-century style, as a marker of disapprobation and distancing, is significant, not least because the association of providentialism and the reformation of manners with 'Puritanism' has been one of the chief barriers, now largely dismantled, to the recovery of the importance of these movements within the post-Restoration and post-Revolutionary Church of England.[16] During that period, of course, the charge was itself part of a struggle over the identity of the Church, not least because of its political overtones during the strife of party (Whigs as Puritans) and the debate over the chief source of danger to the Church (popery or Protestant dissenters, labelled Puritans). Bedford himself felt the adverse consequences of such labelling.

In 1710 Bedford decided not to vote in the Bristol election, but cast his vote for the Whigs instead as a Gloucestershire freeholder. He was then reproached by fellow clergymen, and others, for joining with dissenters and other enemies of the Church. Edward Colston, who had been elected one of Bristol's two Tory MPs (ousting the Whigs for the first time since 1695), wrote a bitter letter of criticism to the trustees of the charity school in Temple parish which he and Bedford had collaborated in founding two years before (Colston putting up most of the money).

In his two letters of response, Bedford explained that his vote had been motivated largely by the question of the playhouse:

> When the play house was set up in this city, I appeared against it both in preaching and printing. And therefore when the patriots of the play house were set up both in city [Bristol] and county [Gloucestershire] to be pillars of the Church, I thought I could do no less than vote in the one place and be neuter in the other. And as by voting I suffer the censure of being against the Church, so neutrality in this case would have exposed me to the censure of being lukewarm or turning about and being for the playhouse … Should dissenters prevail (which God forbid) there will be some religion, but should the profaneness of the play house succeed there can be none at all. And therefore if I apprehend a greater danger to all revealed religion, the ruin of souls, the increase of atheism, debauchery, and the pulling down of God's most dreadful judgments from that quarter which others do not mind, I must be excused for voting differently from others … When men vote for such as are of violent turbulent tempers, and especially when the clergymen shall vote for men of atheistical principles, such who seldom come to Church, promoters of the playhouse, common swearers, cursers, drunkards, whore-mongers, profane and lewd in their conversations, because, to serve a turn, they style themselves pillars of the Church (for this has been the case in some elections) I am afraid it will give too great an occasion of scandal and cause the new converts to return to their old ways … For that which happened at the election, was but the reviving of the old calumnies, which I find I must expect as long as I live.[17]

These calumnies, he explained, related to his earlier collaboration with some dissenters in Bristol's Society for the Reformation of Manners, active between 1699 and 1705. On both occasions, he argued, he had collaborated with a mixture of Anglicans and dissenters to promote a common programme of moral reformation, and thus to reinforce the Church of England by showing its leading role in promoting reformation.

When Bedford referred to the 'patriot of the playhouse' standing in 1710 for Bristol, he was not referring to Colston, but to his fellow candidate, Joseph Earle. Earle's later career and reputation certainly explains Bedford's suspicions. In 1710 and 1713 he appears to have been a candidate acceptable to both parties, but in 1714 Earle broke with the Tory Loyal Society, who bitterly denounced his behaviour, accusing him of being scandalously loose in his principles, ridiculing and profaning the Sabbath and querying miracles, as well as railing against the established Church. The accusations against Earle were repeated in 1715, when Earle stood on the Whig ticket. Earle was re-elected in 1722, but was apparently not chosen by the Whigs as a candidate in 1727. Nevertheless, he joined the contest at the last moment and when 'asked who he chose to manage his election, he answered "The Devil by G-d", polled 2 men and went off'.[18] A more succinct statement of the attitude which Arthur Bedford considered the diabolical fruits of the theatre, can hardly be imagined. In 1730 the Common Council (referring to a 1728 grand jury presentment against Bristol's two playhouses) declared the actors at the playhouse on St Augustine's Back to be in 'open defiance of authority'. The chief constable ordered to apprehend the actors as common players of interludes was apparently abused and assaulted in this task by one Joseph Earle of Bristol esquire, who then died before he could be prosecuted. This suggests that Earle may have been the unnamed 'gentlemen' who had promoted the building of a theatre at Bristol in 1705–07, since this was the same theatre.[19] If so, Bedford's epithet of 'the patriot of the playhouse' to describe Earle in 1710 is understandable.

As Earle's complex political position illustrates, it would be dangerous to read into Bedford's remarks of 1710 the idea that Bristol was simply divided between Whig Puritans and Tory Cavaliers, but this was a language deployed by both sides during the years 1710–15, when the Whigs portrayed the Tories as debauched Jacobites and the Tories the Whigs as Roundheads and Cromwellians. Take, for example, the literature surrounding the trials that followed the Bristol coronation riot of 1714, in which a Quaker was killed during an attack on a Presbyterian meeting house in Tucker Street, Bristol (a building which may once have been a theatre, ironically!). The Whig pamphlets describing the trial, notably that ascribed to John Oldmixon, present the Whigs as the party of decent Protestants, challenged by a hard core of ungodly, drunken and profane crypto-Jacobites who used the dregs of the city and the notoriously uncivilized Kingswood colliers to overawe the 'sober, honest, thriving part'. Bristol had 'several learned and pious divines, who adorn the doctrine they profess, particularly the Reverend Mr Bedford of Temple church, who wrote against the stage, but these are, forsooth, Presbyterians in their hearts. And if a man has any sobriety of manners and sweetness of temper, damn him, say the leaders of the mob, he's a fanatic, as if it was inconsistent with a good churchman to be either charitable or sober.' Clearly the writer was unaware that Bedford had left Temple parish two years before.[20]

Throughout the discourse and practice of 'the reformation of manners' in Bristol, three vices – begging, swearing, and cursing – recur as a way of understanding the common questions underlying apparently diverse issues, such as workhouses to manage poor relief, the education of the poor, the enforcement of oaths of loyalty, the status and support of the Anglican clergy, the effect of the theatre, and the 'rage of party'. The threats posed to 'manners' – that is to say to the fabric of urban society, which was assumed to depend on a common culture based on household, religion, and public order – by the tensions caused by revolution, war, and religious difference were the common currency of urban politics. They found their focus in recurrent debates about how to rid the town of 'beggars' – those whose dependence and idleness challenged the model of independent and industrious householders – and of the vices of swearing and cursing. Yet, at the same time, begging, swearing, and cursing all appeared the inevitable counterparts of ideological division and party politics. Political and religious leaders became dependent on the people for support, seeking to buy or coerce their votes, while recurrent use of oaths to consolidate political support and exclude opponents made oath-taking a central issue; the bitterness of partisan politics made opponents seem damnable. To many contemporaries the closest parallel to this state of affairs was the turbulence of civil war and republic when, indeed, many of the same issues had been fought out, and recourse to the language of that earlier period both expressed and reinforced this viewpoint.[21]

But, as in the 1640–60 period, such issues also lent themselves to portrayal in the language of witchcraft. Not only were begging, swearing, and cursing the central motifs of popular concern about maleficial witchcraft, but strife within a godly state was naturally seen as the work of the devil, working directly and through his agents. To Arthur Bedford, at least, the theatre came to comprehend all these other problems, forming a diabolical anti-Church that threatened to destroy the reformation. The theatre not only symbolized all the evils that needed reform, but its influence, as that of the devil, explained the apparently inexplicable, namely why God's agents, the reformers, were not succeeding in their battle against vice. The campaign for reform became centred on the struggle between playhouse and church, devil and God, for hegemony.

Bedford's writings on this subject arose from his efforts to stop the performance of plays in Bristol. These began with plays performed at the two annual fairs, St Paul's Fair in January, in Bedford's own Temple parish, and St James's Fair in late July and early August, in and around St James churchyard. In October 1694 the Bristol Grand Jury complained of 'the great inconveniences yearly at St Paul's Fair occasioned by plays at the end of Tucker Street', and in December 1704 it again attacked 'the acting of plays and interludes', which would 'exceedingly eclipse the good order and government of this city, corrupt and debauch our youth, and utterly ruin many apprentices and servants'. The magistrates were urged to suppress them totally since 'all the methods to correct and keep them within modest bounds (where they are tolerated) have proved ineffectual'. Such action would further 'the work of reformation', 'so earnestly pressed by Her Majesty's proclamation, whose pious endeavours God hath so signally owned in the great victories with which he hath blessed her arms'.[22] The foreman responsible for this presentment was Walter Chapman, a leading activist alongside Bedford in the Bristol Society for the Reformation of Manners, and in January 1705 Bedford preached against the theatre as part of a series of lectures by Anglican clergy for the reformation of manners, which the Society had helped to establish after persuasion by Bedford. This sermon was published later that year as *Serious Reflections on the Scandalous Abuse and Effects of the Stage*.

Action against the St James's Fair centred around the profits received by the sheriffs and Corporation for letting booths in the Horsefair and Broadmead. From 1699 to 1703 the sheriffs were recompensed by the Corporation for not letting out these booths, although plays were certainly performed at the fair in 1699, and in 1701 the sheriffs only received part of their money because one booth had been authorized. The Corporation advertised in the *London Gazette* of 2 July 1702 that no plays, interludes, or puppets were to be shown at the Fair. The Society pressured the Corporation to take such action and succeeded in getting plays suppressed in 1700 and 1702. However, no recompense was made to the sheriffs in 1703–04 or 1704–05 and both 'comedies and tragedies' were performed in 1704 and 1705. It took two grand jury presentments in August 1706 and a series of Common Council discussions to re-establish payment to the sheriffs for not letting booths, applied retrospectively for 1706; payment was then given for 1707 and onwards, at least until 1775.[23]

By 1704 any early Society success against playgoing was being eclipsed by the danger that the theatre would move from an occasional problem at fairtime to a more permanent presence. By 1703 the actor-manager John Power, who ran a travelling company based at Norwich called the Duke of Grafton's Servants, had established a theatre in Bath and was trying to create a twin theatre in Bristol.[24] On 19 July 1704, the Common Council urged the mayor and aldermen 'by reason of the ill consequences by the introduction of lewdness and idle debauchery by the acting of stage plays, That no stage players be admitted by Mr Mayor and Aldermen to act at any time in the jurisdiction of this city in any public manner'. When he published his sermon later in 1705, no playhouse had been built and Bedford was hopeful that his preaching had 'had its desired effect in some measure at that time'. But by October 1705, a playhouse had been set up on St Augustine's Back.[25]

In response to their critics, the Bristol actors presented themselves as friends to a reformed stage and the reformation of manners, as is revealed in the printed prologue and epilogue to a performance of Timon of Athens, written by John Froude and spoken in 1705. Bedford noted 'When Mr Power and his company came to Bristol he urged this plea, That he would act nothing, but what should be sober and modest, etc. and expressed a great esteem which he had for Mr Collier's works, and design to reform the stage; and that he only selected the best plays, and most inoffensive.'[26] That this playhouse had received some kind of official sanction is suggested by the 1704 presentment's reference to 'the late permission given to the public stage in the liberties of this city, from whence some have conceived hopes it shall be tolerated always, and countenance (or at least connivance) given to acting of plays and interludes within this city'. The grand jury presentment of 15 August 1706 urged the magistrates to show

utmost care and unanimous zeal, to search out and pursue the most effectual

and lawful methods for crushing the newly erected playhouse, that school
of debauchery and nursery of profaneness, where vice and lewdness appear barefaced and impudent, swearing notoriously practised and recommended: the danger and growth of which, we have been seasonably warned
against by our Right Reverend the Lord Bishop and other reverend divines
from the pulpit.[27]

In 1705–06 a city employee was recompensed for his efforts against
Power's stage players. In October 1706 Bedford reported plans for a
petition to the House of Commons against the stage, to be signed by
the chief inhabitants of Bristol, and he recorded acting visits until late
1707.[28] A publication in 1715 gives a dubious version of why the Bristol
players were expelled (for satirizing the mayor and charter), reporting
that the gentleman at the charge of building the new fabric of a
playhouse (probably Joseph Earle) had been forced to let it out as a
warehouse.[29] The St Augustine's Back site was again referred to as a
theatre in 1714, used once more as a theatre in the 1725–31 period,
then became an Assembly Room, before finally being converted into
Lady Huntingdon's Chapel.

Meanwhile, on 13 September 1708, Bedford reported to the Society
for the Promotion of Christian Knowledge (SPCK) that the players
driven out of the liberties of the city had resorted to Stokes Croft (just
beyond the city boundaries in Gloucestershire) in the time of the fair,
whereupon the Gloucestershire JPs had made a sessions order that no
plays should be acted in the county.[30] In December 1709 Bristol's
Common Council established a committee to act with the
Gloucestershire JPs to ensure that the players had no reception within
5 miles of Bristol, and in 1710–11 both Nathaniel Wade and the Town
Clerk were paid for legal advice on how to suppress the playhouse.[31]
By 1715, however, if not before, plays by the Duke of Grafton's Servants
were regularly advertised at the 'Great Booth in Stoke's Croft' during
July and August.[32] This theatre continued to operate intermittently until
the 1740s, though it was overshadowed by the opening of the Jacob's
Well theatre in 1729. The establishment of the latter also followed a
series of skirmishes between theatre companies and the city authorities.
In a 1728 farce, when the Bristol merchant's wife asks liberty to go to
plays, the merchant calls them 'the devil and all his works' and 'a
nursery for the devil'. In 1730 the dying Presbyterian pastor Samuel
Bury urged his Lewin's Mead congregation (including many of the
Whig Corporation) to keep themselves free from the infection of evil

company and haunting playhouses, which he considered the devil's chapels and a school and nursery of lewdness and vice.[33] Although the grand jury in 1728 had presented both playhouses, it was the one within the city, at St Augustine's Back, which was acted against, not that in Stokes Croft. The Jacob's Well theatre, established with funding from a number of leading Bristol citizens, seems to have been an effort to regularize the position, once again by compromise. It was also beyond city boundaries, halfway between the city and the Hotwells, where it could expect a considerable leisured audience for its summer-based season. In 1732 the grand jury returned ignoramus verdicts on a number of presentments against actors as 'common players of interludes' indictable under the vagrancy acts.[34] A modus vivendi had emerged in which Bristol had its theatre, but only as an unofficial presence excluded from the city proper. It was not until 1764 that a licensed theatre, the present Theatre Royal, was built within Bristol's jurisdiction. Those who fought long and hard against that proposal, forcing it to seek statutory protection and delaying it until 1778, looked back consciously to the earlier struggle over the theatre in the 1700s, praising the civic patriots who had defeated the threat. Once again the issue was one that brought together dissenters and Anglicans, although the leading controversialists then were Methodists and in particular Quakers.[35]

Bedford's writings, therefore, were part of a campaign linked to the reformation of manners, which clearly had considerable backing, but ultimately failed to prevent the establishment of a theatrical presence in Bristol, perhaps because most people were not prepared to regard the theatre as a crucial threat to the civic community. Bedford's 1705 sermon was, by his own account, deeply controversial. His lengthy preface is spent defending his arguments against those who had apparently condemned it as both irrelevant and offensive to civic order. In 1706 he published a fuller version of his arguments in a 200-page work, *The Evil and Danger of Stage Plays: Shewing their Natural Tendency to Destroy Religion and Introduce a General Corruption of Manners; in almost Two Thousand Instances, Taken from the Plays of the Last Two Years, against all the Methods Used for their Reformation.* Both these books were noted by the SPCK, which had first taken up the campaign against the playhouses after the storm of November 1703 when the lawyer William Melmoth brought in playbills for *The Tempest*, describing them, as Bedford did, as a flouting of God's judgement and in 1706 Melmoth sent Daniel Defoe a copy of Bedford's *Evil and Danger*. In 1706 the SPCK had to retreat when its call on the bishops to speak out further against the stage was regarded as tantamount to ordering them about, but their interest continued.[36] Bedford described his *Serious Remonstrance* to the SPCK secretary as a work 'against the playhouse which gives a dismal account of their impiety and profaneness sufficient without infinite mercy to rout out all the knowledge of God in the land'. A charity schoolmaster in Bath asked if the SPCK could help him to obtain copies of Bedford's book as he was informed that 'the Society for Reformation have bought several hundreds of Mr Bedford's late book against playhouses to disperse'.[37] In 1729 Bedford recycled the themes of his 1705 sermon for a London congregation faced with the threat of another new theatre.[38]

For Bedford the theatre and reformation were inseparable issues. The theatre corrupted manners and, despite all its claims to the contrary, the theatre of the early eighteenth century was not reformed. Instead, it opposed at every step the agencies of reformation, holding to ridicule the magistrates, clergy, informers, and societies for reformation, and itself propagated all the sins that reforming societies targeted.[39]

> In vain may we pretend to a reformation of manners and a regulation of our youth, when such temptations lie in their way, which, if frequented, will certainly debauch them ... In this case we expect that youth will follow that which is most agreeable to their corrupt inclinations; and whilst the temptations are equally strong on either side, and the heart of man is fully set in him to do evil, we cannot but expect that the consequences hereof will be fatal to some, and the Devil will not be wanting to make use of such opportunities to tempt men to sin, until they are involved in eternal destruction.[40]

In describing the 'misbehaviour of the stage', Bedford initially focused on 'their lewd and filthy communication; their swearing, cursing, blasphemy, profaneness, and lewd application of scripture; their abuse of the clergy, in order to make the religion (which they profess) become vile and contemptible; and also their giving great characters to libertines, or persons who scruple no vice or immorality, and bringing them off with honour and success'. In detailing the harmful effects he begins with 'profaning of God's name by swearing, cursing and blasphemy', and then, after considering murders, adulteries, and 'whoredoms', turns to 'idleness', focusing, like the 1704 grand jury, on the temptations to youth.[41] His extended text of 1706 offers a similar focus, for alongside chapters on the direct threat to Christian religion his chapters concentrate on swearing, blasphemy, cursing, 'virtue exposed', and 'vice encouraged', as well as the abuse offered to those in authority. Systematically, therefore, Bedford is establishing the same evils as the consequences of the stage as those against which the reformation of manners had been aimed, with a particular emphasis on the affront to both God and authority offered by swearing and cursing.

Equally systematically, Bedford undermines the claims of the stage to act as a reformer of manners itself, concluding sarcastically 'if the reformation of manners, which they pretend to aim at should succeed accordingly, God must be dethroned, the devil adored, virtue suppressed, vice encouraged, the churches destroyed, and then the playhouses will be frequented. In short, hell is broken loose among us, and we have schools erected in several cities of this nation, to teach the language of the damned.'[42] One edition of the work contains an alternative opening page suggesting that it might have been entitled, *Hell upon Earth or the Language of the Playhouse*.[43] Bedford presents the struggle for reformation as nothing less than a battle against the devil. Throughout his works there is the effort to establish a clear polarity between good and evil, God and devil, schools of virtue and schools of vice, church and theatre: 'The Church and playhouse are as contrary to each other as Christ and Belial, light and darkness, heaven and hell.'[44]

But, as his writings proceed, there is a shift away from the moral issue of reformation towards the issue of whether the stage was not an anti-Church, a place of devil-worship.[45] In 1705–06 Bedford hoped to invoke a consensus by displaying across a broad range of issues the incompatibility of the theatre with a virtuous and cohesive civic order. By 1719 he felt it necessary to display it as nothing less than an anti-Christian conspiracy, which all Christians must surely recognize as their most deadly enemy. *Serious Remonstrance* subordinates the arguments of Bedford's earlier works to an effort to demonstrate that the plays of the period involve a systematic invocation of the devil and his powers, at the expense of the true worship of God. This was, surely, Bedford's ultimate effort to present an argument which should bring all Christians together in condemnation of the stage, regardless of the complex debates that had frustrated the campaigns for the reformation of manners.

It would be simplistic to present this as simply a polemical strategy, let alone a successful one, though it is interesting that Bedford might have regarded such a strategy as worth pursuing as late as 1719. There is no doubt that Bedford himself believed in the devil. He had written to Edward Fowler, Bishop of Gloucester, another reformer of manners and believer in spirits,[46] in 1703, recording how he had counselled one Thomas Perks who had raised spirits by conjuration, a letter published anonymously in 1704 and much reprinted thereafter.[47] Thus, for Bedford, the invocation of the devil was much more than a metaphor for evil and many of his readers would have shared his literal belief in this respect. Equally, there is little sign that the emphasis on the devil in *Serious Remonstrance* bore fruit for Bedford. His own judgement was that he had 'fully shown the respect paid to the Devil there in direct opposition to the true God but it had no visible effect at that time'.[48]

Nevertheless, Bedford's excursion into demonology offers other insights into the power of demonological language in the early eighteenth century, and perhaps at other periods. The first point to note is the nature of Bedford's own understanding of the demonic. Despite his account of Perks' invocation, Bedford's devil and devils do not feature in his writings on the stage as anything other than spiritual tempters of man to false worship and vice of every description. While Bedford certainly believed in the possibility of witchcraft and contracts with the devil, he shows little concern with the power and activities of witches, let alone their prosecution (just as he makes no suggestion that Perks, whom he presents sympathetically, might have been prosecuted for his conjurations), focusing all his attention instead on the playwrights and actors as the really dangerous servants of Satan. Discussing the play *The British Enchanters*, which displayed the nation, in his words, 'wholly addicted to diabolical practices', he comments 'the design I think is to recommend the study of magick, and he who can patiently see and hear the one, hath made a great step towards the practice of the other'. Lest people 'should not know how to make a compact with the Devil and ruin their souls to all eternity', blasphemous sentences were spoken for imitation, all 'in a playhouse built (as they tell us) for Reformation'.[49] But the real sin here was of blasphemy, making a jest of the sacred story and of Hell, and inviting God to see the British nation collectively as guilty of mocking God's judgements. There was a very real danger that the stage's representations of devils and magical practices would bring about real effects, for this was 'apt to fill the heads of raw and ignorant persons with false and dangerous notions as if the Devil's power and knowledge was much greater than it is, insomuch that they may come in time to think it in their interest to be upon good terms with him, as we hear of many in our own country who hath been so wicked as to make compacts with him'.[50] But this theme is not pursued.

Indeed, it is clear that for Bedford the devil has no real power, being above all the father of lies, and that the sin of witchcraft is its denial of the actual omnipotence of God and his providence. In *Serious Remonstrance* he explicitly focuses on two particular vices, 'the respect and esteem which they pay to and express for the Devil and their exposing and vilifying the great God, the creator of Heaven and Earth', above all in 'the veracity which they ascribe and the reverence which they show to the oracles of Satan and in their contradicting, blaspheming and burlesquing the sacred scriptures, the oracles of the living God'.[51] The danger posed by the devil is not that he will himself cause harm, but that humans will believe that he has power, whether to do good or evil, and so empower him by becoming his servants and acting his will and, above all, that God will react to this false worship and evil by punishing the nation. Throughout his works, it is this theme, of the need to avert God's judgement, which recurs endlessly. Hence, for Bedford, the language and images of the stage, in granting to the devil (and other false gods) the powers to which he pretended, are undermining the epistemological foundations of that true understanding of God without which fallen man, naturally prone to evil, would be bound to err and force God to abandon his mercy for his justice.

Secondly, while I have stressed the shift in emphasis from the harmful social effects of the theatre to its diabolic character, it is clear that, at all times, Bedford was acutely aware of both aspects of the problem. Historians of witchcraft and demonology have frequently sought to contrast popular fears of *maleficia* – acts of harm – as wrought by witches and devils, with learned concern with devil-worshipping and other spiritual issues. The validity of this dichotomy has always been questionable, not least because, within a providentialist view of the world, acts of harm of various kinds were bound to follow from spiritual sins, by the hand of God if not by the hands of human sinners or evil spirits. As noted above, there is no sign that Bedford was concerned with the maleficial acts of witches, nor wished to stir up legal action against them. But he was clearly keen, in all his writings, to demonstrate the maleficent effects of players and playgoers and stir up legal action against them, even though his ultimate priority was clearly the souls rather than the bodies of the nation.

Finally, we need to consider seriously Bedford's contention that the theatre of his period was saturated with the language of witchcraft and depended upon it for many of its dramatic effects. Compared to the attention paid to this issue for the Shakespearean period, there is little work on these later plays.[52] Modern critics have been appalled at Bedford's temerity in attacking the masterpieces of the English theatre, such as *Macbeth* and *The Tempest*: ironically, they seem to find his criticisms almost blasphemous. We should remember that the versions of these plays he attacked were those then current, which offered much cruder and more sensational versions of the magical and witchcraft elements than the originals. To conventional humanist scholars, Bedford's apparent inability to allow for the metaphorical use of language, or to distinguish the views of the dramatist from those put into the mouths of his characters, renders his critique worthless. But Bedford's credentials as a critic might be rather stronger in the current age of deconstruction and cultural studies. Bedford's sense of both the independent power of language and its subversive capacity might be appreciated, even if his conspiratorial understanding of the authors' intentions as satanic might be less acceptable.

Above all, Bedford's work illustrates, by its obsessive quotation (7000 instances in 1719, from the plays published in the previous five years alone), the centrality of the devil and witchcraft as metaphor and language in the plays of this period. In part, as Bedford acknowledges, this was an ironic consequence of the pressure to rid the stage of blasphemy and swearing, since curses and invocations of the devil were not illegal, whereas under the act of 1606 taking God's name in vain was, and had been successfully prosecuted several times around 1700. But Bedford's analysis also shows, by constant juxtaposition of scriptural texts and play passages, how much of the literature of this period proceeded by inversion of biblical passages. While some of his examples seem strained, with Bedford assuming that any use of a scriptural phrase was a deliberate burlesque or inversion of the scriptural original, in many cases the allusion seems inescapable since, without the intertextual force, the language would lose its power. As Bedford argued, 'All the wit consists in the profane allusion and without this there would be no diversion for the audience', or again, 'without the profane allusion all the wit, and frequently the very sense, is lost'.[53] But equally, the endless repetition and reapplication of words away from their scriptural meaning threatened to rob them of their original force. As he notes of the endless use of the word 'damned', 'what such a familiarity with this word upon the stage should mean is unaccountable, unless it is to bring it into contempt'.[54]

Alternatively, playwrights sought to maintain the aura of the sacred and mysterious, but avoid the problem of blasphemy by turning to the classical world and using pagan deities, ceremonies, and theology to make their points. To Bedford, of course, such paganism was an equal affront to Christianity, but it underlines the point (forcefully made by Justin Champion) that even the critics of 'priestcraft' in this period found themselves fashioning a counter-religion of primitive virtue and worship. To legitimate itself and to speak to its audience, the theatre of this period had to approximate to a church, even an anti-Church.[55] It had to sell itself as a reformer of manners and a teacher of virtue. Players and playwrights could not help comparing themselves, favourably, to the clergy: the new Haymarket theatre of 1705, opened under Vanbrugh and Congreve with royal approval as a new start for the theatre, trumpeted in its prologue: 'In the good age of ghostly ignorance, How did cathedrals rise, and zeal advance ... But now that pious pageantry's no more, And the stages thrive, as churches did before.'[56] Presumably, this was intended to contrast enlightened morality with medieval superstition, but its identification of the churches *per se* with the past, and of the theatres as the teachers of the future, understandably convinced Bedford, and his like, that there was a deadly competition under way for the minds and souls of the people.

In short, the intertwining of witchcraft and demonology with the struggles to reform culture after the Reformation was still very much a live issue in the early eighteenth century.[57] For Bedford, indeed, 'reformation', in every sense, was the key concept which held all these concerns together. Even for those he criticized, the image of the reformation was one which they could not ignore, but found themselves bound to imitate or invert, or both. In doing so, all concerned found it hard not to invoke hell upon earth as a way of dramatizing the conflicts around them.

Notes

1. London, 1719, facsimile edn, ed. Arthur Freeman (New York and London, 1974).
2. S. Clark, *Thinking with Demons* (Oxford, 1997).
3. W. Weber, *The Rise of the Musical Classics in Eighteenth-Century England* (Oxford, 1992), pp. 25, 47–56, 69–71, 73, 86, 151, 200–1. See also J. Barry, 'Cultural Patronage and the Anglican Crisis: Bristol c.1689–1775', in J. D. Walsh et al. (eds), *The Church of England c.1689–c.1833* (Cambridge, 1993), pp. 191–208. Bedford's works on music are: *Temple Musick* (London, 1706),

The Great Abuse of Musick (London, 1711) and *The Excellency of Divine Music* (London, 1733).

4. I. Bostridge, *Witchcraft and its Transformations c.1650–1750* (Oxford, 1997), pp. 177–8.

5. J. Barry, 'The Society for the Reformation of Manners 1700–5', in J. Barry and K. Morgan (eds), *Reformation and Revival in Eighteenth-Century Bristol* (Bristol Record Society, vol. 45, 1994), pp. 1–62, and a forthcoming essay, 'Begging, Swearing and Cursing: The Politics of Religion in Bristol 1689–1715', in J. Barry, *Religion in Bristol c.1640–1775* (Bristol: Redcliffe Press, 2001).

6. 'Case of Mr Arthur Bedford', copies in Bristol Record Office and in Wiltshire Record Office, ref. 1178/631; *DNB*.

7. T. Hearne, *Remains and Collections*, vol. 10, ed. H. E. Salter (Oxford Historical Society, vol. 67, 1915), pp. 7, and 305.

8. A. Bedford, *Animadversions on Sir Isaac Newton's Doctrine* (London, 1728), and *Scripture Chronology Demonstrated* (London, 1730). S. Mandlebrote, 'Newton and Eighteenth-Century Christianity', in I. B. Cohen and G. Smith (eds), *The Cambridge Companion to Newton* (forthcoming).

9. Bedford, 'Case'; idem, *Observations on a Sermon* (London, 1736), and *The Doctrine of Assurance* (London, 1738).

10. See, in particular, A. Bedford, *A Sermon at St Mary Redcliffe 21 October 1717 in Celebration of King George's Happy Coronation* (Bristol, 1717). I am grateful to Scott Mandlebrote for discussion of Bedford's Anglican providentialism.

11. G. V. Bennett, *The Tory Crisis in Church and State 1688–1730* (Oxford, 1975); J. Spurr, 'The Church, the Societies and the Moral Revolution of 1688', in Walsh et al. (eds), *Church of England*, pp. 127–42; C. Rose, 'The Origins and Ideals of the SPCK 1699–1716', in ibid., pp. 172–90, 'Providence, Protestant Union and Godly Reformation in the 1690s', *Transactions of the Royal Historical Society*, 6th series 3 (1993), 151–69, and *England in the 1690s* (Oxford, 1999); T. Claydon, *William III and the Godly Revolution* (Cambridge, 1996).

12. Clark, *Thinking with Demons*; C. Larner, *Enemies of God* (London, 1981).

13. Bostridge, *Witchcraft*, and 'Witchcraft Repealed', in J. Barry et al. (eds), *Witchcraft in Early Modern Europe* (Cambridge, 1996), pp. 309–34; P. Elmer, '"Saints or Sorcerers": Quakerism, Demonology and the Decline of Witchcraft in Seventeenth-Century England', in ibid., pp. 145–79.

14. J. W. Krutch, *Comedy and Conscience after the Restoration* (new edn, New York, 1949), pp. 127–31.

15. J. Barish, *The Anti-Theatrical Prejudice* (Berkeley, CA, 1980), pp. 232–3.

16. A. Walsham, *Providence in Early Modern England* (Oxford, 1999).

17. Barry (ed.), 'Society', pp. 53–5.

18. *A Few Short and True Reasons why a Late Member was Expelled the Loyal Society* (Bristol, 1714); R. Grassby, *An English Gentleman in Trade* (Oxford, 1994), pp. 226–7; J. Latimer, *Annals of Bristol in the Eighteenth Century* (n.p., 1893), p. 102; R. Sedgwick (ed.), *The House of Commons 1715–54* (London, 1970), vol. 2, p. 2.

19. Bristol Record Office, 04264, Common Council Proceedings, Feb. 1731; K. Barker, 'Churches and Stages in Restoration and Eighteenth-Century Bristol', *Theatre Notebook*, 45 (1991), 84–93.

20. *The Bristol Riot* (London, 1714), pp. 4–5, 10–11. Authorship of this is discussed in P. Rogers, 'Daniel Defoe, John Oldmixon and the Bristol Riots of 1714', *Transactions of the Bristol and Gloucestershire Archaeological Society*, 92 (1973), 145–56. See also *A Full and Impartial Account of the Late Disorders in Bristol and a Compleat Tryall of the Rioters* (London, 1714); J. Oldmixon, *A History of England* (London, 1735), pp. 611–12.

21. Barry, 'Begging, Swearing and Cursing'.

22. Bristol Record Office, 04452(1), presentments 1676–1700; A. Bedford, *Serious Reflections on the Scandalous Abuse and Effects of the Stage: in a Sermon preached at the Parish-Church of St Nicolas in the City of Bristol, on Sunday the 7th Day of January, 1704/5* (Bristol, 1705) facsimile edn, ed. A. Freeman (New York and London, 1974), pp. 39–44, reprinted in Barry (ed.), 'Society', pp. 49–51.

23. Bristol Record Office, 04026, Corporation accounts, 1699–1775, and 04264, Aug. and Oct. 1706; Latimer, *Annals*, p. 21; Barry (ed.), 'Society', pp. 22, 38; SPCK Minute Books, vol. 1, 15 Nov. 1705; A. Bedford, *A Second Advertisement concerning the Profaneness of the Play-House* (Bristol, 1705) facsimile edn, ed. A. Freeman (New York and London, 1974), p. 3, and *The Evil and Danger of Stage-Plays* (Bristol, 1706) facsimile edn, ed. A. Freeman (New York and London, 1974), pp. 13, 150, 226–7.

24. S. Rosenfeld, *Strolling Players: Drama in the Provinces 1660–1765* (Cambridge, 1939), pp. 45 ff; Bedford, *Serious Reflections*, p. 18.

25. Ibid., Preface; SPCK Minute Books, vol. 1, 25 Oct. 1705. Barker, 'Churches and Stages', correctly identifies the location of the theatre, but is unaware of the SPCK evidence.

26. Bristol Central Library, Bristol collection, items 10633 and 7976, partly reprinted in G. T. Watts, *Theatrical Bristol* (Bristol, 1915), p. 24; Bedford, *Evil and Danger*, p. 12.

27. Barry (ed.), 'Society', pp. 50, 52.

28. Bristol Record Office, Corporation Vouchers, 1706–7, bill of William Danby; SPCK Minute Books vol. 1, 3 Oct. 1706, and vol. 2, 9 Nov. 1707.

29. Rosenfeld, *Strolling Players*, p. 171.

30. SPCK, CR1/1B no. 1394; J. A. Chartres, 'The Place of Inns in Commercial Life of London and West of England 1660–1760' (unpubl. Oxford D.Phil thesis, 1973), p. 68.

31. Bristol Record Office, 04264 and Corporation Vouchers.

32. *Bristol Post-Boy*, 2 July to 27 August 1715.

33. J. Hippisley, *The Journey to Bristol* (London, 1728) p. 7; J. Murch, *History of the Presbyterian and General Baptist Churches in the West of England* (London, 1835), p. 110.

34. Bristol Record Office: 04026, Dec. 1731; Corporation Vouchers 1731–2; 04450(3) May and Sept. 1732.

35. *The Consequences of a New Theatre to the City of Bristol Considered* (Bristol, 1765), pp. 6–8; J. Gough, *Bristol Theatre: A Poem* (Bristol, 1766), p. 6; Bristol

Central Library, Bristol collection, item 4531, fo. 259; P. T. Underdown, 'Religious Opposition to Licensing the Bristol and Birmingham Theatres', *University of Birmingham Historical Journal*, 6 (1958), 149–60.

36. O. B. Allen and E. McClure, *Two Hundred Years: The History of the SPCK 1698–1898* (London, 1898), p. 20; W. A. and R. W. Bultmann, 'The Roots of Anglican Humanitarianism', *Historical Magazine of the Protestant Episcopalian Church*, 33 (1964), 36–7.
37. SPCK, CR1/9 nos 5952 and 5979.
38. A. Bedford, *A Sermon preached in the Parish-Church of St Botolph's Aldgate* (London, 1730) facsimile edn, ed. A. Freeman (New York and London, 1974).
39. Bedford, *Evil and Danger*, chs 1 and 9.
40. Bedford, *Serious Reflections*, pp. 21–2.
41. Ibid., pp. 3, 23–5, 29–30.
42. Bedford, *Evil and Danger*, p. 219.
43. See Freeman's preface (p. 11) and appendix to 1974 edition of *Evil and Danger*.
44. Bedford, *Second Advertisement*, p. 14.
45. Compare, for example, *Serious Reflections*, pp. 30–2, with the parallel passage in the 1729 *Sermon*, pp. 17–22 and pp. 31–9 on Macbeth.
46. A. G. Craig, 'The Movement for the Reformation of Manners 1688–1715' (unpubl. PhD thesis, University of Edinburgh, 1980), pp. 51, 266.
47. *A Copy of a Letter sent to the Bishop of Gloucester from a Clergyman of the Church of England living in Bristol* (Bristol, 1704). Bedford's copy of the original letter is in Bristol Record Office P/Tem Le 7; its later history is noted in J. Barry, 'Piety and the Patient' in R. Porter (ed.), *Patients and Practitioners* (Cambridge, 1985), p. 157.
48. Bedford, 'Case'.
49. Bedford, *Evil and Danger*, pp. 6–8.
50. Bedford, *Serious Remonstrance*, p. 9.
51. Ibid., p. 3.
52. A. Harris, *Night's Black Agents* (Manchester, 1980), devotes only one chapter to the post-1640 period, emphasizing the 'trivialising of the supernatural elements' in post-Restoration adaptations of earlier plays. For the historiography of the earlier period see D. Purkiss, *The Witch in History* (London, 1996), pt 3 'The Witch on Stage'.
53. Bedford, *Serious Remonstrance*, pp. 16, 346.
54. Ibid., p. 252.
55. J. Champion, *Pillars of Priestcraft Shaken: The Church of England and its Enemies 1660–1730* (Cambridge, 1992); A. Williams, 'No Cloistered Virtue: Or Playwright versus Priest in 1698', *Proceedings of the Modern Language Association*, 90 (1975), 234–46; J. Hopes, 'Politics and Morality in the Writings of Jeremy Collier', *Literature and History*, 8 (1978), 159–74.
56. Cited in Krutch, *Comedy and Conscience*, pp. 188–9, and discussed in Bedford, *Evil and Danger*, pp. 20–3.
57. J. Barry, 'Bristol as a "Reformation City" c.1640–1780', in N. Tyacke (ed.), *England's Long Reformation* (London, 1997), pp. 261–84.

Part Three

How Contemporaries Read
Witchcraft

Chapter Eight
Circling the Devil:
Witch-Doctors and Magical Healers in Early Modern Lorraine

Robin Briggs

ny truly rounded picture of witchcraft must incorporate the ways in which certain people established their claims to be able to read – or detect – witchcraft, the ends to which they applied that capacity, and the role that books played in their world. Here, as elsewhere, there are good reasons to move away from the traditional concern with persecution as such, in order to look in greater detail at the complex world of village suspicions, threats, and counter-magic. Witchcraft can then be envisaged as much in terms of therapy as of personal animosity; in many if not most cases, the point of such a diagnosis was to open the way to a cure. The Lorraine cases on which this analysis is based cannot be assumed to be typical of Europe as a whole, yet the duchy was an area of quite intense legal prosecutions, so the very slow maturation of most cases (an important point for the general argument) is rather striking, while the details do seem congruent with those from other parts of Europe. There are even stronger reasons for believing that the mental universe of the inhabitants of villages and small towns in this region must be broadly similar to that across large parts of the continent. If, as the evidence from witchcraft trials suggests, they saw the world as permeated by hidden powers and lines of force, then that is highly significant for our understanding of both their thought and their behaviour.[1]

The crucial role of the local healers and cunning folk in sustaining witchcraft beliefs is obvious, even if we may also see them as the necessary product of such beliefs. To them one must add a certain number of clerics, surgeons, apothecaries, knackers, and hangmen, all seen as possessing some expertise in detecting witchcraft. How many suspicions passed through these agencies is ultimately impossible to determine, partly because there are reasons for thinking that some witnesses preferred not to reveal all the steps they had taken, while others who thought they had obtained healing might opt not to testify at all. My current estimate would be that some kind of expert identification is mentioned in a little under 30 per cent of my 400 or so Lorraine witchcraft cases; as a proportion of all individual accusations the figure would of course be far lower, less than 5 per cent. One point to make here is that one is not really establishing anything about the origin of charges, because it is well known that these experts – even relatively high-status ones – normally proceeded by articulating the client's own preformed suspicions. Their importance may lie rather in forming part of a multilayered structure which validated and sustained beliefs, and helped to turn private, almost unavowable thoughts into public and acceptable ones. At the same time, they generally allowed for the informal resolution of accusations, so it remains a moot point whether their operations did more to encourage or to damp down legal action. There is certainly no sign that these practitioners did anything directly to provoke recourse to the courts; so far as I can tell, not one of the surviving Lorraine trials actually began with an identification of this type. One or two of the accused claimed that their reputations as witches had begun in this way, however, which seems plausible enough.

What the Lorraine records do suggest is that a very high proportion of known witch-doctors ended up at the stake on witchcraft charges themselves; it is hard to believe that any other identifiable group ran similar risks. This phenomenon also needs to be kept in proportion because one is probably dealing with something between a dozen and a score of individuals, out of perhaps 2000 executed in the duchy, and it seems likely that many less-conspicuous operators were more fortunate. In my sample of about 380 accused witches, there are just six individuals who might be classified as witch-doctors, and another 20 who look like semi-professional healers. They were predominantly women, men comprising two of the six and four of the 20; most of the other witch-doctors I have been able to identify were also women. However dry the statistics, it is important to be quite clear about the facts when so many wild claims have been made about the identity of the accused; for this region at least, it is quite impossible to sustain the idea that witchcraft charges were really the cover for a violent assault by the establishment on popular medicine. While a fair number of other accused persons had some marginal claims as healers, these rarely played much role in their trials, and were probably no more than the typical activities of adult women in early modern households, or of herdsmen and blacksmiths. Of my six witch-doctors, two were only accused of illicit or superstitious healing; the woman, Jennon Villemin, was sentenced to whipping and banishment, but the man, Antoine Grevillon, was executed on the grounds that he had made a tacit pact with the devil. These two were apparently semi-itinerant practitioners pulled in by local officials, rather than victims of denunciations by their clients. While a third case, that of Claudette Clauchepied, has some similarities, here there were some witnesses who thought she had bewitched them or others. The other three seem to have gone on trial when there were specific allegations of evildoing, rather than because the authorities disapproved of their practices. There are also a couple of cases where the idea may have been that it took a witch to know one, as when a woman who was a fugitive from the Ban d'Etival was called in after a cow broke a leg. She said this apparently banal incident was the work of evil persons, then asked if Colas Mengin had a reputation as a witch, responding to a negative answer with the comment that 'he was one of the most perfect ones.'[2]

Three other groups can be identified as fairly extensive operators in detecting witchcraft; clerics, medical practitioners, and those who dealt with sick or dead animals. Among the Lorraine clerics was the monk-*devin* Dom Jean de Xanrey, who seems to have been active until sometime in the 1590s. Several witnesses described consultations with him, during which he gave varied advice, but entirely within the traditional repertoire of an ordinary *devin*. While he normally advised how to identify the witch responsible, in one case he merely provided a herbal remedy for a bad hand, which he attributed to witchcraft whose real objective, he alleged, had been to cause the loss of the sufferer's arm – to say that the spell had not been fully effective was a common way for the cunning folk to display their mastery of the situation.[3] The Ambrosian fathers were specialists in exorcism and mental illness, who more than once carried this over into identifying witches, as did some other regular clerics. Then there were a few parish priests who also offered exorcisms and detected spells, displaying a particular interest in strangely twisted feathers found in bedding. One of these, Dominique Gordet of Vomécourt, was tried by an ecclesiastical court in 1631, after several accused persons claimed to have seen him at the sabbat. Although only a fragment of the trial survives, it seems likely that he was put to death.[4] Priest-witches are of course not uncommon, and a number of them practised varieties of magic; the unusual aspect of this case is that Gordet was experiencing the kind of role-reversal usually reserved for the cunning folk. Normally, any witchfinder possessing a certain status appears to have been safe from such a fate, so perhaps the danger for a curé arose from his repeated activities in the local community, which could build up an ambiguous reputation. There is of course no problem in explaining why priests were thought to possess special powers to detect and counter witchcraft; the puzzle is rather why they were not more prominent in this role than actually seems to have been the case.

Much the same could be said of medical practitioners, very few of whom were university-trained physicians; in most of Europe they comprised a motley group of surgeons, apothecaries, and miscellaneous healers. In Lorraine at least, they are very rarely cited in evidence against suspects, so the common charge that they found witchcraft a convenient excuse for their own failures cannot be confirmed from these sources. In one of the very few cases I have found, the doctors treating Jennon Barthelemin around 1615 diagnosed witchcraft because she had a strange lump on her thigh with marks like five claws, some of which they cut away. She suspected Babelon Voirin, and sent a servant to ask for milk at her house, which was refused with the comment 'that if she gave it, people would say she had given the sickness'. Despite Jennon's subsequent death, it was another three years before Babelon was tried, after an identification by another convicted witch as an accomplice. Another witness in this trial, Nicolas Simeon, claimed his wife had died also believing herself bewitched by Babelon; he merely said her sickness was judged not to be natural, but to be witchcraft, because she was emaciated and 'frenetique'. Since he claimed to have spent a lot of money over several months seeking a cure, one might suppose that this diagnosis came from those he consulted, yet he made no explicit statement to that effect. This kind of studied vagueness is normal form for Lorraine witnesses, who repeatedly describe illnesses as unnatural and thought to be witchcraft without locating these suspicions precisely. One should also note how Babelon claimed that one of her accusers had been to the *devineresse*, when there was no trace of this in the original testimony.[5] So while it is very important to count instances, the evidence is decidedly fragile in some respects, and one must be wary of building too much on its many silences.

What one suspects is that there were fairly numerous episodes that we hear nothing about on the lines of one reported against Claudon Bregeat. She had already taken Jacquemin Gerard to court for calling her a witch, then threatened him while they were harvesting. He immediately felt as if surrounded by a whirlwind, lost the use of his right side, and bled from the nose for two days. The apothecary Mre François was called in, only to declare that it was witchcraft and he would not touch it, but they must act quickly or he would die. Jacquemin's wife then helped him out into the street to confront Claudon; she beat the suspect with a stick, while he threatened to kill her if she did not take off the illness. Claudon replied that they did her wrong and the illness was God's doing, but she would cure it, and he recovered within little more than a day. This was the outcome people hoped for, the standard dynamic of witchcraft as diagnosis and therapy; since Claudon had some reputation as a healer she was able to put her own gloss on events by disputing the witchcraft interpretation. With another client she suggested that the surgeons and apothecaries who were also treating him were a waste of money, quite a common attitude taken by the healers themselves towards other medical practitioners, whose competence they were often inclined to question.[6] This obviously relates to the element of self-promotion which was an important part of their stock-in-trade. Sometimes it is easy to sympathize with them, as it is with the elderly healer Nicole Nigal, faced with a doctor who was visiting the town of St Nicolas 'selling waters for certain illnesses', perhaps in the style of Dr Dulcamara. When she heard that Villermin l'Huillier had bought some of these, she told other women he would never be healed unless she put her hand to it, which led the doctor to call her a witch and tell Villermin he had 'un mal donné', so his wife called Nicole in and she treated him periodically over the next two years.[7]

Many other cures involved suspects who had no specific reputation or claims as healers. Jeannon Collignon pressed Mariotte Mengin, who was her tenant and with whom she had previously quarrelled, to take a meal with her at Eastertime. The same evening she became ill, and remained so for six months. According to Mariotte's husband, the treatments recommended by the apothecaries to make her bring up what she felt in her body were unsuccessful. He had then consulted a woman at la Vanolbe, since convicted as a witch, who told him it was a 'mal donné'; she refused to name her, but said he should tell his wife 'that it came from one with whom she had quarrelled, and she would understand very well who it might be'. When he told his wife she immediately suspected Jeannon. At this stage, because she was so ill and losing her speech, she received the last rites, and some nine days later he saw Jeannon slipping into their house; he went back to find her alone with his wife. When asked if she had something to make her evict what was inside her body, she said she had not at present, but promised it for the next day. She sent a girl round next day with a drink like yellow milk, and that evening the sufferer vomited up two large black and white lumps. Mariotte then started to recover, but her arms were still very weak, so she had them rubbed daily by Jeannon, who assured her they would soon be better, as they were after three weeks during which she also brought her gifts of fruit.[8] The same *devineresse*, la Queprotte, was named by Laurent Pacquin, who said that when his mother-in-law was ill, she and her sister went to consult her. She again said it was a 'mal donné', adding 'that it was a woman who had given her the lump she had above her heart, and that if it had been beneath it then she would not have survived even 24 hours'. She then prescribed a nine-day series of prayers to God and three saints, telling them that she would either be healed or die within that time. In fact, she died on the sixth day, which made them suspect Hellevix Magister. Asked to say more about their reasons for suspecting her, he said they had owed her husband money, and she had sworn they owed 7 francs more than was the case. After threats from her they had lost various animals, notably some pigs which they had refused to sell her. What is clear from other testimony and Hellevix's own statement is she had been under suspicion for at least 20 years, during which time she had often visited the sick, made them soups, and taken them food and drink. Her own claim that she had done this for religious and charitable motives may have been a little economical with the truth; a more likely explanation is that such displays of good neighbourliness were a surprisingly effective way of warding off a formal accusation.[9]

Pilgrimages and prayers were very often recommended, either on their own or in conjunction with other kinds of treatment. A number of healers used simple divination techniques to identify the saints who needed to be placated; they might see which candle went out, or measure a forearm until there was an apparent variation – Claudon Charniere was accused of deliberately manipulating this test to pick the saint she wanted. Several witnesses described how she combined this with suggestions of witchcraft, as when she said to Rose Cordier 'that the sickness had been given by an evil person and could she not imagine who had done it'. When the sufferer replied that she could only think of a woman to whom she had refused alms that morning, Claudon asked her name, then said that the woman 'had a bad reputation and that the witness was afflicted by the evil of St Pian, le bel Bernard, and St Denis', which resulted in a series of pilgrimages made by her and her husband.[10] Other treatments were more imaginative. Mongeatte Recouvreur had a fall on the road, then was picked up by Nicole Nigal, but this frightened her because of Nicole's reputation as a witch, and she became very chilled. That evening she was ill, with her arm and thigh so twisted she could hardly walk; the next day she struggled to Nicole's house, where she found her in the porch, with a cat in the garden behind her. Nicole told her she was 'in thrall to an evil person', and should obtain honey and wax from a neighbour, items she brought to her that evening. She was spinning on the porch when Mongeatte came back, then told her to go home and sit on the highest place she could find; she would feel overcome by weakness, but as soon as she felt better she should go to her nearest neighbour and get them to slap her, then put a towel round her head and run as far she could, jumping over the hedges and bushes. She went home and sat on the table, trembling so much her feet were rather like pestles, then followed the rest of the advice, to return home breathless but already recovering.[11]

During the trial of Claudatte Clauchepied, who had evidently worked with another healer called Jeandon Bassat, Mengeon Masson explained how two years earlier her daughter Jacquette had fallen ill, with her left leg becoming red, then this moving up to her shoulder. She first consulted Tante Annon, who recommended bathing with some herbs of St Jean, but things only got worse. Jeandon then came to the house and said, 'it is witchcraft, the work of someone who shows you a fair face and a good appearance, I know a woman who would have healed it if she saw it', so he was asked to bring her. Claudatte looked at the girl, but would not do anything in her father's presence; she returned later and advised a pilgrimage, also that for three days, as the Ave Maria was rung, the witness should stand outside their house with her back to the road, utter the most execrable curses she could against those who had made her daughter ill, and throw salt over her shoulder. Then she should fetch a broom and sweep the salt as far and wide as she could – a performance she duly carried out. Jeandon offered to make a pilgrimage to the shrine of le Bel Bernard, before which he made the girl touch his hand and kiss his staff; he returned with a picture and a small white loaf, which he told her to eat over nine days, after which she started to recover. Claudatte asked for a chemise belonging to the girl and a silver coin, which she would give to the first beggar she met, but the witness gave them to her, saying she did so for the love of God because she begged her livelihood, at which she said she had done well. During the convalescence, the mother said to Claudatte that only Jeandon had said it was a 'mal donné', to which she replied that he had given it himself.[12] The ambiguous relationship between these two healers seems to have included a marked propensity for each to identify the other as a harmful witch.

There is a sense in which matters were different with animals because there was nothing resembling a veterinary profession, and so expertise was widely distributed. One group who did quite frequently diagnose witchcraft were the knackers who cut up the carcasses of dead animals, a trade which was a stand-by of executioners, among others. A very sinister instance came in the trial of Lutschen Mayette, with a story dating back ten years to an occasion when she had found a missing bull belonging to Bastien Charpentier, then unsuccessfully provided a drink to heal it. When the local executioner Mre Simon was called in to deal with the carcass, she refused the loan of a horse to help drag it out of the stable and shut herself up in her house. As soon as he saw the animal he said, 'I am amazed that the magistrates leave so many witches alive in this place', adding not only that Mayette had bewitched it, but that three witches had ridden it. He then pulled away the skin, which was all loose, to show three black places on the flesh. Mre Simon's interest in promoting witchcraft trials is obvious enough, and Bastien was indeed induced to make a complaint, with no success – perhaps Mre Simon was right about the indifference of his superiors. Bastien's left arm then became very swollen, and when the surgeons would do nothing it was again Mre Simon who said it was witchcraft, treating him successfully with poultices and lancing.[13] Again, it is impossible to tell how often some such scenario was played out, because most testimonies are so vague about the identity of the experts who claimed to recognize bewitchment in animals; it is plain enough that in many – probably most – cases, such a verdict came from the afflicted household or from neighbours, and was based on the standard elements. There might have been something odd about the sickness or, above all, it had followed rapidly on a dispute with or threats from an existing suspect, preferably all three.

There were numerous instances where the supposed witch was invited to visit the sick animals; when Nicole le Mercier was thought to have bewitched Vaultrin Jeandel's horse, he told his wife he would go and kill Nicole unless she healed it. She was induced to give it a spiced drink, then thrust her arm down its throat several times; when Jeandel's wife expressed concern, she replied 'that she had not walked three hundred leagues on land without learning a few things', adding the gratuitous claim – or was it a threat – that she also knew how to use onion seed to make a man languish for anything from one to three years. Other witnesses alleged that she had talked of curing a poisoned wound her husband had suffered, while boasting that she could poison a wound herself so that the victim could only be cured by her hand, and that on another occasion, she said 'that if she saw a man urinate, she could dry him up and make him emaciated, by taking up the earth on which the urine had fallen'. Nicole herself said she had treated fevers with small cubes of dried pork made on Ash Wednesday, to be eaten on three successive mornings in conjunction with a nine-day cycle of prayers. Her drink for horses was made with a pinch of pepper and five roots of ginger, mixed up with wine. She said none of this came from the devil, but the judges told her that such cures must come from illicit means and the teachings of Satan.[14] This was a typical piece of judicial bluster, because it is perfectly clear that the courts never sanctioned such harmless practices for themselves. Many witnesses referred to consultations with the *devins*, a much more serious offence in theory, yet at no time did the judges show any concern about such evidence. With that splendid lack of logic one so often finds in legal proceedings, they only did so when it was a matter of browbeating the accused. Jean Jacques Gerardin denied making Catherine Simon ill, but agreed he had said that before giving her the last rites they might find some remedy, and should search for one. He was then asked:

> What remedy did he regard as more helpful for the health of both body and soul than the reception of our Lord's body?
>   Replied that he did not know, apart from the way some had recourse to *devins*, both male and female.

He was reproached that this was a diabolical work, and that all those who went to them damned themselves, then was asked from whom he had learned that the reception of this most holy sacrament prevented the recovery of bodily health, since this was what he seemed to conclude, by the advice he had given that the said Catherine should not take communion.

He said that the common people judged thus.

In this case the perplexity felt by Gerardin is obvious, as he is attacked for advising what everyone else normally does, and sharing a general belief.[15]

Claims about the origins of special knowledge or powers were varied. Catherine Claude said she had learned the prayer with which she healed many people from an old man named Jean Malherbe, whom she promised she would not use it in his lifetime, a delay of only six weeks as it turned out; here the suggestion seemed to be that potency was increased by exclusivity.[16] Jennon Villemin had been married to a doctor, and used a range of techniques, involving seven different herbs, pilgrimages, and drawing out pieces of bone. She did not attribute any of this to her late husband, however, saying she had learned some of it from her first mistress, while other practices were common among women or customary at individual shrines. One of her treatments – le remède flambé, one might call it – included boiling up a mixture of herbs and wine until it caught light, then calling out over it 'witch, witch, you are going to be very ill'; she told one client that the giver of the sickness was in the cauldron and would suffer badly.[17] This can be related to the common practice of thrusting red-hot pokers into cream that would not churn, in order to make the witch responsible suffer terrible agonies, itself linked to the notion that the witch had to put something of themself into the spell, thus becoming peculiarly vulnerable to retaliation. Barbe la Grosse Gorge was one of those who had allegedly been born on Good Friday; one of her charms had come via her brother from a gypsy, another from an uncle who was prévôt to the canons of Metz.[18] Claudatte Clauchepied also said her godmother had told her as a child that since she had been born on Good Friday while the Passion was being read, she enjoyed a special gift of grace which enabled her to identify several illnesses and know if they resulted from evils attributable to the saints or from witchcraft.[19] Antoine Grevillon claimed to have cured a sick girl 'with mithridat from Venice and soap from the same place mixed with white wine, which drink had made her vomit out all the venom, that he had lived with a doctor at Spire who had taught him these remedies'. He also sold people horseflies in boxes as familiar spirits, having bought them on the bridge at Lyon and in other places, partly at least to bring luck when gambling.[20] Chesnon la Triffatte had a book left her by her mother, who had also been a healer, and had taught her how to use a measuring technique to identify the right saint to propitiate.[21] Nicole Nigal used herbal fumigations, and again said this had come from a book, owned by her mistress when she was a young nursemaid.[22] Margueritte Estienne was illiterate, but claimed she had served a surgeon for three years, and that he had given her a piece of paper as large as a cloth, on which there were the pictures of various herbs – she took this to the fields and prayed to God and the Virgin to discover which to use.[23]

It is easy to detect elements of charlatanry in most of these stories, yet these are quite compatible with the view that even those who admitted to deceiving clients on occasion were also true believers in their own powers. Barbe la Grosse Gorge said she had deliberately given one client a worthless potion to secure her a husband, because she thought she would abuse the man she wanted.[24] Several accounts convey similar mixtures of cunning and credulity; the man who fetched Grevillon to attend a patient gave vivid testimony to the various boasts and identifications he uttered along the way.[25] Perhaps the most striking account of all is that from the Nancy healer Nicolas Noel le Bragard, a cobbler in his youth, then a soldier, who was a literate man with a smattering of Latin.[26] On trial in 1593, when he was asked about magical texts found in his possession, he said that he had known nothing about these matters until he came to Nancy. One day he had seen the late Jean Marchal, gatekeeper at the Porte de la Craffe, with:

> a book containing various recipes, such as to find lost property, to have one-self loved by and to enjoy women, and others he did not well remember, which made him envious to acquire that science. To that effect he tore nine or ten pages out of the book, and after this had given him the means and science to do these things, the desire grew on him to know more, so that seeking here and there he met the late Jacques Louys, then a soldier in Nancy, who showed him a book containing various recipes, but would not actually lend it to him. Later – perhaps ten or twelve years back – he encountered a woman who had various old books and papers in a chest for sale, and see-ing these were what he sought he bought them all, which he transcribed and

afterward sold them, or most of them, to the sieur de Precicourt Haulton, who had asked to purchase them ... he had also seen a book entitled *D'occulta philosophia* which the oldest son of the late sieur Baruet showed him, which he thought was the fourth book of Agrippa.

Bragard evidently moved among a whole group of people interested in occult knowledge, for several other names appear in the trial papers, and he had long been protected by the Comte de Salm, one of the most powerful figures at the ducal court.

Bragard described various attempts to use his knowledge; a spell beginning, 'vous incognuz, je conjure et confirme sur vous, o vous tous grands princes d'enfer, Astarothe', was, he said, 'to enjoy a woman, and he had employed it towards Claudine des Prunes, but all his invocations failed to produce any effects'. The next spell was to obtain the favour and friendship of a seigneur, another used nails to cure toothache. He claimed that about 15 years earlier: 'he had drawn a circle with chalk by whose means, and with the words in a spell in a little book he showed us, he intended to make the Sibyl appear so that he could hear from her about the matters he wanted to know ...' This failed because he could not obtain the young child whose presence was necessary, and he had no more success when he drew another circle within which he tried to invoke spirits in the company of his son and another man, whose book of spells they used. He did assert that he had used a spell to find some stolen money, but other attempts at treasure-hunting had not worked. As a healer he used ointments, fumigations, herbal baths and soups; above all he was a stroker, who believed he could draw out the evil within the body with his hands, which would be very painful when he succeeded, while he himself became feeble and could not lift his hand. As he was prepared for the torture, he was asked whether he had caused the illnesses of those whom he had treated by powders, poisons or words, to which he responded 'that he did not know if he had made them ill, that he had not given them any powder or poison, but he feared that the imprecations he had uttered, accompanied by certain invocations of evil spirits following the spells and lessons in his books, by which he prayed that misfortune might befall all his enemies, might have produced such effects'. Little as one trusts such extorted confessions, this curiously hesitant statement might well reflect what Bragard had actually done. Ultimately, he confessed to using spells to make his clients ill, so that they would consult him and buy drink for him, and this was sufficient to send him to the stake, along with his books and other magical materials. Bragard's extensive range of techniques obviously reflected the opportunities open to him in the ducal capital, while he had contacts with people of high status, and a court made up of relatively sophisticated jurists seems to have taken his revelations with deadly seriousness.

Grevillon had some fern seeds, which he said were particularly good for making a horse go well, but which he also used for healing; asked where he got them, he said

> that on St John's Eve two years before he had gone out towards midnight with a German from Sernay who incited him to do this ... that they drew a great circle which they sprinkled with holy water blessed by a chaste and good priest, then placed themselves within it, having a basin containing some of the same holy water and an altarcloth into which the seeds fell, and that during this the devil mounted on a black horse was riding about outside the circle saying they were taking what God had given to him, but they said nothing, and that at midnight the spirit disappeared while they remained until dawn.[27]

More than 30 years earlier, Barbe la Grosse Gorge had described a very similar procedure for gathering fern seed with the aid of various sacramentals for protection against the devil, but she had relied on her uncle to perform this on St John's Eve and supply her with seed. She added that the seed, 'could only serve for the purpose for which one went to collect it, whether for good or ill, and that if she had collected it her intention would have been to get some money'.[28] Hostile interrogators, like those dealing with Bragard, sometimes tried to get the accused to admit that they had been working a kind of extortion racket at the instigation of the devil, making people ill then being paid for healing them. The close relationship between witchcraft and healing was emphasized in many confessions when the witches said the devil had given them powders to heal as well as to harm, which on the face of it seems an absurd and illogical thing for him to do.

One such story was told by Appoline Belz, the 40-year-old wife of a miner tried in 1580, whose healing techniques were described in vivid detail by several witnesses.[29] While she finally admitted that her devil, le Grand Follonde, had helped her by putting powder in the soups she made, her confessions make it clear that she had learned her skills from her late mother, who was a dyer like her. One witness, Marx le Clerc, recounted how when his son Henry was 18 months old, he became ill and remained so for 18 months, with his head twisted back. A neighbour told him and his wife that she had heard Appoline and her mother talking; they said that although he had not wanted to believe them before, if he asked them they would heal the child. They were invited in, and told everyone to leave the kitchen, after putting the child on the table. The maid looked through a hole in the door, then he and his wife did so; they saw them standing at each end of the child and moving from one to the other, in turn they had 'breathed over the body and in the anus of the child', who was cured in a fortnight, and was still well. He then told of the fatal illness of his wife about a year later, which began in her foot and rose to her heart. He had sent to various *devins* for remedies which did no good, then heard from several that the accused had said that he 'went to seek doctors far off and neglected those who were very near'. He called her in, whereupon she put a small piece of oak on the fire, fetched water from the stream, and used the burnt wood to make a tincture with which she treated the bad foot. His wife was able to walk around again after being treated for 15 days; some time later, the accused was making her a soup when his daughter aged 10 saw her put some 'filth and dishonest things' in it and warned her mother, who would not drink it. The next day, which was the first Sunday in Lent, she gave the girl a piece of cake, after which she became ill that day and died the next – she had told her mother that the accused had told her off for informing her about the soup. While he and his wife were crying for her death, Appoline told his wife 'that she should not be sad for the death of her daughter, arguing that she had purchased her own life, and that if she had not died she herself would have done so'. Later, someone asked her if his wife would get well, to which she said 'that she would get well just as she had paid her well'. Seeing his wife getting worse, the witness sent his sister to ask her to come and visit again, with the promise 'that he would pay and content her well and would cause her no harm or discontent'. She said she could not come at present, but might do so tomorrow, and that night his wife died; he was convinced she was responsible for both deaths.

Another failure was with the wife of Pierre Quenault, supervisor in the mines, who thought that Appoline had made her ill by pushing her; when called in to heal her, she made something with bread, honey and other things, which she put on her stomach, and brewed her a herbal drink. She told her she was frightened because she had gone out too soon after giving birth, 'and that there were evil persons who might make someone ill by throwing a bone or a pin in front of them on their path, and she would cure her if she could'. During his wife's final illness, the chambermaid put up a broom over the door, and when Appoline saw this she said angrily, 'was that to test if I was a witch, was that the payment you wanted to make me, if the devil does not carry you off it will not be because you have not done everything to bring that about', after which she would not return to the house despite repeated requests. The point of this exercise was that a broom placed in this way was supposed to identify a witch by preventing them from leaving the room.

During her interrogation Appoline was asked about her technique with children, and said 'that alongside good prayers she blew the evil out of the children'. On the subject of her treatment for one client, Anne Chastenot, she agreed that she had said the woman responsible for her illness was not far away. She added that after she had made 'a recipe with wax, blessed palms and incense, and of moss which grew on the wayside crosses, he or she who had made a sick person ill was forced to come to the house where the sufferer was, and that while she was making that recipe for Anne's child', la Grosse Margo had come to the house twice, and that the second time she had been there herself to see her. This case vividly illustrates the ambivalence surrounding such practitioners. In retrospect her neighbours and clients either thought or were persuaded to think that Appoline was a witch, while by their own accounts they had taken a fairly wary line with her, even when employing her to heal them or their families. She had plainly adopted an aggressive stance, not just in claiming extensive powers, but in defending herself against those who failed to pay her properly or implied she was a witch. She herself had been quite ready to identify others as the cause of illnesses, even if she does not seem to have named them or recommended action against them in most cases, except that of la Grosse Margo. It is hardly too much to describe this as another way of circling the devil, by invoking him and his agents as the cause of disease, pretending to have powers to drive out the evil, and implying that those who maltreated the healer would suffer for it. Another suggestion was that Appoline was the only one who could cure certain people, with other healers having no comparable power; this could rather too easily be turned around into the idea that such unique abilities indicated that she must have inflicted the illness herself. Like several of the other practitioners, she emerges as an astonishingly forceful, domineering character, whose ministrations must have had intense psychological effects, even if she could not actually cure desperately sick people.

It would be possible to produce further examples, and describe roasting young dogs with nine kinds of herbs, burying bottles with specific ingredients under thresholds or in fields, eating food taken from a suspect's house, and so forth. The principles of sympathetic magic and occult powers are well enough known, however, and nothing in these techniques would cause much surprise. The range of objectives is also predictable. The linked purposes of curing illnesses and identifying witches top the list, followed (in no particular order) by a miscellany of practices to defend animals against wolves and other dangers, protect crops and houses, secure love, identify future partners, find buried treasure or stolen goods, protect oneself against swords and bullets, be lucky when gambling or hunting, obtain favour from the powerful, and ensure contraception. While this is certainly not a complete tally, it covers the vast majority of cases. The methods and aspirations imply a flexible and polymorphous vision of the world, whose internal logic was often rickety or non-existent; while it does employ binary polarities of the type Stuart Clark has identified in demonology, the overall pattern is too incoherent and insecure to constitute a system. The implication was that everyday events had multiple meanings, that virtually everything was full of significance, and that there was enormous power available to those who possessed the right keys. One might suggest on the basis of such evidence that the developing combination of formal doctrines and popular beliefs from the later middle ages through to the early seventeenth century tended to produce a super-enchanted world, to which its inhabitants often responded with a mixture of fascination and terror, in ways many of these cases seem to reflect. Such a world would have been quite impossible as a permanent context for ordinary life, however, so it could only exist in parallel with much more down-to-earth everyday attitudes. If we ask whether people really believed in all this, the most plausible answer is that they did so only intermittently, at moments of personal crisis or social excitement. That would have helped to make reading witchcraft amidst the random noise of social intercourse the intensely subjective exercise it ultimately seems to have been. Here then is a special variant of Stuart Clark's polarized binary discourse, although in this instance it is the ease with which polarities could be reversed, and the importance of the transactional space between them, which must be emphasized. Another related point is that the conception of disease that emerges from the examples is of a polluting or malevolent substance which enters the body from outside, and must then be driven out. That is one more instance of how once we stop thinking about witchcraft primarily in terms of persecution, and see it as a language for describing personal interaction in both reality and fantasy, we can also understand how it was a natural idiom in which to understand and manage sickness, and how such ways of thinking have survived into our own times.

Notes

1. Ths essay concentrates on the direct presentation of evidence from the Lorraine manuscript sources; I have treated the subject more generally in Chapter 5 of *Witches and Neighbours: The Social and Cultural Context of European Witchcraft* (London, 1996). There is an excellent general discussion by W. de Blécourt, 'Witch-doctors, soothsayers and priests. On cunning folk in European historiography and tradition', *Social History*, 19 (1994), which emphasizes the comparative neglect of the topic by historians of witchcraft. An outstanding recent contribution touching on many related themes is W. Behringer, *Shaman of Oberstdorf: Chonrad Stoeckhlin and the Phantoms of the Night* (Charlottesville, VA, and London, 1998).
2. Archives départementales de Meurthe-et-Moselle, B8667, no. 7 (1591–92).
3. Ibid., B3317, no. 2 (1599).
4. Archives départementales des Vosges, G710.
5. Archives départementales de Meurthe-et-Moselle, B8721, no. 7 (1618).
6. Ibid., B2192, no, 2 (1612),
7. Ibid., B8945 (1582).
8. Ibid., B8772 (1594).
9. Ibid., B8260 (1584).
10. Ibid., B8939 (1572).
11. Ibid., B8945.
12. Ibid., B3753 (1601).
13. Ibid., B3136 (1619).
14. Ibid., B3801, no. 1 (1615).
15. Ibid., B8708, no. 8 (1611).
16. Ibid., B7279 (1583).
17. Ibid., B7137, no. 1 (1625).
18. Ibid., B7301 (1591).
19. Ibid., B3753.
20. Ibid., B2584 (1625).
21. Ibid., B4077, no. 3 (1596).

22. Ibid., B8945.
23. Ibid., B2211, no, 1 (1625).
24. Ibid., B7301.
25. Ibid., B2584.
26. Ibid., B7309, no. 1 (1593).
27. Ibid., B2584.
28. Ibid., B7301.
29. Ibid., B9554, no. 1 (1580).

Chapter Nine
Witchcraft as Metaphor: Infanticide and its Translations in Aragón in the Sixteenth and Seventeenth Centuries

María Tausiet

The witches of the barrels
smother the children[1]

e cannot hope to understand the peak which the phenomenon of witchcraft experienced in Europe during the early modern period unless we take into account the symbolic extent of the concept of witchcraft itself. Its enormous metaphorical power – an imaginary resort *par excellence*, accessible to those at the centres of decision-making, as well as to those in the remotest corners of the land – was made use of as a pretext, both by institutions and individuals to achieve very different, sometimes even opposite goals. If we analyse life in small rural communities, it will be seen that charges of malevolence brought by neighbours against one another were ways of disguising all manner of conflicts – everything from the purely economic to difficulties in personal relations and matters of inner conscience.

Turning these tensions into witchcraft meant naming them, but also diverting them in another direction. The leap to the extraordinary was an extremely useful resort: on the one hand, it allowed the redirection of problems at an imaginary level, thereby avoiding personal responsibility; on the other, it made the search for a culprit easier, because belief in witchcraft was based on a stereotype that was periodically reincarnated as a scapegoat. One of the motifs which illustrates such a mythical transformation particularly well is infanticide.

As is well known, of all the wickedness attributed to witches one was outstanding: the death of young children. According to the *Malleus maleficarum*, their wish to eliminate every form of human life began long before children were born. First of all, witches tried to prevent the realization of the sexual act. If this had been fulfilled, they endeavoured to make the woman fail to conceive. If she conceived, they tried to ensure that she aborted. If she did not abort, they then aimed to eliminate the newborn child, either by killing it or by offering it to the devil, which thus made it impossible, according to the belief in original sin, for the baby to enter the Kingdom of Heaven.[2]

Reaching an extreme, the authors of the treatise thought that the witches' favourite system of killing children was to devour them:

> Some witches, against the tendency of human nature, and even against the nature of every beast except the wolf, are in the habit of tearing children to pieces and eating them.[3]

According to the description of a witches' sabbath made by Juan de Mongastón, after listening to the accused of Zugarramurdi at the *auto-da-fé* at Logroño in 1610:

> They suck the small children on the backside and the anus, pressing hard with the hands, and sucking they often draw and suck their blood. And with pins and needles they wound them in the temples and the top of the head, and in the spine and other parts and limbs of the body. And they suck their blood elsewhere, the devil saying to them: 'Suck and swallow that which is good for you.' After that the children die, or remain ill for long. Sometimes the witches kill them later, pressing with the hands and biting the throat until they asphyxiate them.[4]

In sixteenth-century Aragón, the deaths of children were at the centre of accusations against witches. Macabre details quoted in the very few surviving secular trials[5] can stand alongside the famous description of the Basque-Navarrese witches' sabbath. In 1534, several women from

Pozán de Vero (Huesca), after being tortured, finally confessed to having killed a great many newborn children by the most cruel methods imaginable. Sometimes they used poison made from skinned toads; these were dried and turned into powder to be mixed with arsenic. Sometimes they simply used their own hands, pressing and suffocating the children. They even roasted them alive in the children's own kitchens. All their deeds had the benefit of the devil's presence and advice, who had gone before, opening every door. As to parental vigilance, they saw to that too, inducing sleep in the parents of their victims by putting henbane leaves under the threshold of the bedroom door.

According to an excerpt from a legal transcript, which includes the confession extracted from Dominica la Coja after she had been subjected twice to torture:

> Some two or three years ago … she was called by Roiz Castellon, a neigh-bour of that place of Pozan de Vero, who asked her to go and see his son who was sick. And she went to see him … And that very Sunday came … Gracia la Nadala … who asked her if she wanted to go with her and they both went to the house of the said Roiz Castellon, and the devil opened the door. And they entered and went to the room where the said Roiz and his wife were sleeping. And they took the said child from the arms of the said Roiz and took him to the kitchen. And the said Gracia la Nadala picked up embers from the fire under the ashes and put the said child there, next to the embers to *roast the small belly of the said child*.[6]

We find many stories like this at a time when the obsession on the part of the civil authorities with female fertility and infant mortality was expressed in countless statutes aimed at making it easier to prosecute those assumed to be guilty. All of them, without exception, include a list of the causes justifying fierce repression: impotence, infertility, abortion, the failure of harvests, the death of animals, and, lastly, of people, 'big and small.' Thus the arguments put forward by the authors of the *Malleus* directly mirrored not only legend but law. According to the *Estatutos y Desafueros contra las hechizeras y bruxas … del justiciado de Gia* [Statutes and Rules against the witches in the Gia district], these women must be punished because:

> they have killed or ordered to have killed or may kill persons large and

small, stout and slight cattle ... have bound or may bind any person or persons with their evil ... have obstructed, may obstruct or have ordered to obstruct that a husband and wife should have carnal knowledge of each other, or that a woman should conceive, or they have harmed or may harm women in childbirth.[7]

The harshness of these statutes was reflected in the fact that they were retroactive: the new laws could and should be brought against those who had committed an offence before they were enacted. And the mention of future crimes was also considered important. Laws against witchcraft were, in fact, written in a language which pretended to encompass a totality that was impossible to express with the words and verbal tenses in common use. The combination of past and future in every clause was designed to refer to a mythical age, an age of mythical vagueness that came into being every time a witch was discovered and judged. Every sentence was thus an updating of the myth through an expiatory rite that consisted in the expulsion of those branded as victims.

Unlike secular justice, enacted in a quick and stereotyped way, ecclesiastical justice (especially episcopal) attached much importance to the provision of information and commissioned all kinds of enquiries. It was thought that, since witchcraft was a crime hard to prove, the path leading to truth should be supported by certain indicators. Of these, the main one, again, was the wake left by the death of children. In order to know if a witch had, or had not, acted in a given place, it was of basic importance to investigate if there were dead children and to establish some link between their parents and the suspect. This was the advice given by the vicar-general of the Archbishop of Zaragoza to one of the parish priests under his jurisdiction in 1591:

> I have been told that in this place there is a woman called Isabel de Garay who is reputed to be a witch and who has done much evil. Since her crimes are difficult to prove, a lot of industry is necessary. I commission the vicar to seek information from witnesses to say what they know, how and why they know it, and if they happen to hear it, from whom; and also the way of conversing of the said woman, if she is a woman who quarrels with her neighbours and other people and, by quarrelling, threatens them; *and if there have been dead children, what marks did they have, and if she had been quarrelling with the parents of these children.*[8]

Obviously, in view of her reputation as a witch, there would be many people willing to attest against her. The fact that there were dead children would be taken as justification for her accusers to state that they had quarrelled with her. Two months after the letter had been sent, the parish priest's answer could not be clearer:

> My Lord: I have tried to get the information that Your Worship ordered with the greatest diligence and secrecy. And in order not to attract attention, it seemed to me prudent not to accept more witnesses than those included in the trial. But if it were necessary and Your Worship agrees that more evidence is needed in order to seize this woman, I shall do it if that is the order of Your Worship, because *I understand that we shall find all the evidence we need to make this crime apparent without the need for big efforts. And if we need to prove that this woman is a thief and guilty of other kinds of crime, we could also obtain much evidence.*[9]

It was enough to interrogate the villagers concerning those marked out as witches in a community to hear stories such as the following:

> Two people known as Juan Lorente and Anna Montañes suffered the death of their child, and when he was laid out for burial they found that his whole body was covered with sores, with much blood in the ears, the mouth, the eyes, the back and calves and arms. And the sores looked like pinches. His parents and all people who were witness to it were astonished because the previous day the child had been healthy. And they are sure witches killed him, and among them the said Isabel Garay, who is reputed as such.[10]

In spite of the total lack of evidence, the accused was jailed, tortured, and eventually sentenced and exiled by the episcopal judges. It is possible to find many variants of such cases in the following centuries. The only reason, as put forward by accusing witnesses, for making suspected witches responsible for the death of the children was that it was the revenge of such women following quarrels with the children's parents. Therefore a simple account of a dispute, which might have taken place long before, was enough to settle the question, the least important matter being the actual reasons for the dispute – spitefulness and rancour were justification enough.

Many times the actual quarrels were not even mentioned, but only nightmares or delirious outbursts which normally took the form of psychological combat with the forces of evil as embodied in the accused.[11] The main support for every line of argument, no matter how weak, was 'public opinion'. Far from having to justify accusations, it was usual to reason the other way round. The only requirement of the statements witnesses made seemed to be that they should prove with new examples what everybody already knew. Every dead infant was fresh proof of what had previously been established by the 'common voice and public reputation'. According to one of many ambiguous accounts relating to the death of a young girl:

> Barbara Serret ... aged thirty ... thinks that Nadalmava ... is a witch and sorceress ... because ten or twelve years ago this witness quarrelled with the said Nadalmava, and some days later, being at home at nine in the evening, with the doors closed ... she fell asleep with her daughter in her arms. And then she awoke and in the dim light she saw the shape of a woman and knew it was the said Nadalmava and she said: – Jesus, Mary, and then the woman disappeared. And one year ago ... a daughter aged six, very healthy and fine, was found dead in the bed. And as this witness had thought and still thinks and has seen her to be thought ... as a witch and be publicly considered as such in the village.[12]

In spite of the fact that the derivations of most people's opinions were explanations of a mythical kind, it should not be forgotten that there existed two other, more rational explanations based on common sense. Both kinds of interpretation could be found in the same criminal proceedings: while the witnesses for the prosecution attributed the deaths of children to the witches, witnesses for the defence would link them more objectively to such elements as climate and illness, or even to the ill-treatment and lack of care suffered by the children.[13] The resounding success of the former kind was due to its manifest usefulness, in that it allowed the community to participate and to take revenge on a certain person (the witch), while evading any personal responsibility. Belief in witches was less a way of thinking and reasoning than a phenomenon of social consensus favouring the weight of public opinion.

Repeated accusations against witches ran alongside the well-established parental custom of getting rid of unwanted children as a way of controlling the size of the family. This practice was in use until recent times. Many historians have concluded that the decrease in infant mortality from the eighteenth century onwards cannot be explained by improvements in hygiene and medical practice alone; the main factor had to be the growing abandonment of the custom of allowing children to die, or helping them to die, when their lives were not wanted.[14]

Tolerance towards the practice of infanticide had been the general rule up to that time, in spite of the legislation then in force.[15] In fact, by most of the population it was not considered a crime at all, but, on the contrary, an aid to survival. Without denying the existence of parental love that many felt for their children, or the much discussed 'sentiment of childhood', it can be asserted that, in general, the lives of newborn children were valued with the same ambiguity as the foetus is viewed today.

In classical Antiquity, the only person with power to decide the life and death of minors was the *pater familias*. Greek and Roman philosophers often compared the situation of children with that of slaves. Both could be sold or done away with, since both were encompassed by the concept of 'family'. No law existed for their defence apart from the *ius vita et necisque* inherent in guardianship.[16] With the official acceptance of Christianity, the situation changed: concurrently with the increasing depopulation of the Late Roman Empire, the authorities began to favour a policy encouraging a higher birth rate. It was at that time that Constantine enacted his famous edict against all forms of parricide.[17] But in spite of the change in the law, not only did infanticide survive, but also, with it, the central idea that children were the property of their parents. In the sixteenth and seventeenth centuries, the Church continued to support this idea through its insistence that parents had responsibility for any malformation of their children. As Jean Louis Flandrin puts it:

> If God punished the child because of the sin of the parents, that was because, both in Frankish society and among the Hebrews of the Old Testament and among the Greeks of mythology ... the child was nothing but a thing of the parents.[18]

Beyond questions of ideology and mentality, it is indisputable that the cost of bringing up children was met not by the state, but by the family and, more particularly, by the mother. It is therefore not surprising that the victims of accusations of witchcraft were almost always women. It was they who were in charge of the survival of children and, it followed, they were also responsible for their deaths. And since total responsibility for new lives was ascribed to the female sex, every woman was considered a potential witch. The connection was manifest most of all in the so-called 'evil eye', that is, the poisonous regard of those women who were detested either because they were menstruating or because they were old and useless. The notion that every woman was a possible child destroyer was widespread both among ordinary people and among the élite. Thus it was not unusual for treatises on obstetrics and children's medicine, without any distinction or qualification, to consider the evil eye as just one more illness among those to which children were susceptible at a tender age.[19]

Concerning this myth, it has to be borne in mind that having children was considered a burden, a feeling that was not uncommon among European women of that time and which would, to some extent, explain why infanticide was so widespread. Yet it was often less a question of deliberate infanticide than of indirect or unintentional forms. The abandonment or neglect of infants was rarely deliberate. On the contrary, it inhabited an uncertain and unnamed territory between intention and oversight, at the borders of wakefulness and sleep. Indeed, one of the most favoured methods of getting rid of unwanted children was to lie on them during the night. In principle, this would be involuntary, even accidental infanticide: the mother put the baby next to her in the marital bed and crushed or suffocated it when turning over in her sleep. The frequency of deaths of this kind was such that in many bishoprics, after it was realized that simple denunciations were useless, adults were actually forbidden to sleep in the same bed as children under two years of age.[20]

Inebriation, a close neighbour of sleep, was another way of gaining access to the territory of unconsciousness. Alcoholism was often linked to accusations of witchcraft, and in particular to the half-involuntary suffocation of children. Pascuala García, an ageing woman of the wine-producing town of Herrera de los Navarros (Zaragoza), was taken before the episcopal justice in 1572. She was accused of causing the deaths of several children in the town, including her own granddaughter, all of them after quarrels with their parents. Nevertheless, according to her defence lawyer:

> It has been seen a thousand and one times that drunken women affected by wine who are nursing mothers have suffocated their offspring at night in bed, while asleep. Senseless because of the wine they have drunk, they sleep

soundly, careless of them ... they are accustomed, and they have been seen many times like this ... to lie upon them and, as they are small and soft, to suffocate them.[21]

One of these women was in fact the daughter-in-law of the accused, Francisca Catalán, who, according to several defence witnesses,

> is a woman who loves wine and in order to get wine and her daily meat she will say anything and commit perjury, especially if she has been annoyed ... Both when she was single and after marrying ... her reputation has been that of a drunkard and a woman addicted to wine.[22]

It should be remembered that one of the most frequent methods of discrediting witnesses for the prosecution was to brand them as alcoholics. Almost always this would be connected with a propensity for slander and deceitfulness, as well as to the unreliability of their statements in court. But the adoption of that recourse on the part of defence lawyers was not always a matter of mere convenience. On the contrary, it is significant that in wine-producing areas, the number of references of this kind is found to be especially high. According to several defence witnesses giving evidence in another trial initiated in the same region – the so-called 'Campo de Cariñena'– almost two decades later, people accusing the woman were not only her sworn enemies, but also individuals

> of ill fame, notorious reputation and infamous life, given to slander and gossip ... depraved in their eating and drinking habits, in such a way that they are drunk most of the time on account of the excessive wine they imbibe.[23]

Drinking alcohol was not something only men did. In spite of the stereotyped image of women's lives given by some texts ('interior beings' who hardly ever went out and had to suppress every physical expression directed outside themselves, such as regarding, smiling, etc.),[24] the truth is that the social life of women often did exist outside the home. Meeting places, apart from the baking oven or the washhouse, were streets, yards, gardens, and also taverns.

In 1571, at carnival time, one of the witnesses in the trial of Pascuala García was present at a meeting of eight women in the local tavern.

While these 'ate and talked', the witness reported hearing an excerpt of the conversation between two of them. If we can trust her account (and there is no reason not to, in that the incident had no direct connection with the objective of the charge), the dialogue confirms the closest correspondence between the death of children and wine drinking; and even more, the identification of harvest time as the period when the highest rate of infant deaths was registered:

> Jordana Ordovas said to her mother: – Mother, there are no witches now. To which the mother replied: – Daughter, now it is not the time for them, because there is little wine, but when there is a lot *the witches of the barrels smother the children.*[25]

Such a statement (whose rhyme and rhythm in the original Spanish, 'las broxas de las cubas ahogan las criaturas', seem to bring it closer to a folk-saying accepted by the community than to an expression of personal opinion) was nothing but the translation into metaphorical language of a reality known to everybody, but only partly accepted. Perhaps it had to do with an old motto, from a time when witchcraft was expressed in plural terms, as a phenomenon more imaginary than real, and as a resource less of the actual than the poetic. In the late sixteenth century, although times had changed and the old 'broxas' had materialized as women of flesh and blood (scapegoats to be hunted down in the name of the common good), popular mentality continued to maintain that indeterminate plural: a plural signifying mythological beings of uncertain origin, old numena which still permitted the naming of realities that were not fully assumed.

Another form of infanticide, not very different from those more-or-less deliberate occurrences taking place at night or under the influence of alcohol, was simple neglect. Bad nourishment, the premature end of breast-feeding – in sum, negligent and indifferent childcare– were responsible for countless deaths due to starvation, dehydration, and the lack of attention essential to the newborn. According to the defence lawyer of Pascuala García, accused of having killed many of the recently deceased children in the village:

> Francisca Jorro says that two of her infants have died, withered and wasted away ... for this, she infers and believes that the accused is responsible ... which is completely foreign to the truth. They died because of poor care and

the bad treatment they suffered ... because it happened that she left them in the morning in their cradle and went to gossip and tell lies and drink with her cronies, and it was very late, later than midday, and she didn't go back to feed the babies ... she left them ... alone crying and they perished of hunger and thirst.[26]

One of the reasons which led many women to be indolent with their children was the ill-treatment they, in their turn, received from their husbands. According to the same lawyer:

Likewise, the said Francisca Jorro, after quarrelling or being slapped by her husband, was observed to have stopped giving milk to the said infant or infants and stopped giving any food to them.[27]

His words were based on certain accounts of defence witnesses. According to a young mother living in the village where all this had happened:

One day, when this witness was talking to Francisca Jorro in the street, who was carrying both her infants in her arms, this witness said to the said Francisca Jorro: – Jesus, Francisca, how is it that your children are so wasted and thin? And the said Francisca replied: – If I liked children as much as you do, they would be as plump as yours, but as I don't like them, they are like this. Because if my husband hits me, I'll not give them the breast for a whole day and I'll not move from my place.[28]

Faced with tales of poisons introduced by witches into their small victims using all manner of orifices (not only mouth and nose, but also ears and even eyes, transmitters *par excellence* of the poison of envy), some defence witnesses insisted on the importance of the mother's milk for the survival of infants. It was generally recognized that the misfortunes of the mother might change her milk even to the point of poisoning it – this accounted for the deaths of many children still being breast-fed. According to the above-mentioned Francisca Jorro, the ill-treatment she herself suffered resulted in the poisoning of one of her children through breast-feeding:

She could find no joy in any of her children because she was rather a chol-eric woman, and with her own milk she killed her children, because when

she quarrelled with her husband and father-in-law ... she didn't feed them
for one or two days, and when she did feed them, her milk was bad, infected
and poisoned, with the result that she killed them.[29]

The enormous influence the mother's state of mind had on the quality
of her milk, and consequently on her children's health, is now
acknowledged and accounted for by scientific arguments that were
unknown in the sixteenth century.[30] Nevertheless, in spite of the lack
of objective explanations that could be demonstrated, the phenomenon
was known at the time and designated by a simple expression that can
be understood both literally and metaphorically, namely 'the evil milk'.
The angry milk – or in other words, an upbringing to some extent bereft
of loving care – was, according to a frequent interpretation given by
witnesses, the origin of countless infant deaths. As the defence lawyer
of another woman accused of witchcraft in 1591 explained, the recent
deaths of several children in the village, in particular the son of a certain
Isabel Alviol, had nothing to do with any supposed acts of the accused:

> The day before the night when the son of the said Isabel Alviol died, the said
> Isabel Alviol quarrelled in the village with the daughters of Mossen Valls
> and they exchanged very bad words, with a great anger and choler, so that
> the said Isabel Alviol herself became very angry and choleric, and after that
> she might have given her angry and vexed milk to the said child and killed
> him in that way with the said milk, as happens very often.[31]

In addition to thoughtlessness, unconsciousness, carelessness, or the
harm indirectly transmitted through the mother's milk, wild aggression
against newborn babies was fairly common. Many of them were hit,
pinched, or injured before being suffocated, as is demonstrated by the
marks known as 'marks or pinches of witches' often referred to in trials.
According to Juan Llorente, the father of a child whose death had been
attributed to the village witch, the baby was completely healthy the
day before, but

> The day after, his mother found it dead. It had been pinched all over, and
> from parts of the body blood was flowing.[32]

Similarly, a girl 'aged about six weeks' had been found one morning
with a crushed nose and 'on the wrists three thumb marks of a person'.

According to several witnesses, the infant had died due to 'the hand of a witch', and the accused was this time Susana Dalmau, nicknamed 'the Burguesa', the daughter of an old woman who had been accused of casting evil spells that very year. According to the statement of Bárbara Alviol:

> On the eve of the past St. Lucy's Day ... having her granddaughter in her arms ... walking in her courtyard, came there Susana, nicknamed Burguesa, having nothing to do ... and she was there the whole afternoon ... and now and then she said: – Such a beautiful girl! And the following night, after the girl had gone to bed very healthy and happy, she was found dead with three spots of blood in her nappies and a crushed nose. And she saw clearly that the witches had killed her. And she was certain the said Burguesa had killed her.[33]

There were exceptional occasions when the accused and the alleged child-killer were the same person. If we believe the account of the father of Petronila (a seven-year-old girl whose age makes her a rather different case from the ones we have been studying so far), his daughter died due to the spanking given her by her own mother, whom he accused of being a witch:

> The morning when the daughter of the witness died, the witness saw that the said Maria Tolon, his wife, spanked her because she had wet the bed. And he saw that the girl died later, after some two hours. And when this witness saw that she was dead he said angrily that his wicked wife had killed her.[34]

Whether the account by the resentful husband is credible or not, according to the few, but none the less telling surviving documents, it is indisputable that a good deal of the aggressiveness of parents towards children was diverted in the direction of witchcraft. An immense and privileged territory for the secret and the unmentionable, the limitless world of witchcraft could encompass a wide range of clandestine behaviour and feeling. Infanticide itself, so often condemned by divine law and the laws of men, came to be considered by the representatives of the church in Zaragoza as 'involuntary homicide', simple oversight or negligence, so long as it stayed within the sphere of the private. In 1557 Archbishop Don Hernando of Aragón granted one of the priests

of the diocese the right to absolve, among other sins previously
reserved,

> the guilt or negligence through which children are found suffocated, pro-
> vided this was kept private and did not come about deliberately: because if
> it were known publicly, we would want the guilty to make public penance
> in the cathedral of Zaragoza in the usual form.[35]

Once again, what matters are appearances. What counted above all
was public opinion, the chief bestower of fame and reputation. The
domain of the intimate and the private, confined almost entirely to the
home and family circle, remained a woman's world. Some women, the
witches, played an even more arduous role, shouldering the weight of
the inadmissible at a period of growing ideological control. The varied
translations of infanticide – at the same time tolerated and condemned,
permitted and detested – were nothing but masks, in terms of the
language of witchcraft, for a conflict barely capable of resolution.

Notes

1. Trial against Pascuala García. Herrera de los Navarros (Zaragoza), 1572.
   Archivo Diocesano de Zaragoza (ADZ), C. 42–12, f. 7.
2. See María Tausiet, 'Comadronas-brujas en Aragón en la Edad Moderna:
   mito y realidad', *Manuscrits*, 15 (1997), 377–92.
3. Jacob Sprenger and Heinrich Institoris, *Malleus maleficarum* (n.p (Paris?),
   n.d. (1510?)), p. xi.
4. Juan de Mongastón, *Relacion de las personas que salieron al auto de la fe ... de
   Logroño ... de 1610, y de las cosas y delitos por que fueron castigados*, Madrid
   Biblioteca Nacional, V/C 248–71.
5. During the sixteenth and seventeenth centuries, crimes of witchcraft were
   judged by various different bodies in Aragón. In addition to aristocratic
   justice and what was commonly known as 'popular justice' (lynching
   outside the law), the three most active institutions were: Inquisitorial
   Justice, Episcopal Justice, and Secular Justice. The *inquisitorial tribunal of
   the Holy Office*, created specifically to eradicate heresy, based its
   persecution on accusations of apostasy. Yet despite the infamous cruelty
   associated with the Black Legend, trials for witchcraft became increasingly
   infrequent, and eventually almost non-existent as the sixteenth century
   developed. This reflects the interests of an institution whose main task
   was the social and political control of those groups which were thought
   to be the most dangerous; given the inquisitors' increasing scepticism

towards crimes attributed to witches, such crimes soon came to be regarded as minor issues which could be dealt with by the so-called 'ordinary' judge, that is, a judge who acted as the representative of a bishop. Witchcraft and superstition, which occasionally appeared among the crimes dealt with by the *episcopal tribunals* from the end of the fifteenth century, were increasingly present in the last decades of the sixteenth century, along with other types of behaviour considered irreligious (cohabitation, homosexuality, usury, etc.), and they gained greater importance after the Council of Trent. Both the Inquisition and the episcopal judges used proceedings based on Canonical Law, which tended to be long drawn out on account of the search for evidence. The *secular tribunals* in Aragón, on the other hand, whose authority was limited to one district or borough, held very brief trials based on lawless statutes which were specifically drawn up so as to persecute certain criminals (invariably witches and thieves) without observing the jurisdiction or laws of the kingdom. These local judges regarded witchcraft mainly as a problem of public order which should be controlled as expeditiously as possible. Aragón's true 'witch-hunt' occurred particularly in small isolated or mountain villages; however, given the rapid nature of the method and the dispersal of documents, it has traditionally been the least well known type of justice. See María Tausiet, *Ponzoña en los ojos. Brujería y superstición en Aragón en el siglo XVI* (forthcoming).

6. Trial against Dominga Ferrer, La Coja. Pozán de Vero (Huesca), 1534. Archivo Histórico Provincial de Zaragoza (AHPZ), C. 31–2, f. 91.

7. *Estatutos y desafueros contra las hechizeras y bruxas, hechos y otorgados por los Jurados y Concejo General de la villa y lugares del justiciado de Gía.* 1592. Archivo Diocesano de Barbastro (Huesca), f. 3.

8. Trial against Isabel Garay. Cosuenda (Zaragoza). 1591. ADZ, C. 33–23, f. 6.

9. Ibid., f. 20.

10. Ibid., f. 37.

11. See María Tausiet, 'Terrores nocturnos', in *Ponzoña en los ojos: Brujería y superstición en Aragón en el siglo XVI* (Zaragoza, 2000).

12. Trial against Catalina García, La Dalmava. Peñarroya de Tastavins (Teruel), 1591. ADZ, C. 18–17, ff. 102v.–103r.

13. See María Tausiet, 'La presencia de la muerte en los procesos por brujería en Aragón en el siglo XVI', in Eliseo Serrano (ed.), *Muerte, religiosidad y cultura popular (siglos XIII–XVIII)* (Zaragoza, 1994), pp. 305–20.

14. See Philippe Ariés, *L'enfant et la vie familiale sous l'ancien régime* (Paris, 1973); W. Langer, 'Infanticide: A Historical Survey', *History of Childhood Quarterly*, 1:3 (1974) 353–365; L. Miniturn and J. Stashak, 'Infanticide as a Terminal Abortion Procedure', *Behavior Science Research*, 17 (1982) 70–90; Jean-Louis Flandrin, *Le sexe et l'Occident: Evolution des attitudes et des comportements* (Paris, 1981); Glenn Hausfater and Sarah Hardy (comps), *Infanticide: Comparative and Evolutionary Perspectives* (New York, 1984); Jean Gaudement, *Le mariage en Occident: Les moeurs et le droit* (Paris, 1987), pp.

367–68; Marvin Harris and Eric B. Ross, *Death, Sex and Fertility: Population Regulation in Preindustrial and Developing Societies* (New York, 1987); and A. Bideau, B. Desjardins and H. Pérez Brignoli (eds), *Infant and Child Mortality in the Past* (Oxford, 1997).

15. Although it is true that tolerance of infant mortality and infanticide began to decrease from the eighteenth century onwards, certain customs continued well into the nineteenth century, such as eliminating a considerable number of children taken to the poorhouse, or simply allowing them to die. In his *Disertación sobre la muchedumbre de niños que mueren en la infancia y modo de remediarlo* (Zaragoza, 1812), Arteta de Monteseguro recounts with horror how village courts handed over abandoned children to 'a man who is often the most idle and despicable in the town' to be taken to the orphanage: 'He carries them in a basket or knapsack ... without an ounce of compassion for the new-born child; on the contrary, he smacks or beats them if they cry or wail (and sometimes, as has been seen in this province, throws them into a well or river) until finally he hands them over, drenched in their tears and excreta, to the district Mayor or Judge, who then does the same ...'

16. See Jean Louis Flandrin, *Familles, parenté, maison, sexualité dans l' Ancienne Societé* (Paris, 1976); and Paul Veyne, 'L'empire romain', in Philippe Ariès and Georges Duby (eds), *Histoire de la vie privée* (Paris, 1985).

17. This constitution, which regarded those who approved the death of their children as guilty of parricide and sentenced them to the 'leather-sack penalty', still existed in Spain in the thirteenth century in the *Partidas* by King Alfonso X, which specified that such criminals should be drowned in a sack along with a cockerel, a dog, a monkey, and a viper (VII, Art. 8, Law 12).

18. Flandrin, *Le sexe et l'Occident,* p. 180.

19. See Francisco Núñez, *Libro intitulado del parto humano* (Alcalá de Henares, 1580).

20. See W. Langer, 'Infanticide', p. 356; and Flandrin, *Le sexe et l'Occident*, pp. 192–4. Well into the eighteenth century, the pastoral visits of the Tarragonese archdioceses revealed that this custom was still in force. One of the commands of the Archbishop of Tarragona on his visit to the district of Vilabella in 1737 stated: 'To avoid the deplorable misfortune of many new-born infants who are suffocated in their parents' bed and, worse still, that this often occurs before they have received the baptismal sacrament, so that parental injustice deprives the souls of their offspring from entering eternal bliss: we therefore order them most strictly and in the name of Jesus Christ to be more merciful with their children, and take greater care to protect them from such misfortune, and therefore keep them in separate beds or cradles. And when poverty prevents them from doing this, at least try to give them more special care.' (Archivo Histórico Archidiocesano de Tarragona, Abadía de l'Espluga de Francolí, 'Decrets en Santa Visita', c. 10–41).

21. Trial against Pascuala García. Herrera de los Navarros (Zaragoza), 1572.

ADZ, C. 42–12, ff. 137–8.

22. Ibid., ff. 148 and 168.

23. Trial against Isabel Garay. Cosuenda (Zaragoza), 1591. ADZ, C. 33–23, f. 50.

24. See Marie-Christine Pouchelle, 'Le corps féminin et ses paradoxes: l'imaginaire de l'interiorité dans les écrits médicaux et religieux, XIIe–XVIIe siècles', in Yves-René Fonquerne and Alfonso Esteban (eds), *La condición de la mujer en la Edad Media* (Madrid, 1986) pp. 315–31.

25. Trial against Pascuala García. Herrera de los Navarros (Zaragoza), 1572. ADZ, C. 42–12, f. 7.

26. Ibid., f. 144.

27. Ibid., f. 14v.

28. Ibid., f. 265.

29. Ibid., f. 267v.

30. According to modern manuals of obstetrics, the influence of the mother's psyche on breast-feeding is evident and can be explained by the secretion of prolactin and oxytocin by the central nervous system. Given that human milk contains natural antibodies like immunoglobin A or lactoferrin (an iron binding protein), it is easy to understand the close link between the mother's state of mind (which conditions the quality of her milk) and the child's health.

31. Trial against Bárbara Blanc. Peñarroya de Tastavins (Teruel), 1591. ADZ, C. 31–34, f. 72.

32. Trial against Isabel Garay. Cosuenda (Zaragoza). ADZ, C. 33–23, f. 78.

33. Trial against Susana Dalmau. Peñarroya de Tastavins (Zaragoza), 1591. ADZ, C. 74–30, f. 56.

34. Trial against Francisca Castán y María Tolón. Peñaflor (Zaragoza), 1609. ADZ, C. 5–10, f. 166v.

35. ADZ, Registro de Actos Comunes (1554–58), f. 126v.

Chapter Ten
Witchcraft and Forensic Medicine in Seventeenth-Century Germany

Thomas Robisheaux

n 28 February 1672, the barber-surgeon and bather from the princely court at Langenburg was requested to carry out an autopsy on the body of a peasant woman from the nearby village of Hürden. Anna Fessler, a poor servant who had worked at the court, had died suddenly and mysteriously just a few days before, and alarmed villagers feared that a witch had poisoned her. These court functionaries were not so certain. Fessler's untimely death puzzled them. The case, they argued to Dr Georg von Gülchen, the Court Advisor, required a physical inspection of the corpse to determine the cause of death. A formal forensic medical examination of Fessler's body might provide a convincing medical explanation for her untimely death. In the meantime villagers denounced the Hürden miller's wife, Anna Elisabeth Schmieg, for witchcraft. According to witnesses, Schmieg's daughter had brought a basket full of cakes to the Fessler house on Shrove Tuesday, and, in a suspicious gesture, urged Fessler to eat one large and appetizing cake in particular. After wondering whether she should accept the gift, Fessler accepted it, and took several bites. The young maid, satisfied, then returned home. Later that evening Fessler began to complain of stomach pains. She paced restlessly about the house, while waves of heat and sweat broke over her body. Intense fears and anxiety overwhelmed her. Her mother and sister, who were present during the

197

terrible ordeal, reported that her torso, neck, and legs swelled to grotesque proportions. When her husband came home late that night, she was writhing in pain in bed, and calling out: 'Lord Jesus, I must die!' At midnight she did.[1]

The death of Anna Fessler and the trial of her neighbour, Anna Elisabeth Schmieg, for witchcraft were the pivotal events in one of the last small waves of witch-hunting in south-west Germany in the late seventeenth century. The peak of witch-hunting in the region had been reached in the 1620s, but witch trials surged in several territories between 1660 and 1680. The trials around Langenburg in the county of Hohenlohe represented a part of this wave of trials. Between 1668 and 1678, ten individuals from around the small residential town of Langenburg were accused and tried for witchcraft.[2] The momentum of the Langenburg trials turned on the long and difficult trial of Schmieg. She would become the last woman successfully prosecuted for witchcraft in the territory.

At a time when trials were relatively few in number, and judicial scepticism increasingly more common, just how did villagers and public authorities come to view the case as one involving witchcraft? The question is not an easy one to answer. Interpreting disturbing crimes or misfortunes was a complex process. General understandings about witch trials often break down when trying to explain individual cases, where it becomes critical to distinguish how perceptions of supernatural or diabolical causation were actually triggered and became convincing. A suspicious death could be explained in many ways, and usually was, without any recourse to witch beliefs.

Understanding witchcraft in a case like this one from Langenburg therefore requires understanding the mental or cognitive worlds of seventeenth-century villagers, court officials, jurists, surgeons, and physicians as they sorted through the disturbing and confusing events. How were the events to be read? What signs pointed to witchcraft? What distinguished those signs from others that simply pointed to the mundane or natural? Common folk and public authorities were quite skilled and experienced in reading the signs surrounding odd, unexpected or distressing misfortunes, and could call upon a wide variety of explanations. Witchcraft was actually a comparatively rare explanation, especially in the late seventeenth century. An answer to these questions requires understanding how those involved in the events rejected common criminal behaviour as an explanation, and became convinced instead that the uncanny and demonic powers of a witch were at work.

The victim's body plays a particularly prominent role in the Fessler case. Fessler's body was more carefully scrutinized for signs of witchcraft than almost any other piece of evidence in the case. Just how was the body read for signs of witchcraft? At its simplest level, this scrutiny of the victim's body for signs of witchcraft required gathering a variety of evidence: eyewitness testimonies, physical evidence, and, of course, the condition of the corpse itself. Finding a convincing pattern of explanation for all of this evidence was no easy matter, for the evidence was actually created at different times by different individuals, all of whom relied upon quite different modes of perception or ways of sifting the evidence for its meaning. Some perceptions were arrived at swiftly, even instantaneously as when the witch was initially cried out, but others that were generated through a forensic medical examination were distilled through more deliberate forms of reasoning.

Building a legal conviction of witchcraft therefore required reconciling evidence gathered in quite different ways. The Schmieg case offers the rare opportunity to study this process at work in detail. The process of accusing and successfully prosecuting a person for witchcraft was fraught with difficulties by the late seventeenth century, and could and frequently did break down. This was especially the case as magistrates began to meet not only stricter applications of the law, but also, on occasion, the high standards demanded by forensic medical investigations.[3] When public officials ordered a forensic medical examination in a witch trial, they were drawing into the legal process surgeons and university-educated physicians, and the specialized knowledge that only Renaissance anatomy and physiology could provide. The outcome of the Fessler case – and the Langenburg witch trials surrounding it – therefore hinged in the end not on politics or social dynamics, but on the investigative methods of seventeenth-century forensic medicine.

The Law

Forensic medicine began to develop in the sixteenth century in the Holy Roman Empire, a century or so behind the earlier developments in Italy, but a good two centuries ahead of England and France. The stunning achievements of Vesalius, and other Renaissance anatomists, played a part in generating public interest in anatomy and its practical applications, but a more direct spur to the development of German forensic medicine came with the promulgation of the new criminal law code for the Holy Roman Empire, the *Constitutio Criminalis Carolina*, or *Carolina*, in 1532. While applied unevenly in the mid- and late sixteenth century, many German territorial states made the *Carolina* into an integral part of criminal law practice and procedure in the seventeenth century.[4]

How did the law influence the development of forensic medicine? The *Carolina* required in the cases of suspicious death that a careful visual inspection of the victim's body be carried out. The key provisions were spelled out in §147 and §149 of the *Carolina*. Article 147 required two different types of examiners – a surgeon and lay witnesses close to the victim – to inspect the body, and provide testimony to the court. 'When someone is struck down, and over a period of time dies, and it seems suspicious whether the person died from the blow that was administered or not, in such cases one should take testimony about the matter from both sides, as the wise saying goes, and especially [get testimony from] a surgeon ...'[5] The law did not require the technical expertise of a physician. In the mid-sixteenth century university-trained physicians in Germany concerned themselves primarily with theoretical questions in medicine. Naturally, they advised and treated patients, usually the wealthy and privileged, but the writers of the law understood that surgeons were more widely available and more likely to have direct experience with wounds.

Particularly noteworthy is the prominence that the law assigned to lay witnesses in inspecting the body. Article 147 required that the magistrate gather testimony from people close to the victim at the time that the injuries were inflicted, or who knew the victim's circumstances intimately, that is, '... other people who know how the deceased carried himself after the blows were given, and can give evidence about how long the deceased lived after receiving the injuries ...'.[6] The law did not privilege the views of the surgeon, or other medical authorities, above the lay witnesses. Surgeons naturally had specialized knowledge of wounds, but friends and relatives of the victim brought the authority of direct visual knowledge of the victim's body and spirit at the time of the crime. Since women managed so much of the day-to-day healthcare in early modern Germany, lay witnesses were frequently women from the victim's family. In the eyes of the law, women witnesses could be as significant as any medical authority consulted in a suspicious death.

What of the body itself? How was a medical investigation to be carried out? The law required a careful visual inspection of the body, or corpse, and all of its wounds. Article 149 required that the presiding magistrate, two representatives from the court, and 'one or more surgeons carefully inspect the corpse, and look carefully at all the wounds that have been administered, note them, and write them up.'[7] The law considered it important that the magistrate himself visually apprehend the wounds, the assumption being that a direct observation placed him closer to the truth. Magistrates were therefore envisioned as part of the 'inspection team' that went to a public viewing of the victim's body.

By the seventeenth century, two important changes had occurred in the application of the law. First, the law was increasingly interpreted to include physicians in forensic medical investigations. The change can be traced to the higher visibility and status of Renaissance anatomy, and the increasing role of German university faculties in advising public authorities in legal matters. Renaissance anatomy had also increased in public importance after Vesalius.[8] Because of Vesalius's influence at Padua, and Padua's importance in training many German students in medicine, anatomy rose in public awareness and esteem as students returned to Germany and took up their medical practices, public posts, and university positions. Some began to carry out public dissections. The connection between Padua and Renaissance anatomy and the Fessler case was a direct one. When the Langenburg magistrate needed medical advice on the autopsy, he wrote to the medical faculty at the Nuremberg University at Altdorf. The report came to the attention of Moritz Hofmann, a physician trained at Padua and one of the leading German anatomists of his day. Hofmann had founded the university's anatomical theatre in 1650.[9]

Territorial states had also begun drawing university-trained physicians into forensic medical investigations by the seventeenth century. The medical faculty at Leipzig, for example, became the most prominent in Germany in the area of forensic medicine and was widely consulted.[10] By the late seventeenth century, forensic investigations engaged not only surgeons, but also physicians with specialized knowledge of the body derived from Renaissance anatomy and physiology.

The second change in forensic medical investigations involved the method of inspecting the body. The law required only an external visual inspection of the body and its wounds. No article mentioned dissection of the corpse, let alone carrying out a full autopsy and a visual inspection of the body's internal organs. By the seventeenth century, however, public dissections and private forensic autopsies were common in many parts of the empire. Universities and cities took the lead. Moritz Hofmann routinely carried out public dissections at the Altdorf Anatomical Theatre and the city's humanists praised him for his skill and knowledge.[11] In practice, it therefore became common to extend the visual inspection of the body to include, where necessary, a visual inspection of the internal organs and parts of the body. Here, it was thought, one could see the handiwork of God's creation in magnificent complexity.[12] In cases of witchcraft, this offered the opportunity to see the physical imprint of the devil on the body as well. It was this modern knowledge of anatomy that would be brought to bear to decide whether Anna Fessler had died from poisoning and witchcraft or not.

To read a body for signs of witchcraft was to become involved in a complicated process involving villagers, magistrates and consulting jurists, and medical authorities. Not everywhere was it followed, of course, but three points are worth making about the procedure where it was carried out. First, the law prescribed no single way to understand a cadaver, its wounds, or any other signs that the internal organs might display. It simply prescribed that evidence be gathered about the body before and after the wounds were afflicted or the poison ingested. There was complete confidence that a visual inspection of a body would yield up sure signs about the cause of death. Second, magistrates were obliged to turn to certain kinds of witnesses for sure knowledge about the victim's bodies. The law mentioned surgeons, but the law made it clear that those who were closest to the victim also provided direct visual evidence about the condition of a victim's body. Implicitly, this meant that lay opinion – very often the testimony of women – weighed equally with that of expert medical opinion. Typically, women provided the most detailed knowledge about a victim's state of health before a crime was committed. Implicit in the process, then, were at least two different methods of reading a body for signs of witchcraft.

Finally, detecting the signs of poisoning and witchcraft was notoriously difficult. German jurists who commented on the *Carolina* repeatedly warned their readers that poisonings were especially troublesome to detect without specialized medical knowledge. Benedict Carpzov, the great Saxon jurist and one of the leading commentators on the *Carolina* in the seventeenth century, cautioned his readers that reading the signs of poisoning and witchcraft was exceedingly difficult. He strongly advised judges to consult medical authorities in these cases.[13]

Village Women and the Body

Before the Langenburg magistrate engaged the surgeons and physicians in the Fessler case, a commonplace understanding of the crime was already well established among villagers from the region. The general opinion is less important in this context than the particular knowledge of those villagers who actually saw the crime, and could give firsthand visual testimony about Fessler's physical health. How did these villagers read her body for signs of bewitchment? The answer revolves less around the coherence, or incoherence, of popular beliefs about witchcraft than around the question of how perceptions were actually triggered and shaped in response to the subtle clues of the environment. The recent work of cognitive anthropologists on how cultural perception actually works offers a useful starting point for understanding how witch beliefs were applied in very particular contexts.[14] Witchcraft was, after all, only one of several explanations for misfortune at hand, and an unlikely and rare one at that, and so a convincing reading and interpretation of a suspicious death like Anna Fessler's was not at all obvious. What was critical in perceiving witchcraft at work was the conjuncture of several separate cognitive perceptions of the events within their specific contexts. In this case, four perceptions or readings of events coincided.

First, the Fessler case involved not just any type of misfortune, but one around which an accusation of witchcraft might be credibly made under the right circumstances: the sudden illness and death of a woman in the lying-in period after childbirth. Lyndal Roper and Ulinka Rublack have shown recently just how great the fear of witchcraft was for women after childbirth and during the lying-in period.[15] One cannot know for sure how often witchcraft suspicions actually arose around these circumstances. Certainly, the few cases of witchcraft from the city of Augsburg grew out of the worries and anxieties common to the lying-in period.[16] Impressions of the many other trials from south-west Germany, however, suggest that this circumstance occurred in only a minority of cases. Among the witch trials that took place around

Langenburg, the Schmieg case was the only one involving childbirth and the lying-in period. Still, it is striking how quickly the cry that Fessler died through witchcraft gained credibility within the village.

One might best understand the lying-in period – the period between childbirth and churching – as a moment of ritual time and place separate from everyday experience. Attention was keenly focused on the new mother's physical and spiritual health, as well as that of her baby, so much so that one might say that the women attending her developed a heightened awareness about all of the mundane affairs and events surrounding her recovery. She was understood to be vulnerable to forces that were unseen and malevolent.[17] One of the critical factors that raised suspicions of witchcraft in the Fessler case was that she had died during the lying-in period. In January a child had been born to Fessler, and since that time, as was customary, a small circle of women, most of them kinswomen and close neighbours, had tended her. This circle included her mother, Anna Trückenmüller, her sister, Barbara Trückenmüller, and a neighbour woman Fessler knew and trusted. Each of these witnesses gave detailed testimony about Fessler's state of health in the weeks before her death, and even more detailed information about her emotional, physical, and spiritual state on the day and evening that she died. They all agreed that Fessler had experienced a normal childbirth. She had suffered briefly from an illness, possibly hepatitis, but she then recovered rapidly, was eating normally and heartily, and displayed no signs of illness before the fateful evening of her death. On the evening she died, she had no signs of illness until she ate the Shrovetide cake. What was uncanny to each of these women was how quickly she had shown distress after eating the cake. She screamed out with pain, her body began to swell, and then came vomiting and a burning, unquenchable thirst.[18] Such signs before the churching might easily point to bewitchment.

A sudden and seemingly inexplicable death following childbirth, however, might have raised suspicions of witchcraft, but a convincing accusation would still not have been likely. The experience of poor health following childbirth, even illness, poor spirits, and death was common enough in rural areas like this one around Langenburg. A credible interpretation of the events required one additional quality: the authority and respect of the people making the accusation. In a village like Hürden *who* raised the alarm about witchcraft was just as important as *what* was said. Villagers did not accord credibility to just anyone, or to just any accusation or rumour of witchcraft.

A brief examination of the witnesses involved in the case shows that socioeconomic or legal status was not the key to credibility in the initial accusation of witchcraft. Instead, closeness to the victim, especially a close visual perception of the victim and the events surrounding her death, was the most important factor lending weight and authenticity to the accusation of witchcraft. The women close to Fessler were all poor. They were cottagers' wives, not kinswomen of powerful or wealthy peasants or townspeople. None of them stemmed from the region's élite. All of these women, however, had tended Fessler during the lying-in, and were present during the distressing events on Shrove Tuesday. What gave them the most credibility before the Langenburg court was that they all offered convincing and detailed visual testimony about the state of Fessler's body and spirit.[19] Their credibility, no doubt, was enhanced by the timing of their accusation as well. By sending out the alarm at night, immediately upon her death, and not waiting for other rumours to circulate, the accusation gained even more credibility. Accusations of foul play could lose credibility the longer one waited after a sudden and mysterious death.

The roles that girls and village men played in spreading rumours of witchcraft are illuminating about the importance assigned to close visual apprehension of the victim and her death. In the summer of 1671, the village cattle maids had sent around the rumour that Anna Schmieg was a witch. That rumour, however, never gathered enough momentum to make an accusation stick. As for the important village men, the full members of the village commune, they were naturally questioned about the suspicious death of Fessler and the accusation of witchcraft. Many mentioned Schmieg's bad reputation, but their answers were vague, and they seem not to have been central to the process of crying out Schmieg as a witch. When the pastor was asked, for example, he simply said he knew about Fessler's death from his wife.[20] This pattern naturally raises intriguing questions about how rumours circulate and gain credibility in a village, and the role of gender, age, and status in that process. One must be careful not to generalize, however. What gave this accusation credibility was the women's personal familiarity with Anna Fessler, and their firsthand visual knowledge of her and her body.

Even these two conditions would never have provided sufficient grounds for a successful accusation of witchcraft had not a third condition been present: a field of social relationships saturated with enmity. Interpreting a suspicious death depended on social knowledge, that is, knowing firsthand the relationships of the victim with her neighbours and family. Witchcraft only made sense through a prism of personal enmity. This point has been made many times, but one should stress here that these judgments rested on an acute and personal understanding of the field of relationships around the victim.[21] In this case, the enmity between Anna Fessler and Anna Schmieg was well known. Had someone else died at that time, someone not presumed to have enmity with Schmieg, or even someone like a spouse or close kinsman, villagers may not have suspected witchcraft. Spousal deaths or murders were often read through a different frame, and there was likely to be understanding and, perhaps, even sympathy in some quarters for this crime.[22] Murder was usually just murder and not witchcraft.

One final factor established clues in the environment for reading misfortune: time. German villagers, Protestant and Catholic alike, were keenly attuned to the rhythms of ritual time.[23] Different cognitive schemes and experiences were triggered by the experience of specific ritual times. The perception of particular associations, or even explanations themselves, might therefore be triggered or made more or less persuasive depending upon the time in which the events were experienced. Certainly, the lying-in period represented one such experience of ritual time, in this case, a time of heightened fears of witchcraft. To this was added the fears and anxieties surrounding another moment in ritual time: Shrovetide Eve. In this Protestant land this feast day no longer had associations with carnival, but the feast retained its significance as a liturgical day charged with unusual significance and dangers. In popular culture it was the day when women baked cakes for their neighbours, and when they presented their baked goods they affirmed ties of friendship and solidarity. At the same time, the day brought with it heightened fears of witchcraft, especially around sunrise and sunset.[24] Schmieg's daughters, the witnesses said, appeared suddenly on Fessler's doorstep just as the sun was setting. Exchanging gifts of food on a day charged with such high expectations and fears about friendship and enmity only heightened concerns. Solidarity mixed with exclusion, anticipation and friendship with fear and worry. Food exchanged that day might nourish or it might kill. The lines between food and poison, fuzzy even in normal times, blurred even more. One reason why memories were so vivid about the events of that Shrove Tuesday was that this was a day of ritual danger within another ritual cycle (the lying-in) filled with its own worries and dangers.

Medicine

While these perceptions quickly won over villagers after Fessler's death, a more deliberate and carefully reasoned reading of the events was beginning. Villagers read the suspicious signs of witchcraft within a dense forest of local social relationships and firsthand experiences with the victim. Perceptions distilled quickly. The medical authorities, however, moved slowly and deliberatively in gathering and sifting through the evidence. Forensic medicine required studying the evidence within the context of learned understandings of anatomy and physiology. Medical findings had also to be transformed into legal evidence. Working through the medical semiotics concerning a suspected poisoning was especially complex. By the seventeenth century the medical knowledge about poisons was, in fact, becoming a specialized subfield of forensic medicine, thanks in large part to the work of Italian physicians.[25] Conducting a forensic medical examination required time, in other words, and in the Fessler case, the Altdorf medical faculty did not deliver their final report to Langenburg until July of 1672, more than four months after Fessler's death.

In cases of poisoning and witchcraft, naturalistic and occult powers mixed in unpredictable and even surprising ways, and increasingly required the expertise of physicians trained in anatomy and physiology to be diagnosed properly. When the Langenburg surgeon initially refused to pronounce witchcraft or poisoning as the cause of Fessler's death, he was probably not expressing scepticism about witchcraft. Skilled and experienced surgeons realized that reading the body for symptoms of poisoning was no easy task.[26] Specialists in forensic medicine were even more cautious. A sure diagnosis required not only considerable skill and patience in dissection, but detailed knowledge of anatomy and physiology. Leipzig's medical faculty warned that surgeons were often ill equipped to understand how a wound was made, let alone read properly the signs of poisoning and bewitchment. They therefore demanded that forensic autopsies be carried out in consultation with university physicians trained in physiology and anatomy.[27]

The association of poison with witchcraft was a commonplace in the seventeenth century. What makes the Fessler case, and so many of the other accusations of witchcraft in the late seventeenth century, especially intriguing, however, was that in forensic medicine the association was loosening.[28] When the Langenburg surgeon sent off his report to Altdorf, there was no way of telling how the medical faculty would read the autopsy findings.

How did the Altdorf physicians read the surgeon's report and the trial protocols, and then think through the physical evidence that they presented? The answer depends on understanding something about these physicians' education, the schools of medicine they belonged to, how they understood physiology and anatomy, and what medical texts they were likely to consult in puzzling through a difficult case.

The Altdorf physicians clearly drew their views from medical ideas common in the 1660s and 1670s. By this time, older views about poison as infused with demonic powers were clearly out of date. In the Altdorf physicians' report, for example, one finds no evidence that they had turned to the major work on poison by the Venetian physician Baptista Codronchi, *De morbis veneficis libri quattuor* (1595), which interpreted all poisonings as demonic in origin.[29] Given the Galenic tendencies in their thinking, however, it is possible that they were influenced by Avicenna's *Canon* or the works of Girolamo Cardano. Also likely, given Altdorf's close ties with Lutheran Saxony and its universities, would have been a familiarity with the collected works of the Wittenberg physician Daniel Sennert. Sennert treated occult causes of death in expert detail in *De morbis occultis*, developing in this treatise a Galenic approach stressing poisons as substances that attacked 'the entire substance' of the body (*de tota substantia*).[30]

What is certain, however, is that the members of the medical faculty knew and read the most important work in forensic medicine of the seventeenth century: Paolo Zacchia's *Quaestiones Medico-Legales* of 1630.[31] Zacchia had served two popes as personal physician and the papal state as a medical advisor. He was among the most widely respected public physicians in early seventeenth-century Italy, and his *Quaestiones Medico-Legales* firmly established his reputation throughout Europe as a leading authority in forensic medicine. If the Altdorf physicians did not consult the work directly during the Fessler case, their method of inquiry mirrored closely the one that Zacchia recommended concerning poisoning. At the beginning of Book 2 of the *Quaestiones Medico-Legales*, where Zacchia treated poison and forensic medicine, the great Roman physician argued that poisons worked through occult properties, and therefore agreed with the view that some poisons were demonic in origin.[32] As his discussion progressed, however, Zacchia tended to play down the association of poisons with demonic powers, arguing more forcefully for a Galenic view that these substances always had natural properties, and that every poison mixed occult and natural properties in complex ways. On the whole, Zacchia tended to reduce the association of poisons with occult powers and stressed the natural properties through which poisons worked.[33]

For physicians trying to identify poison at work in the body, Zacchia's semiotics of poison, a guide to the symptoms of poisoning and how to read them, would have been especially important. His purpose was to help a physician determine whether poison was at work, what kinds of poisons caused different symptoms, and whether occult powers were at work in the poison or not. Zacchia's method divided the signs into three types: (1) the victim's general physical and spiritual health; (2) the symptoms at the moment of poisoning; and (3) the victim's responses after taking the poisoned food or drink.[34] He pointed out that the victim might show immediate signs of poisoning, and reject all food, vomit, develop heart tremors, and feel intense anxiety. In addition, her body might emit strong and noxious smells, lesions might develop on the skin or strange discoloration appear around the mouth. There were many types of poisons, Zacchia cautioned, and he discussed them all. Each one displayed different signs. Even more perplexing was that individuals might show different symptoms. One person might die quickly, but another might not die for weeks or months, making diagnosis particularly difficult.

Zacchia assigned an important role in detecting poisoning to eyewitness accounts of those who knew the victim well. This trust in lay witnesses grew out of a general practice among seventeenth-century physicians to include patients and those close to them in diagnosis and treatment.[35] This aspect of his diagnostic method also accorded well with the requirements of German criminal law in the *Carolina*, and may have made his approach appealing to physicians engaged in a forensic investigation. This emphasis on close visual inspection of the victim by lay witnesses figured prominently in the Fessler case as well. Not only did the court magistrate carefully gather firsthand testimony, but the medical faculty at Altdorf gave great weight to this testimony in its final report. The testimonies accorded almost exactly with each other. The three women witnesses all agreed that Fessler had been in good health, that she showed no serious signs of illness before the evening she died. One witness mentioned an episode of weakness – possibly hepatitis – but the episode passed quickly. This last point was critical to the Altdorf physicians. In their report they considered whether the poison was generated internally, a point of controversy among specialists interested in poison. They concluded, however, that a 27-year-old mother in good health would be unlikely to die this way.[36]

Following death, a postmortem investigation of the corpse was essential in detecting poison. At this point Zacchia assumed that the physician would be familiar with anatomy and physiology. An external viewing of the body, after all, rarely turned up the critical evidence that a close inspection of the internal organs would reveal. In the Fessler case, the Langenburg court advisor knew that in Moritz Hofmann he was engaging a leading anatomist, one celebrated in the Protestant world for his public dissections and his contributions to anatomy. His opinion was as authoritative as one could find anywhere in the Holy Roman Empire.[37]

How did Hofmann go about studying the evidence of poisoning and witchcraft in the Fessler case? In general, Renaissance anatomists like Hofmann were known for stressing the importance of direct empirical observation in acquiring reliable knowledge about the body. The Paduan anatomists Hofmann had worked under had certainly drilled into him the importance of personal visual inspection. Written medical texts carried less weight.[38] Anatomical research took place under ideal conditions, however. Forensic autopsies rarely did. A body decomposed quickly in warm weather or, as in the Fessler case, the corpse was too far from the university for the physician to take part personally in the autopsy. He would have to rely on the reports of the surgeon who would carry out the autopsy and send a report. The medical investigation had begun in exactly this manner in the Fessler case. All of the evidence that the Altdorf physicians actually had was given to them second-hand in the form of a short report scrawled out in a difficult hand by the Langenburg court surgeon. To make sense of this report, they would have to draw on their own experience with dissections, descriptions of poisonings from textbooks, and their imagination to picture what the body might have looked like given the few facts at their disposal.

The dissection of Fessler's body was probably carried out in the Fessler house itself, in the presence of her immediate relatives. This was common practice at the time. Indeed, by 1600, in German towns family members often requested autopsies and they actively participated in them. Family members of the deceased crowded around the table to watch the dissection, their own observations and reactions to the dissection obviously affecting the surgeon or physician as they formed their opinions.[39] Controversy sometimes arose about whether surgeons had the proper knowledge of anatomy and physiology to carry out a competent forensic autopsy, but in practice physicians had to rely on surgeons in carrying out a dissection. In the Fessler case, the Altdorf physicians raised no questions about the surgeon's dissection.

The Langenburg surgeon, following common practice, probably did not dissect the entire corpse. Because of the suspicions of poisoning and witchcraft, attention would have focused on the abdominal cavity and the condition of the internal organs, the heart and the stomach in particular. The brief report on these organs provided Hofmann and his colleagues with evidence for their report.

Did the final report from Altdorf, then, really describe Fessler's corpse? From the language of the report, one has the impression that Hofmann and the other Altdorf physicians had carefully inspected the corpse themselves. The poor body, they wrote, 'looked repulsive'. The 'body or stomach was large, and collapsed like a drum'. In addition, large swellings extended down to the thighs and up to the neck and head. Down the left side, suspicious red and blue spots were noted. Suspicious looking foam had oozed from the mouth.[40] The report was written in the keenly visual and empirical language of a Renaissance anatomist, creating the illusion that it was actually describing the body as it would have appeared at the time of the autopsy.

Hofmann and his colleagues were not trying to fool anyone at Langenburg with this language. They wrote their report so as to fit the requirements of the law, and the law demanded visual evidence about the body. The question remains: where did this detailed description of the corpse come from? Were Hofmann and his colleagues simply glossing textbook descriptions of poisoning? One of the interesting clues to this puzzle are the passages describing the physical condition of the heart, the blood around it, and the contents of the stomach. The blood around the heart had congealed in a suspicious way, they wrote, suggesting that it had been 'corrupted' by poison. The suspicious substance removed from her stomach, they noted, was arsenic. None of these details appeared in the original surgeon's report. These passages, with their careful attention to the quality of the blood and heart, read more like descriptions of poisonings taken right out of Zacchia's *Quaestiones Medico-Legales* or Sennert's *De occultis morbis*. Significantly, their report does not reference any authoritative medical texts in arriving at its conclusions, a style of academic writing quite different from reports in law or theology. The report, in other words, was written to give special weight to the visual observations of the body, even if those observations may only have taken place in the imagination.

Was the cause of death then natural, or supernatural? The question is wrongly put because physicians like Hofmann and his colleagues would not have regarded these qualities as mutually exclusive. Seventeenth-century medicine, in general, left considerable room for the interplay of natural, supernatural, and preternatural causes in creating illness.[41] Indeed, Zacchia and Sennert observed that poisons contained complex combinations of natural and occult properties. Besides, the devil, it was known, had wide-ranging mastery over naturalistic processes: he could instruct a witch in the use of poison or make use of natural processes himself to cause misfortune. Some strands of thinking in the new mechanical medicine – a school of medicine alien to Hofmann and Altdorf at the time – could still make room for demonic influences at work on the body. Even later in the century, the great Halle physician Friedrich Hoffmann, known for a more mechanistic approach to medicine, still left room in his physiology for the devil to use completely natural processes in the body to bring about illness and death.[42] In any event, the medical report from Altdorf accorded well with the popular rumours around Langenburg about bewitchment in the Fessler case. The presiding magistrate ruled that the death had occurred through poisoning and witchcraft.

The seventeenth century was a great age of semiotics. What makes the cultural historian's task regarding witchcraft challenging is that common people, legal authorities, and medical authorities deployed different systems of reading signs. Some read the signs quickly, piecing together clusters of associations in very particular circumstances, and thereby arriving at their convictions firsthand. Others, like the surgeon, the physicians, and the jurists in the Fessler case, considered the signs much more deliberatively, interpreting them within specialized learned discourses. If one considered carefully all of these different modes of perception, as magistrates were likely to do in the late seventeenth century, arriving at a consensus conviction of witchcraft was no simple matter. Not surprisingly, a great many prosecutions failed to do so and collapsed.

The Fessler case illustrates just how difficult and time-consuming a successful prosecution could be in the late seventeenth century. The brake on witch trials like this one was not scepticism about supernatural effects on the body or the filtering down of more enlightened and scientific understandings about nature to the educated. Seventeenth-century forensic medicine, and the specialized fields of anatomy, physiology, and iatrochemistry that it drew on, remained compatible with the belief in witches late into the seventeenth century. What slowed a witch trial like this one, what made conviction difficult for the authorities, was the legal process of reconciling so many different and complex ways of readings the signs of bewitchment. The Langenburg case of 1672 ended with the conviction of Schmieg for witchcraft, but it took eight months to get there, and she would be the last witch ever successfully prosecuted in this region of Germany.

Notes

1. The records of the case are collected in the Hohenlohe Zentralarchiv – Neuenstein, Archiv Langenburg, Gemeinschaftliches Archiv Langenburg 529 and 530.
2. On the witch trials in south-west Germany, see H. C. Erik Midelfort, *Witch Hunting in Southwestern Germany, 1562–1684: The Social and Intellectual Foundations* (Stanford, CA, 1972); and Sönke Lorenz (ed.), *Hexen und Hexenverfolgung im deutschen Südwesten*, 2 vols (Karlsruhe, 1994). On the last trials in Langenburg, see Elisabeth Schraut, 'Fürstentum Hohenlohe', in Sönke Lorenz (ed.), *Hexen und Hexenverfolgung im deutschen Südwesten*, vol. 2, *Aufsatzband* (Karlsruhe, 1994), p. 278.
3. For a general history of German forensic medicine, see Esther Fischer-Homberger, *Medizin vor Gericht: Gerichtsmedizin von der Renaissance bis zur Aufklärung* (Bern, 1983).
4. Ibid., pp. 25–8.
5. Ibid., p. 27.
6. Ibid.
7. ibid., p. 26.
8. Andrew Wear, 'Medicine in Early Modern Europe, 1500–1700', in Lawrence I. Conrad et al. (eds), *The Western Medical Tradition, 800 BC to AD 1800* (Cambridge, 1995), pp. 280–92.
9. J. G. Puschner, *Amoenitates Altdorfinae oder Eigenliche nach dem Leben gezeichnete Prospecten der Löblichen Nürnbergischen Universität Altdorf ...* (Nuremberg, 1710), pp. 2–3.
10. Fischer-Homberger, *Medizin vor Gericht*, pp. 49–50.
11. Georg Will, 'Hofmann, Moritz', in his *Nürnbergisches Gelehrten-Lexicon oder Beschreibung aller Nürnbergischen Gelehrten beyderley Geschlechtes nach Ihrem Leben, Verdiensten und Schrifften ...* (Nuremberg, 1756), pt 2, pp. 170–4.
12. For one effort to understand the cultural importance of Renaissance anatomy and dissection, see Jonathan Sawday, *The Body Emblazoned:*

Dissection and the Human Body in Renaissance Culture (London, 1995).

13. Benedict Carpzov, *Practicae novae imperialis Saxonicae rerum criminalium, Pars I* ... (Wittenberg, 1670), Qu. 21, pp. 99–104.

14. The following analysis makes an implicit use of schema theory in its more recent connectionist form. For a theoretical introduction to schema theory, see Roy D'Andrade, *The Development of Cognitive Anthropology* (Cambridge, 1995), pp. 122–50; and Claudia Strauss and Naomi Quinn, *A Cognitive Theory of Cultural Meaning* (Cambridge, 1997), pp. 48–88.

15. Lyndal Roper, 'Witchcraft and Fantasy in Early Modern Germany', *History Workshop Journal*, 31 (Spring 1991), 19–43; and Ulinka Rublack, 'Pregnancy, Childbirth and the Female Body in Early Modern Germany', *Past and Present*, 150 (1996), 84–110.

16. Roper, 'Witchcraft and Fantasy', p. 21.

17. Rublack, 'Pregnancy, Childbirth and the Female Body', pp. 93–7.

18. Archiv Langenburg Gemeinschaftliches Archiv Langenburg 529/42, May 23, 1672.

19. Ibid.

20. Ibid.

21. See especially, Rainer Walz, *Hexenglaube und magische Kommunkation im Dorf der Frühen Neuzeit: Die Verfolgungen in der Grafschaft Lippe*, Westfälisches Institut für Regionalgeschichte, Landschaftsverband Westfalen-Lippe, Forschungen zur Regionalgeschichte, vol. 9 (Paderborn, 1993).

22. Ulinka Rublack, *Magd, Metz' oder Mörderin: Frauen vor frühneuzeitlichen Gerichten* (Frankfurt am Maine, 1998), pp. 315–23.

23. Robert Scribner, 'Cosmic Order and Daily Life: Sacred and Secular in Pre-Industrial German Society', in Kaspar von Greyerz (ed.), *Religion and Society in Early Modern Europe, 1500–1800* (London, 1984), pp. 17–33.

24. 'Fastnacht', in Hanns Bächtold-Stäubli, *Handwörterbuch des deutschen Aberglaubens*, vol. 2 (Berlin, 1987), cols 1246–61.

25. For a general history concerning poisons in Renaissance medicine, see Fischer-Homberger, *Medizin vor Gericht*, pp. 353–406.

26. The great Renaissance surgeon, Ambroise Paré, devoted separate long chapters to witchcraft and poisonings. See his *Wund Artzney oder Artzney Spiegell* (Frankfurt am Main, 1635).

27. Fischer-Homberger, *Medizin vor Gericht*, pp. 49–50.

28. Ibid., pp. 377–86.

29. I have used the 1618 edition; Baptista Codronchius, *De morbis veneficis, ac veneficiis, libri quattvor* (Milan, 1618).

30. Daniel Sennert, 'De Morbis Occultis', in his *Operum omnia*, vol. 3 (Lyon, 1650), pp. 521–693.

31. Paulus Zacchia, *Quaestiones Medico-Legales, in quibus omnes ex materiae medicae, quae ad legales facultates videntur pertinere, proponuntur, pertractantur, resoluuntur* ..., 4 vols (Leipzig, 1630).

32. Zacchia, *Quaestiones Medico-Legales*, vol. 2, pp. 194–200.

33. Fischer-Homberger, *Medizin vor Gericht*, pp. 379–85.

34. Zacchia handled most of this problem about the signs of poisoning in Question 7 'De signis propinati veneni, & de fallacia, ac validate eorum signorum', in *Quaestiones Medico-Legales*, vol. 2, pp. 248–66.
35. Wear, 'Medicine in Early Modern Europe', pp. 238–40; and espcially Barbara Duden, *The Woman Beneath the Skin: A Doctor's Patients in Eighteenth-Century Germany*, trans. Thomas Dunlap (Cambridge, MA, 1991).
36. Archiv Langenburg, Gemeinschaftliches Archiv Langenburg 529/44, [July 1672?].
37. Will, 'Hofmann', p. 171.
38. Wear, 'Medicine in Early Modern Europe', pp. 290–2.
39. Robert Jütte, *Ärzte, Heiler und Patienten: Medizinischer Alltag in der frühen Neuzeit* (Munich, 1991), pp. 116–18.
40. Archiv Langenburg, Gemeinschaftliches Archiv Langenburg 529/44, [July 1672?].
41. Wear, 'Medicine in Early Modern Europe', pp. 242–4, 261–3, 310–11.
42. Lester S. King, *The Philosophy of Medicine: The Early Eighteenth Century* (Cambridge, MA, 1978), pp. 202–8.

Chapter Eleven
Reasoning with Unreason: Visions, Witchcraft, and Madness in Early Modern England

Katharine Hodgkin

o study witchcraft is for most of us to study something we do not believe in; the active power of malevolent magic, the physical reality of the devil, night flights to the sabbat are no longer realities to be taken for granted. This, however, is true of other fields of study too. Among the consequences of history's increasing preoccupation with religious and magical world views has been the need to engage with events at odds with everyday notions of the possible: conversations with God, visits from spirits, angels and devils, bewitchments, visions. Such magical and spiritual events and experiences take place in different contexts, and have different meanings – divine inspiration, prophetic trance, possession, witchcraft, madness. In their extraordinariness to our own categories of thought, they seem to mark out our difference from the mentalities of the early modern period, and perhaps to offer a way into that difference. We cannot understand them straightforwardly as literal descriptions of real events (however problematic such notions have become, even for historians); the need to be aware of our own interpretative moves, our presuppositions, our methodologies, is much more insistent where we are dealing with something not self-evident.[1]

This interpretative instability is the starting point for my exploration:

confronted by a woman and a vision, what determines the meaning we give to it? How did her contemporaries decide whether she was a witch, or a prophet, or insane, and what routes do historians take in establishing their own categorizations? Extra-natural phenomena, in early modern as in modern society, posed problems of interpretation. We are not dealing with a culture in which seeing spirits or hearing voices was entirely normal and everyday, but one in which within certain limits and at certain points, it was explicable as a phenomenon of the real world rather than simply an internal delusion.[2] The explanatory frames are various – medical, theological, philosophical; but although medical discourse has a place in these debates, the question of how to interpret encounters with spirits did not pose itself entirely, or even primarily, in terms of the difference between madness and sanity. A further set of differences was organized around the meaning of the spirits themselves – good or bad, angels or devils? – and around the identity of the person – a witch, a saint, possessed? genuine, deluded, dissembling? Sir Thomas Browne, early in the seventeenth century, is astonished that anyone should question the real existence of spirits and witches; at the same time it is not to be credited in all cases. 'I hold', he says, 'that the Devill doth really possess some men, the spirit of melancholy others, the spirit of delusion others; that as the Devill is concealed and denyed by some, so God and good Angels are pretended by others.'[3] Devilry, delusion, melancholy, deception: the problem is always to work out which one in a given case. Standard works on witchcraft debated not whether apparent witchcraft might sometimes be attributed to melancholy, but what proportion of it and under what circumstances.[4]

For historians, too, it has become increasingly necessary to be attentive to context, to the meaning of 'spirits' and of what they appear to be saying, to the place and identity of the person in the culture. Historical thinking about subjects such as witchcraft and prophecy has undergone an important shift in the last few decades: there has been a move away from insanity as an explanatory category, towards attempts at interpretation that would be more historically understanding, less culture-bound. Neither witches nor prophets are any longer likely to be dismissed as mad or hysterical. If a given culture accepts the reality of magic, recent scholarship has assumed, then our most useful path is not to seek to explain away magical happenings, but to accept them and attempt to make sense of them by way of folklore, gender relations, symbolic structures, and so forth. Similarly the study of women's prophetic activities emphasizes serious engagement with the content of their speech and writings so as to understand these practices positively, thinking about the doors opened to public discourse, the language provided for disputing questions normally closed.[5]

And yet the relationship with madness cannot be fully exorcized; there is something intrinsically odd about much of what is being described, and this strangeness continues to haunt our attitudes to the study of witchcraft and prophecy. It is also significantly related to questions of gender. You will notice I say a woman and a vision; the prophet I am talking about is gendered female, a prophetess. This is because – again both for the contemporary and the historian – the question is one that seems to pose itself with peculiar starkness in relation to women, or perhaps more properly, the feminine. Because witches (notwithstanding individual exceptions) as a category are gendered female, the proximity of prophesy to witchcraft has an immediacy for the female prophet that is absent for the male. Because femininity is analogically associated with unreason, the connection with madness is also readily made; also, because the cultural constraints on appropriate behaviour for women are much more insistent on containment (emotional and physical), excessive or excitable behaviour in women is too easily attributable to mental disorder.[6]

These three figures, then, the witch, the female prophet, and the madwoman, seem to me significant in their relationship. In their own time, and in ours, they pose a series of related problems around the constitution of rationality, and the establishment of boundaries between different categories of apparently non-rational behaviour. Seen separately, there are many different interpretative possibilities: witches and prophets have been represented as victims or heroines, deluded or astutely manipulative; madwomen as simply mad (in a way that transcends history), or as victims of their society's constraints on female autonomy. But the circumstances of their separations and their connections are not as simple as they have sometimes appeared. In this chapter I want to bring the three figures together again, juxtaposing three cases which, in different ways, circle about this central question of (in a large sense) unreason and how it can be interpreted – not so as to say that the three were all the same, but so as to think about witchcraft in relation to other discourses with which it was seen at the time to have something in common, and with which it retains a complex and often submerged relationship. I thus offer you 'a witch', 'a madwoman', and 'a prophet', in the hope that to re-examine their relations may be a useful way of thinking about historical interpretation; and I will briefly return to that problem at the end.

Night Visits

I begin with three parallel night-time encounters. This is how Susan Swapper of Rye in Sussex, whose trial for witchcraft began in 1607, described the first visits of her spirits:

> Susan Swapper the wife of Roger Swapper of Rye aforsaid Sawyer saieth that about Midd Lent last past she beinge in the Chamber where she did lye with her husband in bed in the night time about the howers of Twelve and one of the clock there appeared to her fower spiritt[s in the] Leiknes of two men and two woemen … [She describes their clothes and general appearance. A few nights later] the woman in the grene petticoat called this examinate Sue come and goe with me or els I will carry thee, whereuppon she this examinate beinge a fearde with that vision and the calling of her by her name, Called to her husband and waked him and willed him to hold her And he Awakeinge turned to her and Answered her wherefore should I holde thee and she Replied unto him againe and said here is a thinge that will carry me away and he said againe unto her I see nothinge and so turned about from her.   Rye 13/1[7]

Earlier the same year Dionys Fitzherbert, daughter of a gentry family living in the household of the Countess of Huntingdon, fell into a state of mental disorder. Writing subsequently of a night near the beginning of her illness, she describes how she was convinced she was about to die:

> & with perfite memory desposed of thos things I gave away as I thought best. & called upon god with great fervency espeshly with thes words. come lord Jesus come quickly. sharply reproving the maid that waicht with me for puting me in hope of life … & most instantly entreted her to bere wittnes that yet I died the true servant of Jesus christ the which she promysed to do with many teres I often enquiring of her if it were day fuly perswading my self that then I shuld dy. but when they informed me it was day I fell into strang & fantasticall Imagnations such as I think are not mete to be repeted for I confes they were both wiked & prosumtious.[8]

Finally, some 40-odd years later, Anna Trapnel describes a couple of nights at the beginning of a sickness from which she was to be miraculously recovered:

> a bright light shined round my head visible, and in the midst of that light stood one all in white, in the likeness of a creature all covered with brightness ...
>
> And thus God came in the first night, the flood of Divine excellency shined down mightily, that some Saints standing by me could not but conclude that certainly I was going out of the body ... they were amazed that stood by me, and that night I still continued speaking, or rather the spirit in me.
>
> ... this Scripture was presented, Hosea 6.2, which voice was from God, my thoughts not being on it, nor none speaking of it but God alone; it came thus, after two daies I will revive thee, and the third day I will raise thee up, and thou shalt live in my sight, and with a full perswasion that I should recover; but I said Lord, this Scripture holds out my resurrection, or the restoring of the Jews; I was answered it was to manifest my recovery ... [9]

For all of these women, night-time is the moment when strange experiences come; the borderlands between sleep and waking open the doors of perception, to let in spirits, angels, fantastical imaginings. But the consequences of these nights for each of the three were to be very different. Susan Swapper would be tried for witchcraft, convicted, and sentenced to death, though ultimately pardoned; Dionys Fitzherbert would spend six months under treatment for insanity, before recovering to write a lengthy account of her experiences; Anna Trapnel would forge ahead as a visionary prophet, undergoing periods of imprisonment, publishing accounts of her experiences and visions, achieving fame in radical circles of the 1650s.

It's very tempting, looking at these three together, to imagine a game of bed-swapping: what would have been the consequences if they could have been switched around in the night, to wake up in the circumstances of one of the others? Would Swapper with her white-clad spirits, or Fitzherbert with her unrepeatably wicked and presumptuous imaginings (they could hardly have been more presumptuous than Trapnel's replay of the Resurrection), have been hailed as a prophet? Tempting; but perhaps not that simple. The reasons for identification as prophet, madwoman, witch are complex and many-layered. Class, location, period, in these three instances, are all crucially important; but I would hesitate to go from there to the assumption that it's all just a matter of labels, that what's happening is fundamentally the same. There are significant differences as well as similarities in the cases I'm dealing with. What I find suggestive are the points at which other possible outcomes seem to be hinted at in the records, but not followed up, or not successfully; it's in these that we can perhaps see elements of a shared structure of unreason at work, and yet also think about the limits on what is shared, the way that these cases formally are differentiated from one another, on what terms and what grounds. The question of whether Swapper was indeed a witch, Fitzherbert mad, Trapnel divinely inspired, and the circumstances under which those encountering them seemed to allow for the possibility that each of them might have been truly something else, are the submerged accompaniments to narratives which attempt to position them firmly in their attributed or claimed identities.

Seeing Things, Hearing Voices

So what might these disparate cases have in common, either to those who saw them at the time or to those who study them now? In the first instance, this combination of a woman and a vision. All three are concerned with problems of reality and perception; each of them sees or experiences something that is neither seen nor experienced by others, that puts her perceptions at odds with those of others around her. The response of Susan Swapper's husband Roger, 'I see nothing', can stand as an emblem for the bewildered responses of families, friends, and indeed antagonists. But if what sets these three apart is the difference of their perceptions, it is also clear that to see visions does not in itself *mean* any one thing in particular. The bare fact of seeing something – a sign or a wonder – outside the range of the normal does not automatically mean that you are mad, or inspired, or messing around with the black arts; visions, in the early seventeenth century, do not necessarily imply any state of being out of the ordinary.

Thus both the Swapper and the Fitzherbert cases include material about visions which are seen by other people and have no sinister implications, at least initially. The prehistory of the Rye case reaches back to visionary experiences shared not only by Ann Taylor (later accused of witchcraft along with Swapper), but also her husband George, and possibly others: 'the Glasse windowes of Mr Fowkes', it emerges, had become a gathering point for members of the town élite to gaze at apparitions and extraordinary sights, and to speculate about their possible significance. To find visions in the glass windows of a neighbour (expensive novelties as they were) may be out of the way, 'above the course of nature', but carries no sinister connotations; one need not hesitate to admit having seen things. George Taylor describes the extraordinary sights – 'A grave man in shewe ... A deathes heid appearing leik A scull newly taken out of the grounde, with div'se psons standing round about the scull ... A pson Apparrell in very rich Attire', and so on – without any apparent concern that this might be incriminating.[10]

Glass windows offer themselves up to the public eye. The spirits Susan Swapper sees, by contrast, are visible to nobody but her, despite suggestions that Ann Taylor knows more about them than is healthy. Swapper's spirits are commoners: they have ordinary names and ordinary forms of speech (Richard is called 'sirrah Dick' by the other spirits), they make requests for food, they're interested in treasure, they're noisy. (Roger Swapper attributes their loud bangs to weasels in the roof.) The window spirits, on the other hand, are pure vision: they imply a symbolic weight, but they don't declare themselves; they are to be interpreted. And they appear to be portents of significant events – particularly deaths – rather than crude instrumentalists looking for treasure. The argument for the guilt of Swapper's co-accused Ann Taylor was largely organized around the evidence of Susan and others that she was obsessed with treasure, that she encouraged Susan to make the spirits welcome, gave them food and other sinister items, endangered her own children by exposing them to these strange visitors. It seems that only retrospectively did neighbours cast their minds back to the visions in Mr Fowkes's window and conclude that it was all part of the same pattern.[11]

Unlike Swapper and Trapnel, Fitzherbert does not mention any type of visionary experience during the six months of her disorder. Her delusions concern her apprehension of the world and her relationships within it; they also focus on the nature of death and mortality, the divine and the demonic. But rather than conversing with devils or angels in person, she suffers from the confusions the devil inflicts on her. These delusions around the nature of the world, life and death are typically expressed not as visions or voices which make suggestions, but as mistaken apprehensions; and the vocabulary she uses to describe her condition ('disordered perceptions', 'conceits'; phrases such as 'to my thinking', 'to my belief', 'I was persuaded') reiterates this sense that it is a problem in her psychic rather than her visual or auditory relation to the world that is at issue.

However, Fitzherbert does claim to have experienced innocuous vision as well as delusion, though some years later: a paper attached to her narrative describes a vision seen in the skies around 1615, interpreting it as a sign of crisis in the Church. This vision seems to represent no threat to the sanity she has been at such pains to establish through her narrative (her argument is that although distracted and tormented by Satan, she was not in fact mad). Like the visions in Mr Fowkes's windows, it is not a sight seen by one person alone: the other witnesses are not specified, but she refers repeatedly to 'we', and mentions also that it was seen in more than one place – warding off any suggestion that it might be just her madness again.[12] Not only is it a public sight; it also has a public meaning, relating to the events and fears of the times, to move it beyond the inner delusions of one person into the sphere of public knowledge. For Fitzherbert there can be no safe claim to visionary status on her own; the disruption of perception has been too acute. But with others to act as guarantors of the truth of what is visible, she is able to mark a separation between madness as disordered perception, and the seeing of visions.

For Anna Trapnel, voices and visions were the basis of her career: she gained fame by them, published pamphlets, and drew crowds to hear her (as well as suffering imprisonment and illness). Her visions signify a special calling, and the pleasure she takes in that calling and in her visionary experiences is repeatedly evoked – 'oh how sweet are true visions!'.[13] In the London of the 1650s, an environment where people were predisposed to believe in the reality of the visionary experience, the solitariness of her visions marks her out, but she experiences that solitariness not as undermining her sense of self, but as constitutive of it; it is precisely her ability to see what others do not that makes her what she is.

To be in a visionary state, for Trapnel, was a matter of ecstasy. Entering a trance, she loses touch with the physical body; the place where she sees strange sights is not in her everyday world, but in the specific state which sets her outside ordinary consciousness. At times of visionary encounter she is, she insists, absent from her body. A letter written during her imprisonment in Cornwall describes her state: 'these cruel Rulers ... pulled me off my pillow, and rung me by the nose, and caused my eyelids to be pulled up, but no harm I felt, nor nothing interrupted me.' She is absent herself so as to be the voice of one who speaks from elsewhere.[14]

The injunction to feminine passivity works to support the construction of the visionary woman as channel, as passive voice.[15] By contrast, the woman who has supernatural encounters without being in trance is too easily seen as colluding with (rather than yielding to) overwhelming and mysterious forces, which may readily become demonic. But visionary trance has its own perils; it is closely mirrored by demonic possession, and the woman whose passivity allows her to become a channel for the words of another is also at risk of speaking for the wrong other, for being deceived as to the place from which she speaks. To guarantee Trapnel's spiritual credentials, her commentaries must be validated not only by her own condition, but also by the clearly biblical foundations and public significance of the visions themselves, and the socially worthy witnesses of her trance who testify to its reality. At the same time, the public invective which threatened to accuse her of witchcraft or distraction registers the potential instability in the meanings of vision and trance.

Susan Swapper's visitors are not referred to as visions, any more than Fitzherbert's disordered perceptions are. The mysterious visions in Mr Fowkes's window are called 'strange and miraculous sightes', or 'Apparicons'; Susan's visitors, seen by nobody but herself, are called merely 'spirits' (and presumed demonic).[16] Moreover her visions and voices leach into her daily life, so that there is no boundary between trance (in which strange things happen) and ordinary consciousness (in which one can be in control). She sees mundane spirits with no special messages; she is apparently in a normal state of mind rather than a trance; one might speculate that it's the sheer ordinariness that condemns her. If she had seemed more like somebody swept away by powerful spiritual forces, she might have been regarded as bewitched herself – or possessed, mad, or divinely visited.

Fitzherbert is similarly unable to establish a boundary between the state of normality and the state of disrupted perception. At the same time, though, like Trapnel, she is not herself, spoken by forces outside her control, as if possessed. During her disorder she raved and blasphemed against Christ, threatened to become a Catholic, and called herself Antichrist (then went through her narrative deleting the word). It is necessary for her to insist that she cannot be supposed to have been speaking in her own voice. On the contrary: 'I knew not that I said nor understood the sencabels things that be ... I apele to them all that have knowen me if I were like to geve such a reson if I had bene in my right sences no shurely I hop I shuld inded rather have plocked out my own eies and tong ...' She speaks, in distraction, for the devil, not for herself; but the possibility of possession does not seem to have been directly raised, even though this was a time of intensive activity around the question of exorcism (and she does refer to herself as having been possessed by false opinions).[17] Her state was perhaps regarded as so extreme as to be outside the categories of active and passive; rather than being a voice for another, so many disrupted voices flowed through her that no single agency could be attributed, and unreason alone remained as an explanation. Her own retrospective account, meanwhile, attempts to foreground and interpret the religious elements in her delusions (thus the conviction that she was to be burned, she argues, indicated her fear of hell), leaving the strangeness of her speech a site of anomalous unease.

The meanings attributed to vision, then, imply many different factors: who sees it – one or many, and of what reputation; how often, and whether it is repeated; in what condition – trance, sleep, ordinary daily life; whether there is communication between the seer and the vision; if so, whether it seems holy or blasphemous or mundane; whether what is seen has a larger social meaning, or is halted at the level of individual significance. In relation to all these questions, contemporaries might identify witchcraft or madness, prophecy or possession – and of course might disagree. In the three cases under discussion, the placing of each under her approved sign seems to have been a relatively unquestioning process; at the same time there are hints at other, unrealized possibilities. I turn now to the question of how these women were constructed and constituted, both by themselves and by others, and by what manoeuvres of assent and dissent, compliance, subversion, and denial they attempted to negotiate their positionings as witch, madwoman, and prophet.

Acts of Knowledge

While Susan Swapper's evidence displays an increasing volume of incriminating material against Ann Taylor, Ann Taylor's evidence (like that of her husband) attempts to exculpate herself by discrediting Swapper. In terms of the body of evidence, Swapper is more successful. The wide repertoire of witch-associations that she draws on give Taylor a convincingly witchlike profile – lacking in affection to children, taking unreasonable offence at small occasions, excessively interested in treasure, spiteful on the subject of public figures and their vices, too knowledgeable for her own good. For the Taylors to discredit Swapper is more difficult, not so much because her credit is better – it clearly isn't – as because they don't know what direction to give their accusations. They can't decide whether to represent her as a deluded fool or a devious witch; whether the spirits should be treated as real or as figments of her imagination. '[M]y masters yow that be of the jury', writes Taylor, seizing the initiative by writing down his own statement of evidence, 'I beseche yow mark and thinke what Creddence is to be geven to so Lewde a pson as this Swaffers wyfe' – then he thinks better of it; deletes the sentence after 'mark', and substitutes, 'how many devices this Swaffers wyfe had' – to delude and entrap others, presumably.[18] Meanwhile, Ann Taylor's strategy is basically to deny everything: either it is not true (and Swapper is a liar or a fantasist), or she doesn't remember, or Susan was herself the prime agent.

If the Taylors do at any point concede that they might have been interested in the spirits, it is only by presenting them as (at least potentially) divine portents, and hinting that this was their only motive for attending to stories. According to Ann Taylor, Susan told her the spirits had shown her six candles in the sky and two angels in her chamber, and 'that these two Angells had each of them A prophett ... and that there comeing was to cutt of the wicked from the yearth And that this examinate and her husband should see the Angells hereafter.'[19] Similarly, Ann Taylor's husband George says that Susan told him her spirits were vexed with him for his incredulity, 'And untill Eleven monthes were Expyred I should never have any more Reveled unto mee: But at Eleven months Ende I should have that Reveled unto mee that never Abraham nor Salloman hade nor any man Lyvinge upon the Earthe'.[20] Thus, while it may be preferable to know nothing of spirits at all, a second line of defence may consist in an attempt to challenge the meaning given to the encounters. Ann Taylor implies that if she was interested in Susan's spirits at all, it was in the same way that she was interested in the spirits in Mr Fowkes's windows, as divinely sent signs or tokens.[21]

Susan, in the Taylors' various accounts, hovers uneasily between different identities: she's a deluded uneducated fool with a rough husband and poor health; she's a devious and manipulative liar with unknown, but no doubt sinister (and witchlike) motives; she's a visionary with access to a world normally hidden, whose meanings are not fully elucidated but may be godly. The case hangs on the meaning of what is seen, but it seems impossible to attribute any fixed meaning to Susan Swapper's spirit visitors: good or bad, divine or demonic, witch, fairy or angel, they are as unstable in their significations as Susan herself. Despite the volume of her evidence it is impossible to decide what Swapper thought about her spirits, what she understood by them, whether or not, indeed, she saw herself as a witch. The absent subject of her own narrative, she asserts no identity. Of course, neither Swapper nor Taylor controls the form in which their words are recorded. Swapper's narrative is full to excess, endlessly reiterating and supplementing evidence, but it remains a court record, with all that implies. Ann Taylor's curt refusal to engage in the court process (constant repetitions of 'this ex. knows nothing') seems to recognize far more than Swapper's loquacity the potential dangers of free speech under such circumstances.[22]

Dionys Fitzherbert leaves her own record of her life, and has in mind a very definite identity which she wishes to assert: that of sanity. What looked like madness to those around her was, in fact, she argues, a special spiritual trial. She acknowledges that she was distracted, out of her right mind; but she was not, in fact, mad. God was allowing Satan to torment her, in punishment for her sins, and – as these included, she hints, intellectual arrogance – he was doing so in the most painfully appropriate way. Her narrative thus attempts to organize and give a coherent meaning to behaviour ranging from the mildly eccentric or depressed to the completely bizarre.[23] Her argument is not so much about whether or not she was in a distracted condition, as around meaning and truth: how to read the meaning of statements made in a state of distraction, and how to read the distraction itself. Her own speech when she was disordered, Fitzherbert argues, has no meaning; it was simply the product of the devil's wiles, to reduce her to despair. Her true self is the one who writes and controls the meanings of the past, redirecting them into spiritual channels.

At the time of her affliction, there was no room for alternative accounts. The early parts of the narrative show her at the mercy of doctors: taken with her hands bound from one place to another, placed under constant supervision, visited by people she feared, obliged to take medicines. As far as can be gauged, those around her were in no doubt that she had lost her mind. By the time she comes to write her account, however, she has clearly found sympathizers who will confirm her version of the disaster as spiritual rather than mental, who help her to circulate it and write encouraging prefaces.[24] But her wish to have her experience located within a theological rather than a medical discourse does not mean that she suggests the claims made in that early delirious night should be validated: she is not arguing for any prophetic status, nor for any privileged access to spiritual knowledge in her ravings. What her narrative attempts to establish is rather that while she was indeed in a state of mental disturbance, it was not that of madness. The devil can produce the symptoms of distraction, but this needs to be subtly differentiated from madness itself.

Thus despite the extremity of her symptoms (to be eating coal and failing to recognize your brothers is now hard to interpret outside the categories of madness), in her own time madness clearly was not the only possibility. The boundary between the darkness of the soul and the darkness of the mind was widely acknowledged to be doubtful; contemporary treatises devote much space to arguing out the relationship, and explaining how to tell one from the other.[25] Other spiritual narratives later in the century offer accounts of behaviour scarcely less extreme than Fitzherbert's, but which, located in a narrative of seeking and ultimately finding God, becomes a rite of passage rather than a defining identity.[26] Another time and place, then, might have given a different meaning to her experiences.

Anna Trapnel was explicitly haunted by both alternates, mocked or threatened as witch and madwoman; the need to refute attempts to re-entangle her prophetic truths in a more generalized category of unreason, and to separate herself out from these other potential identities, is a recurrent theme. Nor was she by any means the only sectary to be called mad by sceptics and detractors, of course. Enthusiasm, as the century progressed, came to be seen as at best one step away from insanity; and sectaries, regarded by religious orthodoxy as almost universally insane (except when malevolent), were also quite capable of using the accusation against one another. Alternatively, however, the meanings of madness could be reappropriated. The notion of the holy fool, opposed to those who are wise in this world, alongside the sense that to be fully reborn into faith required a wholehearted abandonment of self, meant that madness, or at least distraction, was both a dangerous possibility haunting the gathered churches, and a demonstration of that abandonment misunderstood by the worldly and self-seeking. Thus Trapnel (in trance) declares herself:

one that was simple, an Ideot, and did not study in such things as these ... They
will say the spirit of madness and distraction is upon her, and that it is immodesty; but thou knowest Lord that it is thy Spirit; for thou hast cast thy servant
where she would not, and hast taken her contrary to all her thoughts ... [27]

The emphasis on her own passivity and modest reluctance, juxtaposed
to accusations of immodesty, reminds us of the gender dimension here.
The accusations of witchcraft which Trapnel also faced do so even more
directly. Perhaps surprisingly, though, witchcraft for her seems to have
rather little effective weight as a threat. On the one hand, it appears as
a term in a general catalogue of abuse. 'And if handmaids in these
dayes pray and weep for their Lord' she comments in the preface to
her *Report and Plea*, '... England's Rulers and Clergie do judge the Lords
handmaid to be mad, and under the administration of evil angels, and
a witch, and many other evil terms ...'[28] Insanity, possession, witchcraft
are all terms that demonstrate the failure of the rulers and clergy to
understand what is really happening: their worldly knowledge cannot
encompass the spiritual dimensions of her visions. Similarly, in
Cornwall, a place of spiritual darkness, it is 'devout Women, learned
Clergy, Self-seeking Rulers' who count her powers 'foolishness,
nonsense, witchcraft, and a white Devil', or who call her 'witch, deluder,
imposter, and other vilde terms'.[29] And while the threat seems more
immediate when she mentions calls for 'the witch-tryer-woman of that
Town ... with her great pin which she used to thrust into witches', this
threat never materializes.[30]

Witchcraft thus functions in her narrative, on the one hand, to denote
the spiritual ignorance of those who make the charge and, on the other,
as an opportunity for her to demonstrate her unlikeness to a witch,
and to display God's power working in her (she says good things, as
witches reputedly cannot; she rebukes the magistrates). But as an
immediate threat to her prophetic identity, she does not seem to take it
very seriously. Her 'Defiance' at the end of the *Report and Plea* devotes
four lines to refuting the accusation of witchcraft (and imposture the
same amount), compared to a full page each to deny that she is either
a vagabond or a whore.[31] If madness and witchcraft are named as
theoretical possibilities, then, in practice they seem to be more rhetorical
strategies aimed by her enemies at discrediting her, and used in her
own account to discredit them; these apparently convergent identities
remain, after all, readily separable.

Voice, Naming, History

Swapper's account differs in two significant ways from those of Fitzherbert and Trapnel: it is not self-authored, and her life is at stake. The problems of the place of speech and knowledge in these narratives must be most intense in an account written down at second hand from a woman facing the death penalty.[32] Speech and knowledge, however, are very much in question for both Trapnel and Fitzherbert as well. The relation of the writing to the written self is problematic: by definition, both of them must attempt to give voice to a place in which they as subjects were elsewhere. Trapnel cannot write while she is in a state of trance; she is not there to write it. Her own writings thus relate her travels, her decisions, her arguments; but they relate her trances only as told to her by onlookers, and the songs and speeches that pour from her in trance are recorded for publication by others. Similarly, Fitzherbert can frame her argument that she was not mad only after she has emerged from the condition in which she was held to *be* mad; she does not speak the lost language of unreason, she attempts instead to draw reason out of it. And if at times her authorial voice appears less firmly in control of the difference between previous madness and present sanity than she might wish, none the less it is a voice that exists on condition of a distance which seems unbridgeable.[33]

Knowledge of the self is problematic; at the same time, the knowledges proposed by others are being evaded or denied. If the dialectical drama of interrogator (physician, judge, bishop) and interrogated (patient/lunatic, criminal/witch, heretic/prophet) is ideally intended to produce an 'agreed version', and to govern the language in which whatever happens can be spoken, in all these cases that claim to knowledge and authority is challenged.[34] Swapper does not repudiate the accusation of witchcraft by saying it's all lies, as Ann Taylor does; but nor does she ever admit to it; she simply describes, at length and in detail, her spirits, ignoring – subverting – any attempt to bring them back into the demonological fold. Fitzherbert's narrative is structured around a denial of medical (and, indeed, some religious) knowledge, and a counterclaim which relocates her sufferings in the sphere of the spiritual rather than of the organic. Trapnel enacts her rebuttal of those who doubt her claims in a sequence of dramatic courtroom encounters in which she conclusively gets the better of her challengers, not only staged but written in the form of a play.[35] The process of naming is not as straightforward as might be desired; and the thing itself changes as it is named.

The knowledge of the historian in these cases, too, can hardly be straightforward. To read such accounts is to find oneself oscillating between the familiar and the unfamiliar, between the sense that this is 'just the same' as some modern parallel, and that it is sharply different.[36] I suggested earlier that historiography has had two main strategies in dealing with material of the type I have been describing: broadly, either to attribute it to madness in some form or another, or to deny that it is peculiar at all. From the first perspective, it is the individual's mental imbalance, unrecognized by contemporaries trapped in their own lack of scientific knowledge, that produces the 'symptoms' of vision, voice, hallucination; with our greater knowledge we can see where they went wrong, and make our diagnosis. From the second, by contrast, we start from the presumption that the 'commonsense' reading – these people are all crazy – is ahistorical and patronizing; we try conscientiously to explore the cultural contexts in which such behaviours, far from being a mark of madness, made entire good sense, functioned as rational strategies or interpretations at the time. In this sense, we can argue that reading witchcraft presents no greater problem than reading any other trace of early modern society. Attentiveness to contexts, conventions, beliefs, power relations, strategies, language are required no less in the study of other forms of evidence: court records and depositions, diaries and letters, pamphlets and books, all benefit from such analysis, whether their subject matter is witchcraft, religion or agricultural techniques. Here, indeed, we make it possible to tell ourselves that we have found the real meaning of this phenomenon; we have interpreted it into good sense.

But interpreting it into good sense at times risks losing sight of its relation with unreason.[37] Interpretation lays claim to a knowledge of what is *really* happening; the subject of possession, madness, witchcraft does not understand the meaning of her acts until they are named and classified by the theologian, the doctor, the judge (or, indeed, all three in conflict). And this can also be the activity of the historian. If we look at witchcraft or prophecy with the aim of uncovering the real underlying meaning, inaccessible at the time, we may miss the thing itself – like editors of early modern medical books who annotate them with the 'real' illnesses suffered, the interpretation illuminates briefly, then loses sight of its object.[38]

What do historians do, or what should they do, when faced with the problem of unreason, the impossible? After all, interpretation can hardly be avoided, however we might resist the structural parallels between our position and that of the demonologist. But perhaps to think more directly about the specific problems posed by an engagement with materials of this kind reminds us that the problems of reason, and how it is defined and constituted, are not only historical, but continuing; and that to study unreason involves studying more than the history of madness. If for contemporaries the boundaries between insanity, possession, witchcraft, and divine inspiration were places of unease, potentially blurred even if only in theory, then to retrace those boundaries reminds us that the difference between their knowledge and ours may not be as great as at times we might like to suppose.

Notes

My thanks to Kate Chedgzoy, Laura Gowing, Susannah Radstone and Sue Wiseman for helpfully reading and commenting on drafts of this chapter.

1. This point has been addressed by numerous recent commentators. See, among others, Robin Briggs, '"Many Reasons Why": Witchcraft and the Problem of Multiple Explanation', in Jonathan Barry, Marianne Hester, Gareth Roberts (eds),*Witchcraft in Early Modern Europe: Studies in Culture and Belief* (Cambridge, 1996); Stuart Clark, *Thinking With Demons: The Idea of Witchcraft in Early Modern Europe* (Oxford, 1997), esp. ch. 1, 'Witchcraft and Language'; Lyndal Roper, *Oedipus and the Devil: Witchcraft, Sexuality and Religion in Early Modern Europe* (London, 1994); James Sharpe, *Instruments of Darkness: Witchcraft in England, 1550–1750* (London, 1996). See also the review feature 'Witchcraft and the Historical Imagination', *History Workshop Journal*, 45 (Spring 1998), 265–77 (Lyndal Roper, 'Witchcraft and Fantasy'; Katharine Hodgkin, 'Historians and Witches').
2. See Clark, *Thinking with Demons*, esp. pt 2, 'Science'.
3. Thomas Browne, *Religio Medici and other works*, ed. L. C. Martin (Oxford, 1964), p. 30.
4. See Clark, *Thinking with Demons*, ch. 13, 'Believers and Sceptics', for extended discussion of this.
5. On women and prophecy, see, among others: Elaine Hobby, *Virtue of Necessity: English Women's Writing, 1649–1688* (London, 1988); Phyllis Mack, *Visionary Women: Ecstatic Prophecy in Seventeenth-Century England* (Berkeley and Los Angeles, CA, 1992); Hilary Hinds, *God's Englishwomen: Seventeenth-Century Radical Sectarian Writing and Feminist Criticism* (Manchester, 1996).
6. This is a very large topic, for which perhaps the most useful starting point is Natalie Zemon Davis's classic article 'Women on Top', in her *Society and Culture in Early Modern France* (Stanford, CA, 1977). On gender and

mental disorder in early modern England, see Katharine Hodgkin, 'Dionys Fitzherbert and the Anatomy of Madness', in Kate Chedgzoy, Melanie Hansen, Suzanne Trill (eds), *Voicing Women: Gender and Sexuality in Early Modern Writing* (Keele, 1996).

7. The records of this case – over 20 witness depositions and examinations, as well as articles for interrogation – are in the Rye record office, Rye 13, along with a typewritten transcript made in the mid-1980s by Annabel Gregory. Quotation from Susan Swapper's first examination, Rye 13/1.

8. Dionys Fitzherbert's manuscript autobiography exists in two versions, both in the Bodleian Library, Oxford. Ms.e.mus. 169 is her original, in an italic hand and eccentric spelling; Ms. Bodley 154 is a copy for circulation, in secretary hand and more regular spelling. There are minor variations of wording, and some interesting omissions in the second version, which also includes an additional preface not found in the holograph. Quotations are from Ms.e.mus. 169; here p. 3v.

9. Anna Trapnel, *A Legacy for Saints; being several Experiences of the dealings of God with Anna Trapnel*, (London, 1654), pp. 26–7. Most of the half-dozen publications under Anna Trapnel's name – some written by her, some transcripts of her speeches in trance – date from 1654: *The Cry of a Stone, Strange and Wonderful Newes from Whitehall, Anna Trapnel's Report and Plea*, and *A Legacy for Saints*. She also published *A Voice for the King of Saints*, in 1658, and there is a 1000-page untitled book of prophetic verse in the Bodleian Library, an expansion of the same material.

10. Articles for Mr Taylor, Rye 13/2, and examination of George Taylor, Rye 13/6. See also the evidence of Ann Taylor, Rye 13/5, and Margery Convers, Rye 13/25.

11. See George Taylor's written deposition, Rye 13/6; examination of Roger Swapper, Rye 13/3. Neighbours implicating Ann Taylor include most of the witnesses, in brief or at length. For excessive interest in treasure, e.g., Philip Williams, Rye 13/15; for general cursing and ill will, Elizabeth Bysshopp and Martha Higgons, Rye 13/24, 13/25; for heartlessness concerning her dead children, Margery Convers, Rye 13/25. More generally, there are hints at obscure but sinister dealings with money, ailments, Roger Swapper, and pieces of beef and cloth, from Susan Swapper and others.

12. It was seen at Amesbury in Wiltshire, and 'Shemam' in Berkshire; 'we were continually coming and going for as I think the space of two hours in which it appears' she notes, 'yet could none discern how it vanished away so sudden' (Ms.e.mus. 169, loose paper in front of book).

13. *Legacy for Saints*, p. 14. For discussion of Trapnel's life and activities see Hobby, *Virtue of Necessity*; Hinds, *God's Englishwomen*, as well as her own writings, n. 12 above. See also Kate Chedgzoy, 'Female Prophecy in the Seventeenth Century: The Instance of Anna Trapnel', in Suzanne Trill and William Zunder (eds), *Writing the English Renaissance* (London, 1996).

14. *Legacy for Saints*, p. 55. Her editors and commentator insist on it as much as she does.

15. For the various paradoxes of women's position as channel or voice, see

works cited in n. 6 above. Also Diane Purkiss, 'Producing the Voice, Consuming the Body: Women Prophets of the Seventeenth Century' in Isobel Grundy and Sue Wiseman (eds),*Women, Writing, History, 1640–1740* (London, 1992); Suzanne Trill, 'Religion and the Construction of Femininity', in Helen Wilcox (ed.), *Women and Literature in Britain, 1500–1700* (Cambridge, 1996).

16. Evidence of Margery Convers, Rye 13/25. The articles for the husbands of the two accused women ask Roger Swapper about 'the Apparicon of spirites familers or Fayries'; George Taylor is asked 'what Apparicons or sights extraordinary or above the course of nature have you at any tyme seene in the Glasse windowes of Mr Fowkes' (Rye 13/2). The difference between noun and verb form is significant.

17. For instance, e.mus.169, p. 8v; p. 11r. Quotation in text from e.mus.169 pp. 23r/v, where she also speaks of 'the desaite the hart was posest with' (23r) and the conceit 'with which he [Satan] knew I was fully posest' (23v). ('Conceit' here means something between a fancy and a delusion, see Katharine Hodgkin, 'Conceits of Mind, Conceits of Body', in Stanley Porter (ed.), *The Nature of Religious Language*, Sheffield, 1996.) On possession and exorcism, see Daniel Walker, *Unclean Spirits: Possession and Exorcism in France and England in the Late Sixteenth and Early Seventeenth Centuries* (London, 1981); Sharpe, *Instruments of Darkness*, ch. 6; Clark, *Thinking With Demons*, chs 29 and 30.

18. Deposition of George Taylor, Rye 13/6.

19. Interrogation of Ann Taylor, Rye 13/5.

20. Deposition of George Taylor, Rye 13/6.

21. Annabel Gregory, in a fascinating and wide-ranging discussion of the case and its background ('Witchcraft, Politics and "Good Neighbourhood" in Early Seventeenth-Century Rye', *Past and Present*, 133 (1991), 31–66), locates its origins in factional divisions, in which religion played a part, and precarious economic conditions; the question of the Taylors' attitudes to godliness and millennial beliefs may have been significant in town conflicts.

22. Ann Taylor was examined twice, and the articles for interrogation take up more space than the evidence; she favours answers along the lines of 'To the xvith xviith xviiith she can say nothing', occasionally varying it with 'To the xxiiith she saieth that she can say no thing for that she knoweth not any thing conteyned in that inter' to be trowe'. Interrogation of Ann Taylor, Rye 13/5.

23. On this aspect of the narrative, see Katharine Hodgkin, 'Dionys Fitzherbert and the Anatomy of Madness'.

24. The Dean of Bristol (lecturer there at the time of writing), Dr Edward Chetwind, wrote an encouraging preface. A long letter to 'Mr Hall', which follows the main narrative, gives detailed instructions concerning its circulation, specifying the various friends and preachers she is anxious should see it.

25. Among others, Timothy Bright, *A Treatise of Melancholie* (London, 1586); Richard Burton, *The Anatomy of Melancholy* (1621); William Perkins, *The*

Whole Treatise of the Cases of Conscience (Cambridge, 1606). See also John F. Sena, 'Melancholic Madness and the Puritans', *Harvard Theological Review*, 66:3 (1973); and John Stachniewski, *The Persecutory Imagination: English Puritanism and the Literature of Religious Despair* (Oxford, 1991).

26. Such as the Fifth Monarchist preacher John Rogers, in *Ohel or Beth-Shemesh: a tabernacle for the sun* (London, 1653). On this subject in general, see also Stachniewski, *The Persecutory Imagination*; Owen Watkins, *The Puritan Experience: Studies in Spiritual Autobiography* (London, 1972).
27. *Cry of a Stone*, p. 67.
28. *Anna Trapnel's Report and Plea* (London, 1654), preface (no page number).
29. *Legacy for Saints*, p. 59.
30. *Report and Plea*, p. 22.
31. *Report and Plea*, 'Defiance', pp. 49–51.
32. Swapper was sentenced to death – an early victim of the 1604 witchcraft statute, which made dealing with spirits a capital offence even in the absence of maleficium. After spending several years in prison, she was released under a general pardon in 1611. Presumably the execution was delayed while Ann Taylor was engaged on an unsuccessful attempt to deny the rights of the Rye magistrates to try the case, and then subsequently acquitted by a local jury. See Gregory, 'Witchcraft, Politics and "Good Neighbourhood"'.
33. Compare Michel de Certeau's comments on Jeanne des Anges, discussing possession as a condition defined by orality, 'Jeanne des Anges can *speak* but she cannot *write* as a possessed woman ... she describes an object that is distant from her, about which she can utter the discourse of knowledge'; *The Writing of History*, trans. Tom Conley (New York, 1988), p. 254.
34. Several historians have commented on the ways in which the document of a confession or similar is the outcome of a sort of negotiation, although between spectacularly unequal parties. See, for instance, Roper, *Oedipus and the Devil*; Gustav Henningsen, *The Witches' Advocate: Basque Witchcraft and the Spanish Inquisition* (Reno, NV, 1980); Diane Purkiss, *The Witch in History: Early Modern and Twentieth-Century Representations* (London, 1996).
35. She does this extensively in *Anna Trapnel's Report and Plea*; see the extract in Graham et al. (eds), *Her Own Life*.
36. Arguments around anorexia are a classic instance. Compare the approaches and discussions of Rudolph M. Bell, *Holy Anorexia* (Chicago, IL, 1985), and Caroline Walker Bynum, *Holy Feast and Holy Fast: The Religious Significance of Food to Medieval Women* (Berkeley and Los Angeles, CA, 1987).
37. To quote de Certeau again: the act of interpretation is one which declares, 'I know what you are saying better than you ... My knowledge can position itself in the place whence you speak. Certeau, *Writing of History*, p. 250; see, in general, pp. 246–55.
38. For example, explanations in this style of a seventeenth-century doctor's notes: 'She was probably suffering from manic-depressive psychosis and her hissing breathing would probably indicate a terminal broncho-pneumonia'; *Willis's Oxford Casebook (1650–52)*, intr. and ed. Kenneth Dewhurst (Oxford: Sandford Publications, 1981), p. 127.

Index

96
infanticide
theme of witchcraft accusations, 15, 180–92

James VI and I, 47, 108, 121, 130
justices (magistrates), *see under* law

Kapferer, Jean-Noel, 46
Keeling, John (judge), 115
King, Peter, 22
Knewstub, John, 130
Knightley, Richard, Sir, 107
Krutch, J. W., 142

Lambarde, William, 24
Lancashire, 25–6, 32, 34, 59, 63, 66, 115
Langenburg (south-west Germany), 197–213
Larner, Christina, 141
'latitudinarians', 112–14
law
    Constitutio Criminalis Carolina (1532), 200–3, 209
    and forensic medicine in Germany, 199–203
    justices (magistrates), 24, 42–3, 56–71, 115, 201
    legal evidence, 21–35, 55–72
    legal miracles, 65–6
    legal records and narratives, 21–35, 41–53
    legal truth, 21–35, 66–72
    in Scotland, 82
    and witchcraft in Aragón
Leipzig (university), 201, 207
Logroño, 180
Lorraine, 161–77

Macbeth, 41
Macfarlane, Alan, 5, 46–7, 120
madness (unreason), 16, 217–33
magical healers, *see under* witch-doctors
Malinowski, Bronislaw, 2
Malleus maleficarum, 180–1
Manning, Samuel (preacher), 115
Manwood, Roger, Sir, 135
Marsh, Christopher, 131–3, 135

medicine, 28, 29, 218
    detectors and healers of witchcraft, 15, 163–8
    disease, 177
    forensic, 197–213
    Galenic, 208–9
    of melancholy and madness, 217–33
    see also animal healers; autopsy; evil eye; witch-doctors
Melmoth, William (lawyer), 149
memory
    recovered memory debate, 95
Mongastón, Juan de, 180
Montaigne, Michel de, 120

narrative, 9–12, 21–35, 41–53, 55–72, 81–96
New England, 31, 57–72
Newton, Isaac Sir, 140–1
Niclaes, Hendrick, 119, 129–30, 131, 132, 133, 135
Nicodemism, 131, 133
Nonconformists, 112–15
North-East England, 21–35, 58–66, 111
Northern Circuit, 57
Nuremberg (university of Altdorf), 201–2, 207–13

oaths, 24–6
Oldmixon, John, 144–5
ordeals, 63–4, 67

Pacey, Samuel (Nonconformist), 114
Padua (university of), 201
Parsley, Edward (bricklayer), 110
Patterson, Annabel, 120, 125, 131
perfectibility (of human nature), 124, 127, 129–31
poisoning, 202–3, 207–13
Potts, Thomas
    Wonderfull discoverie (1612), 32, 47, 52
Power, John (actor-manager), 147–8
prophecy, 16, 217–33
Puritans (Puritanism), 107–10, 130, 133, 135, 142
Purkiss, Diane, 6, 12

Quakers, 111

Randall, Anthony (vicar), 130